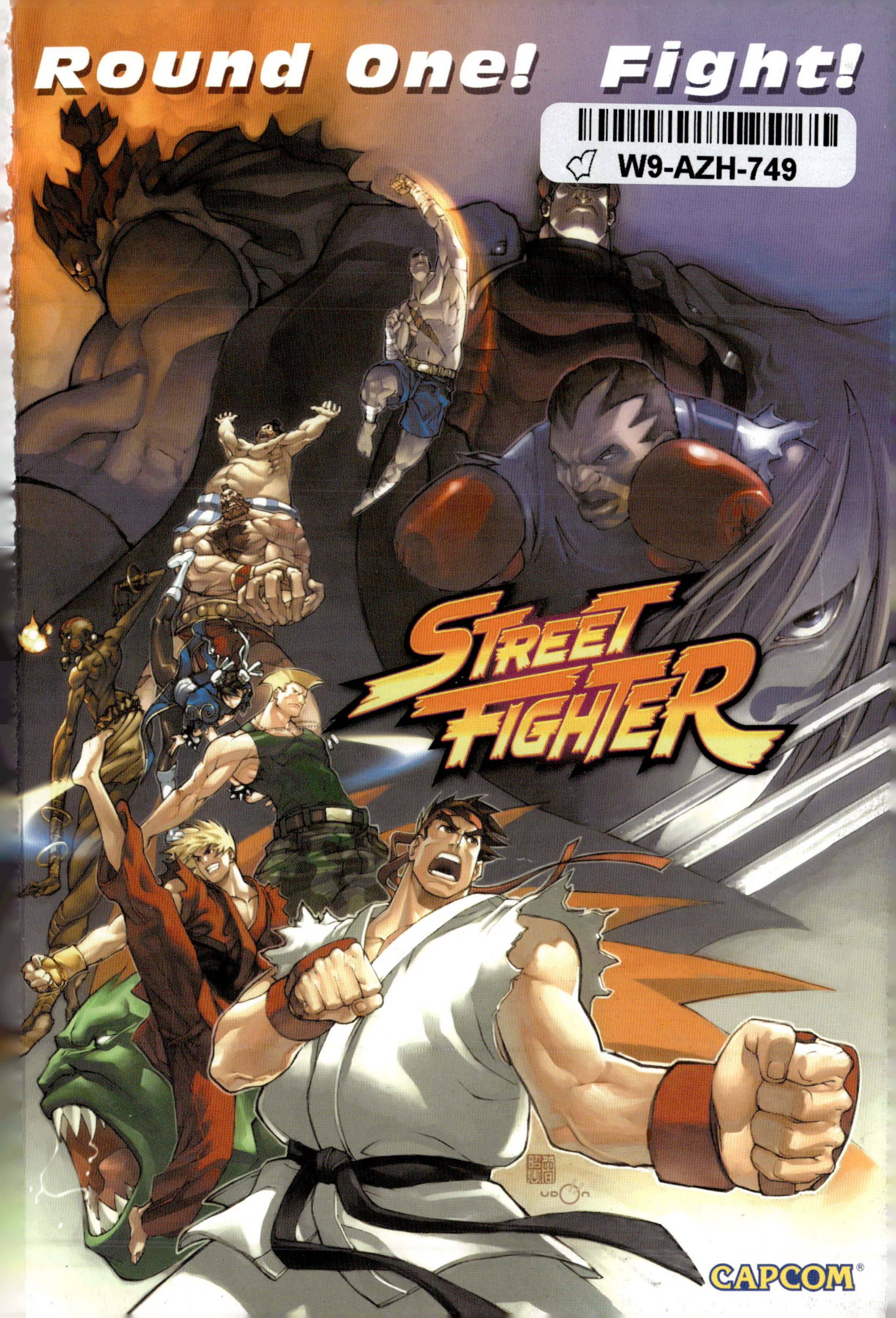
Round One! Fight!
STREET FIGHTER
UDON
CAPCOM®

Cover Art by: Arnold Tsang

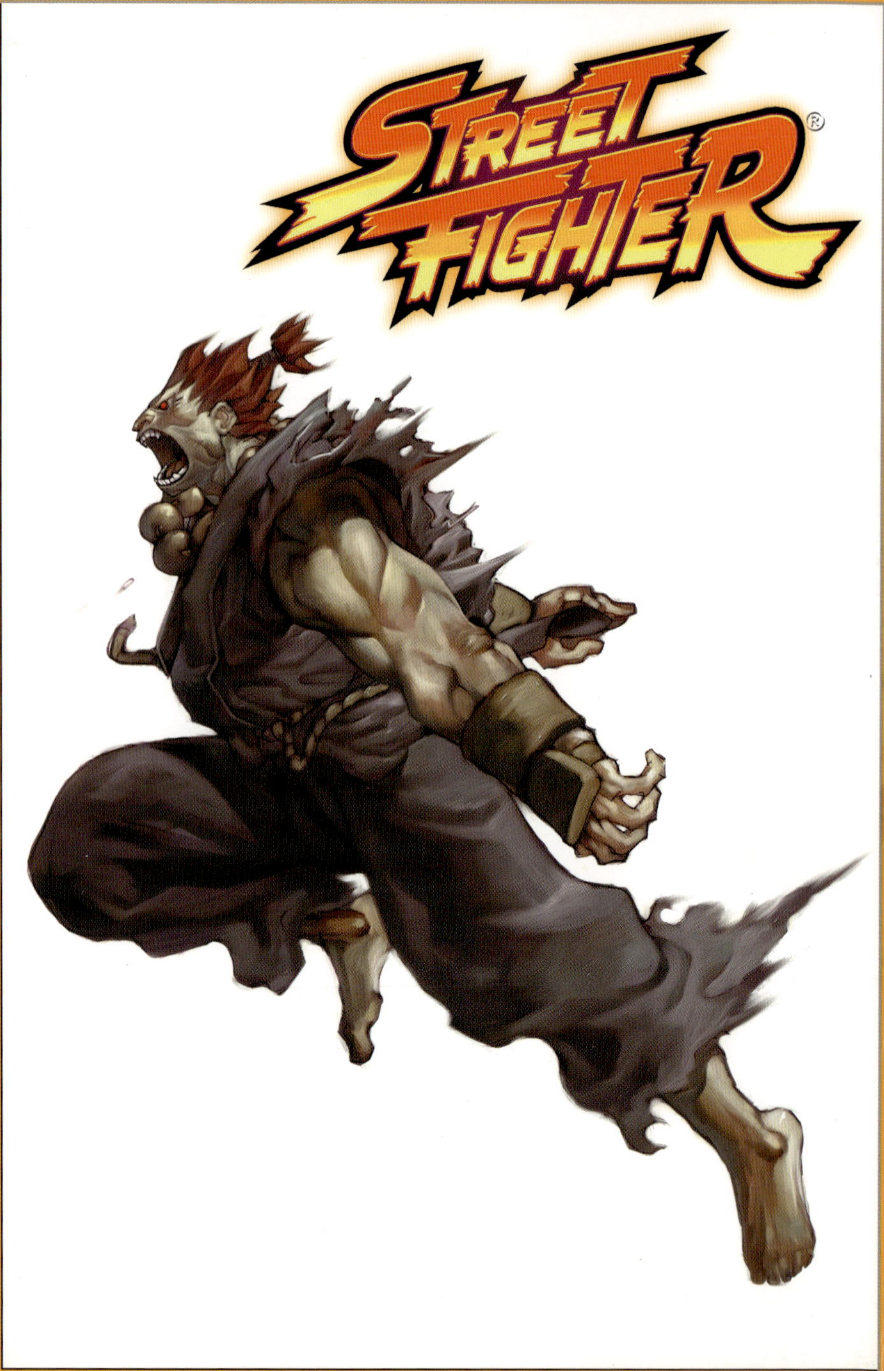
STREET FIGHTER®

Chapter 00: MASTER

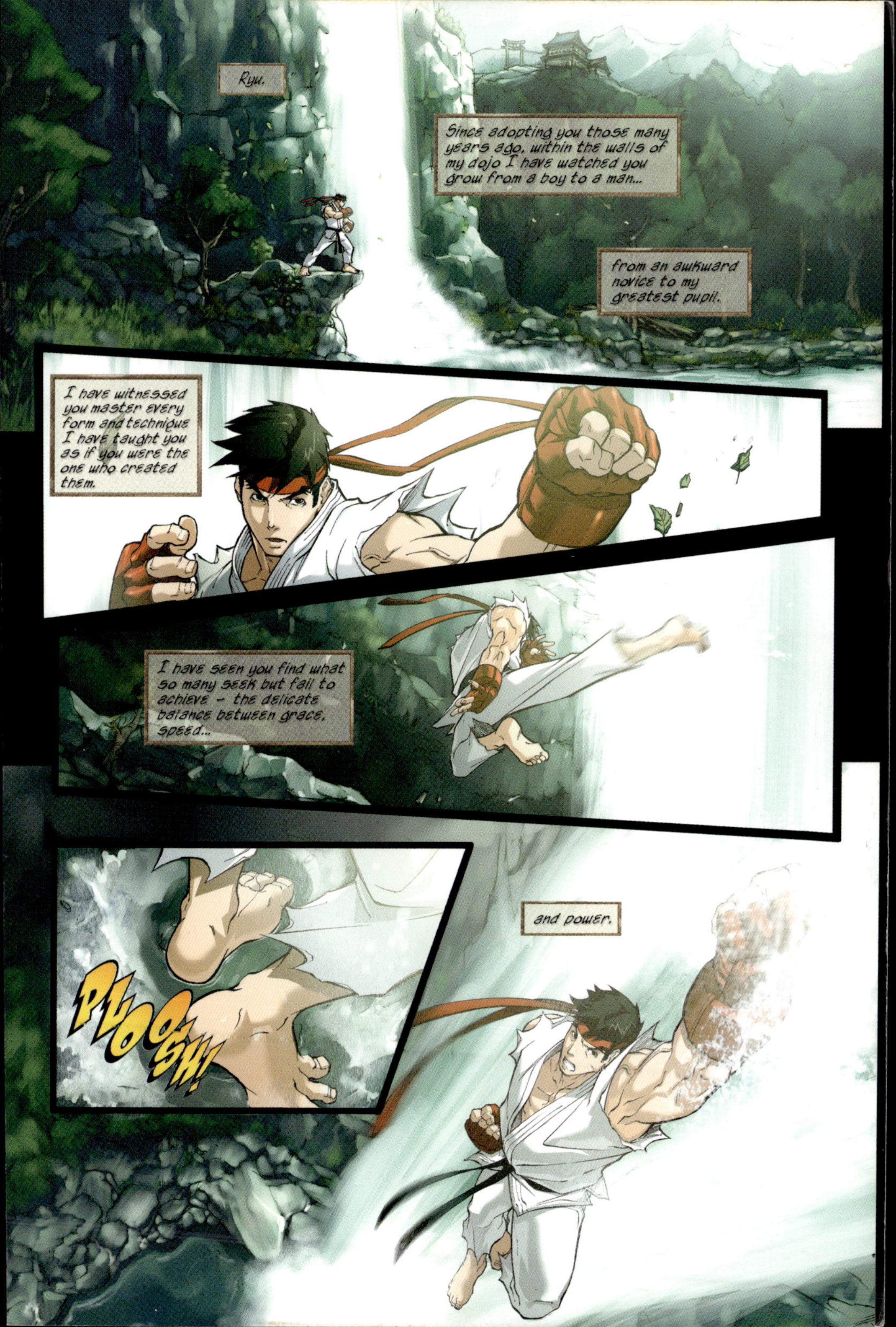
Ryu.
Since adopting you those many years ago, within the walls of my dojo I have watched you grow from a boy to a man...
from an awkward novice to my greatest pupil.
I have witnessed you master every form and technique I have taught you as if you were the one who created them.
I have seen you find what so many seek but fail to achieve - the delicate balance between grace, speed...
PLOOSH!
and power.

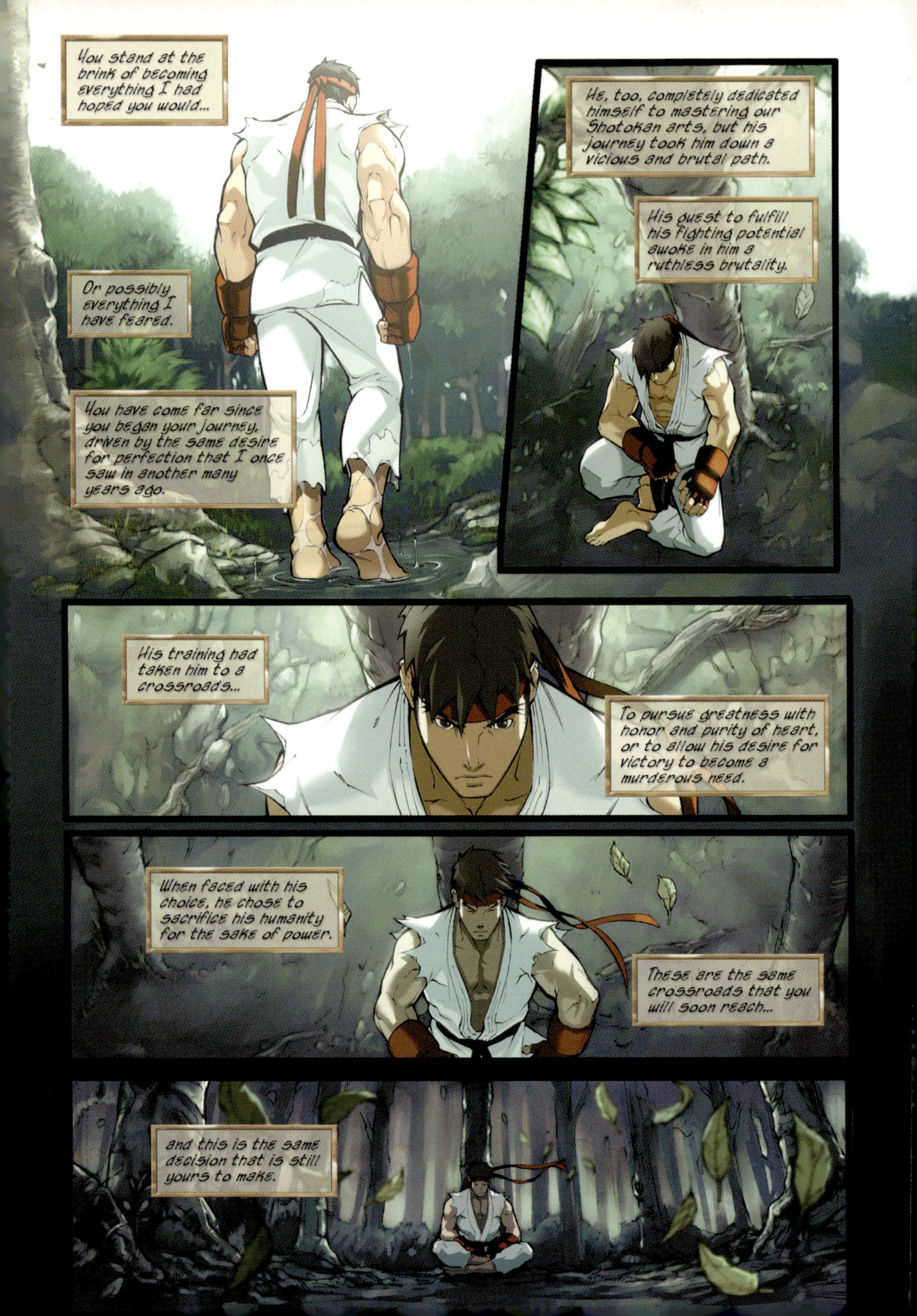
You stand at the brink of becoming everything I had hoped you would...
Or possibly everything I have feared.
You have come far since you began your journey, driven by the same desire for perfection that I once saw in another many years ago.
He, too, completely dedicated himself to mastering our Shotokan arts, but his journey took him down a vicious and brutal path.
His quest to fulfill his fighting potential awoke in him a ruthless brutality.
His training had taken him to a crossroads...
To pursue greatness with honor and purity of heart, or to allow his desire for victory to become a murderous need.
When faced with his choice, he chose to sacrifice his humanity for the sake of power.
These are the same crossroads that you will soon reach...
and this is the same decision that is still yours to make.

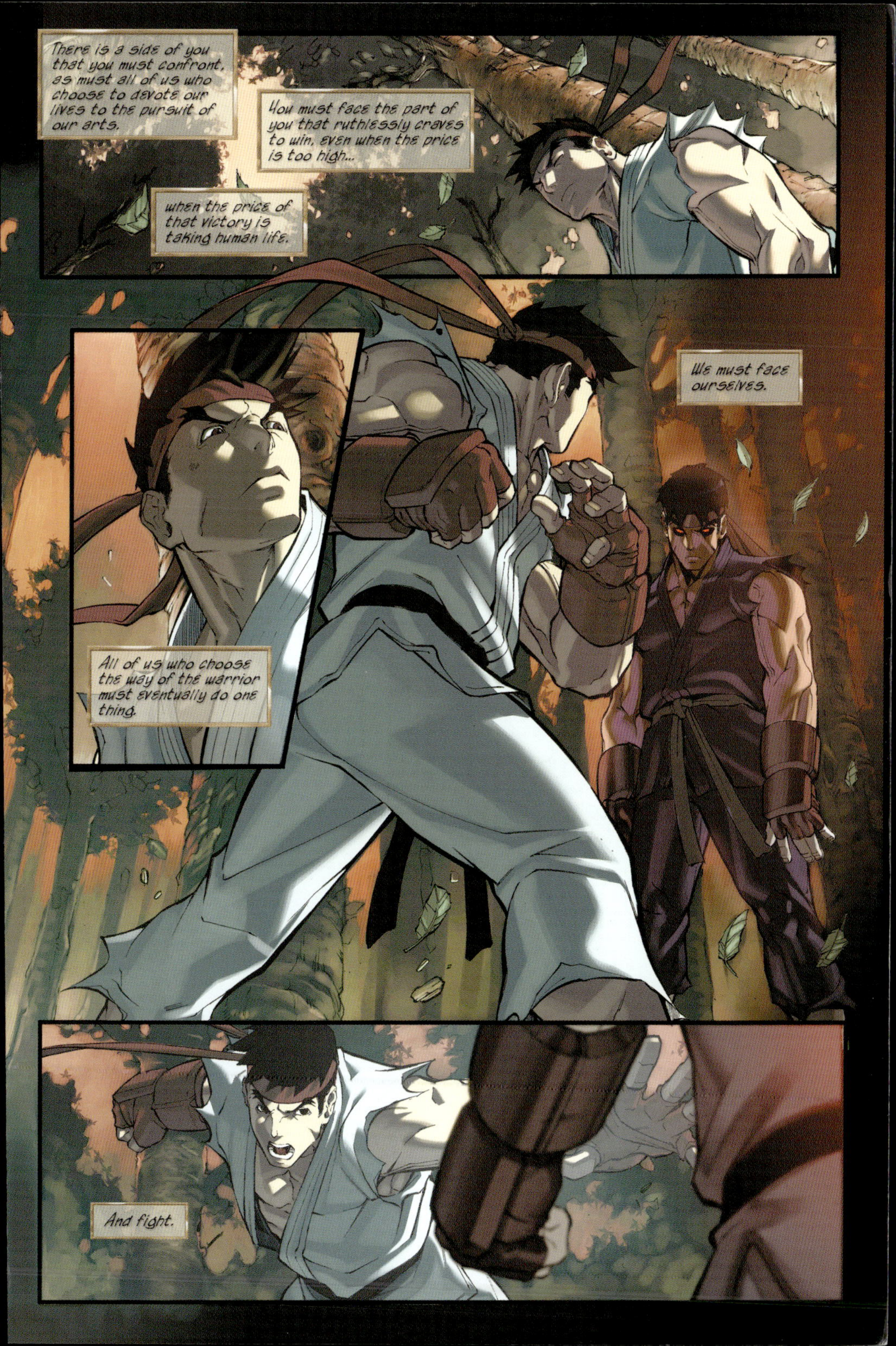
There is a side of you that you must confront, as must all of us who choose to devote our lives to the pursuit of our arts.
You must face the part of you that ruthlessly craves to win, even when the price is too high...
when the price of that victory is taking human life.
We must face ourselves.
All of us who choose the way of the warrior must eventually do one thing.
And fight.

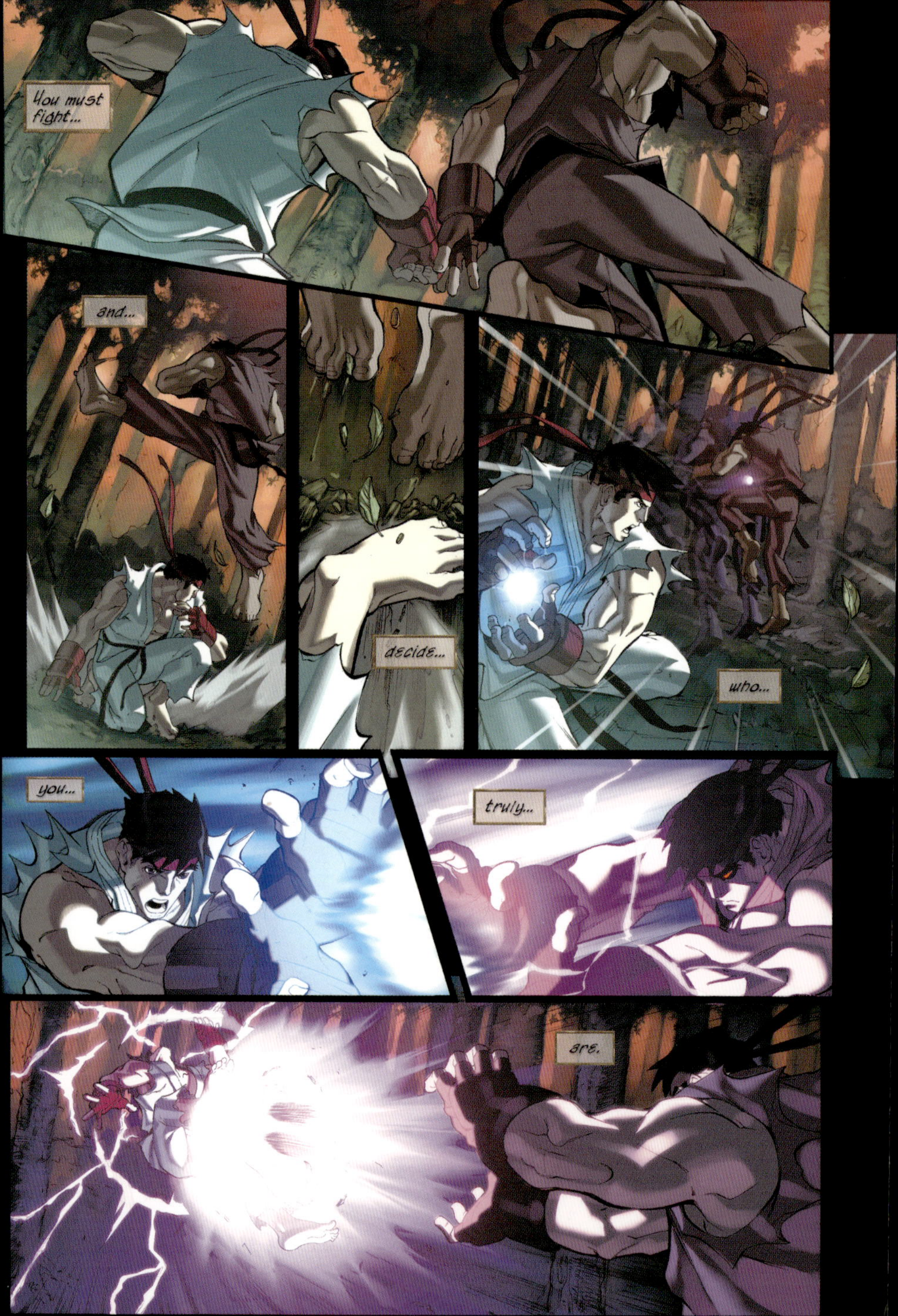
You must fight...
and...
decide...
who...
you...
truly...
are.

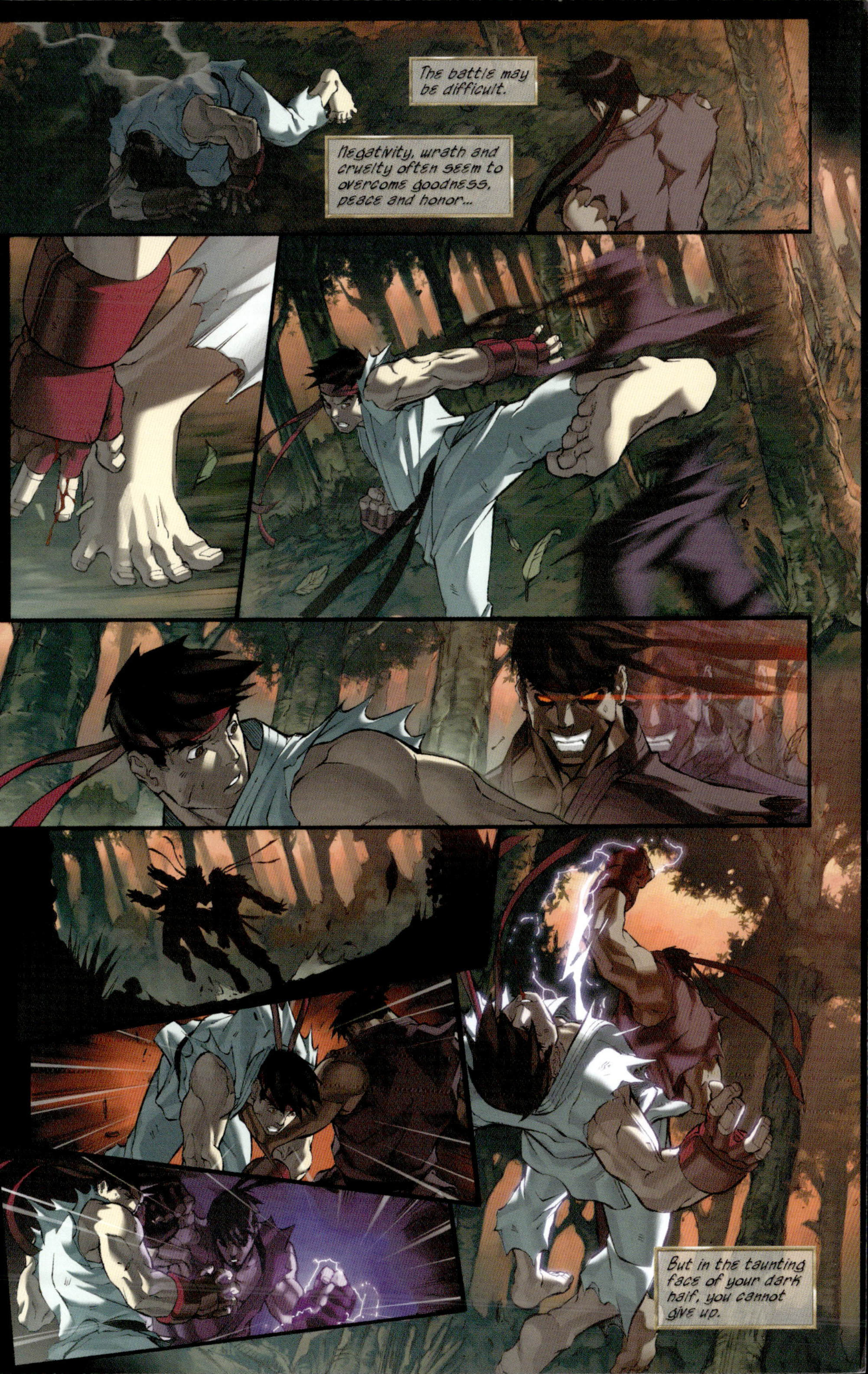
The battle may be difficult.
Negativity, wrath and cruelty often seem to overcome goodness, peace and honor...
But in the taunting face of your dark half, you cannot give up.

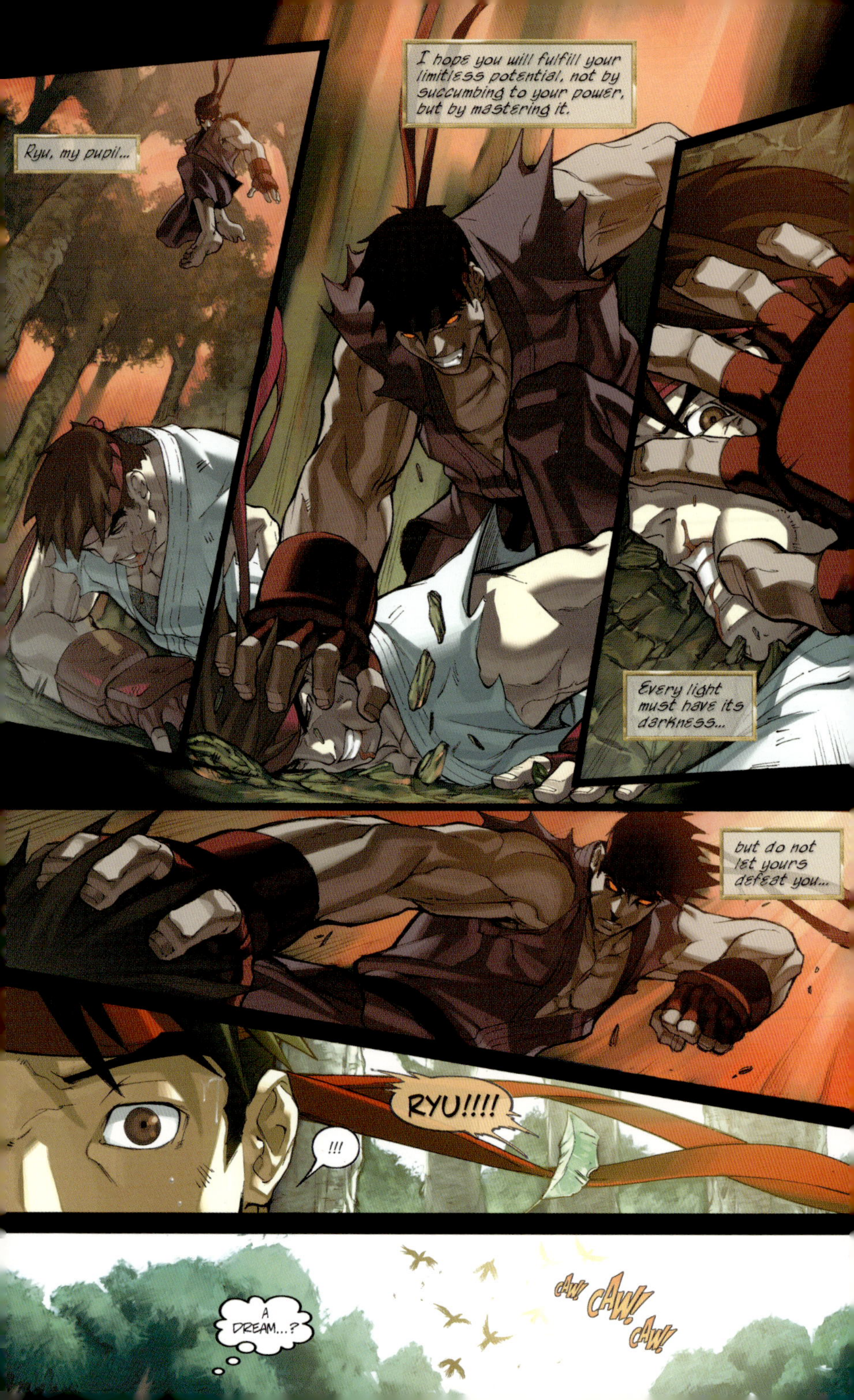

Ryu, my pupil...
I hope you will fulfill your limitless potential, not by succumbing to your power, but by mastering it.
Every light must have its darkness...
but do not let yours defeat you...
RYU!!!!
!!!
A DREAM...?
CAW! CAW! CAW!

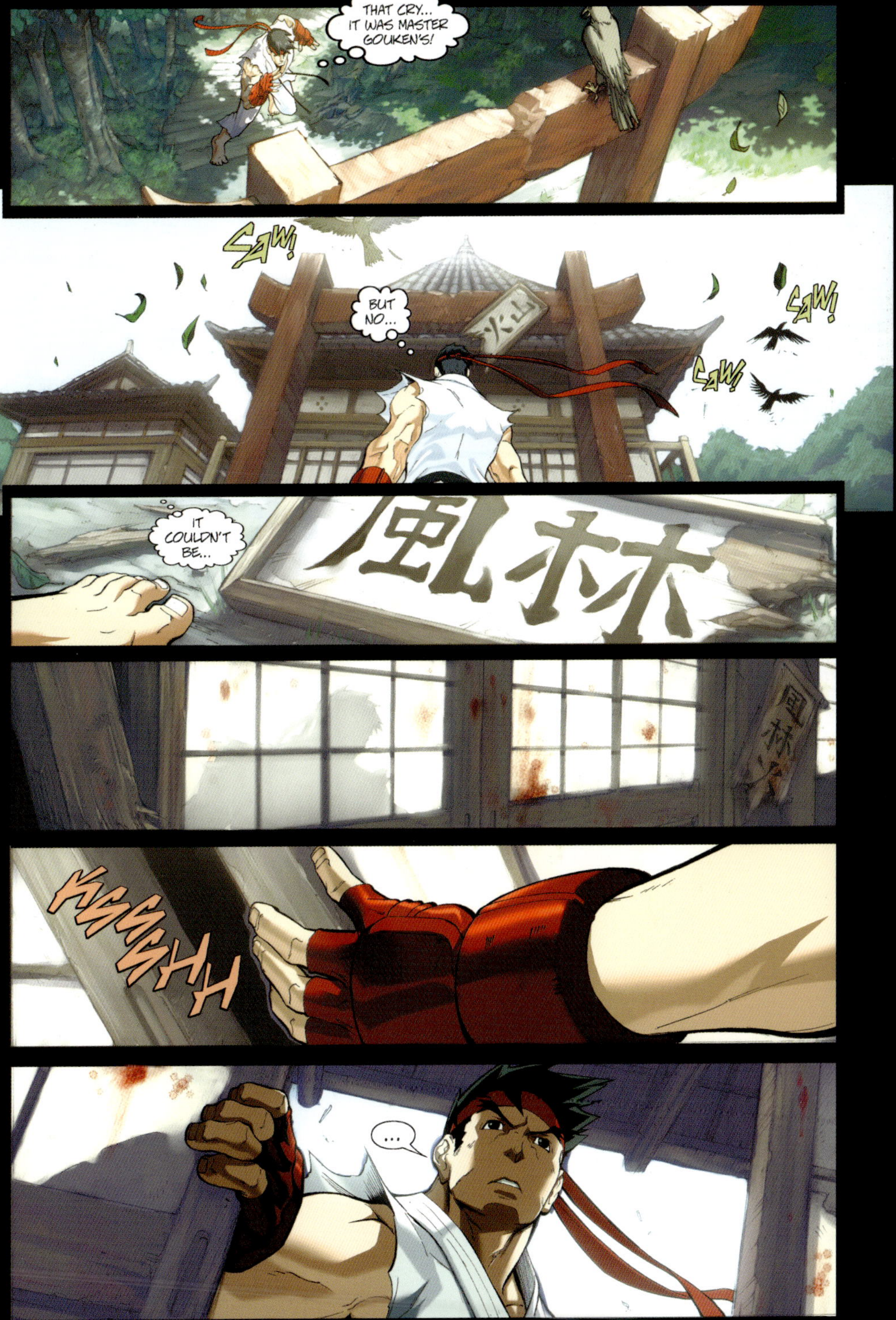
THAT CRY... IT WAS MASTER GOUKEN'S!
SAW!
BUT NO...
SAW!
SAW!
IT COULDN'T BE...
風林
KSSSHH
...

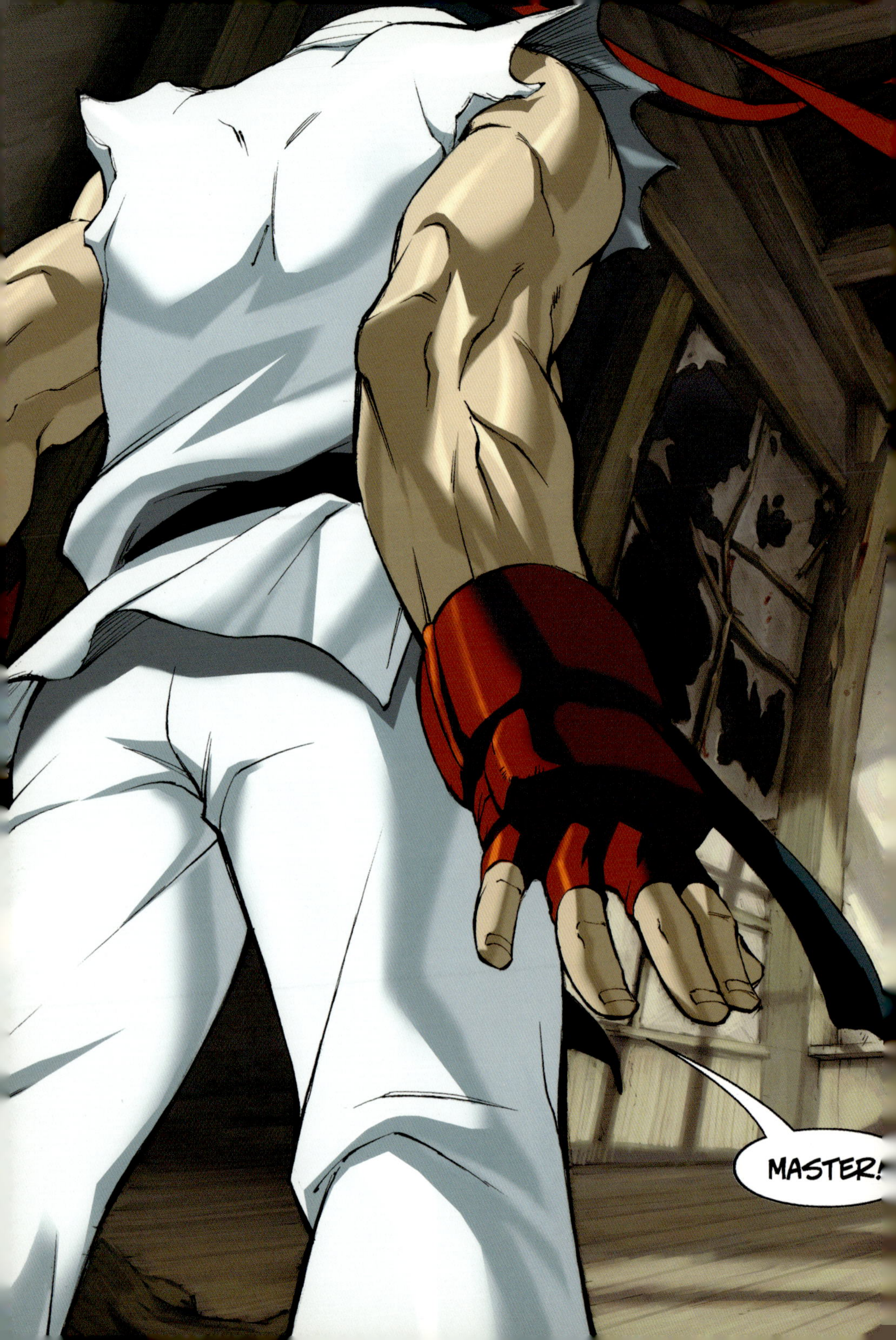
MASTER!

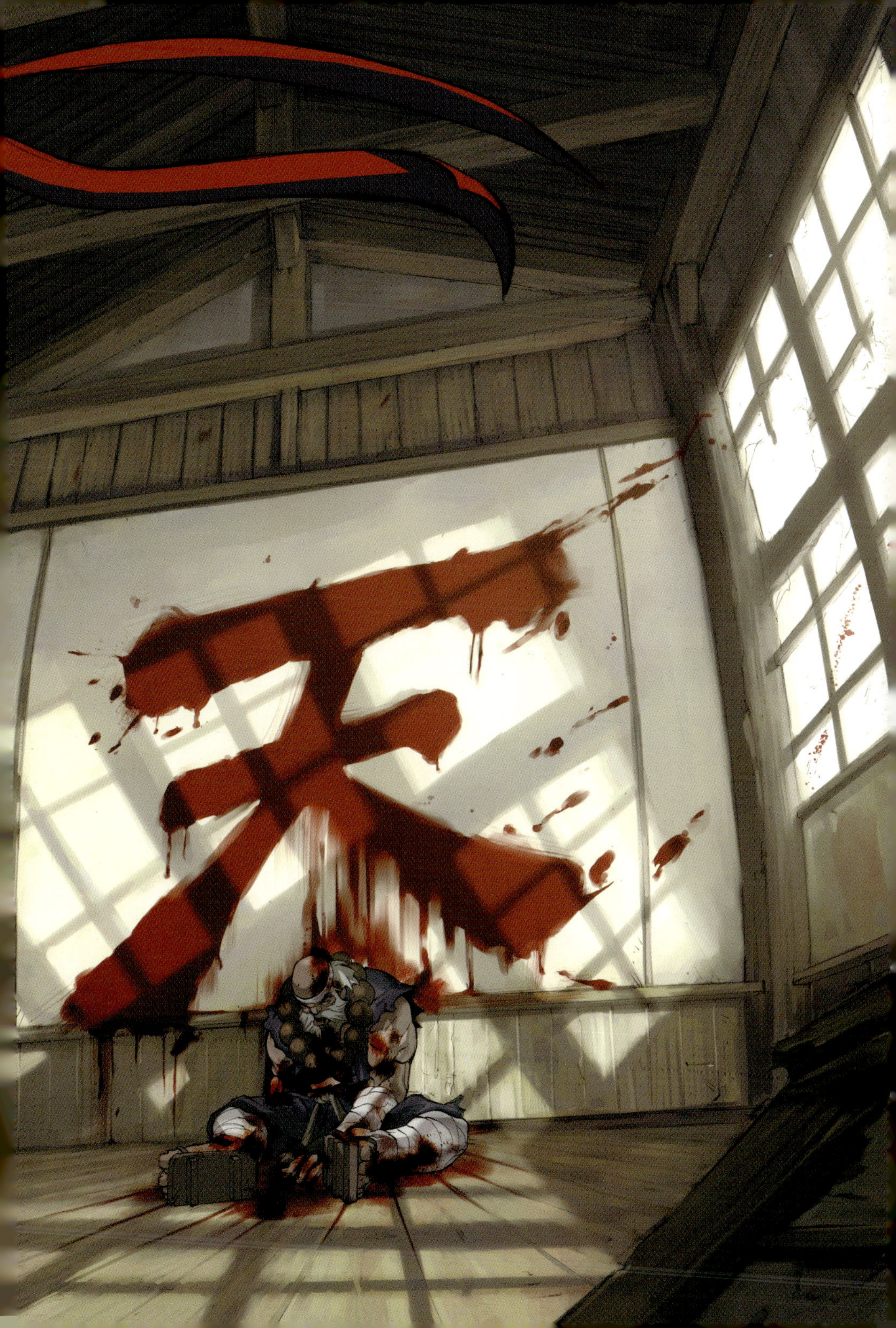
天

Cover Art by: Arnold Tsang

Chapter 01: OLD FRIENDS

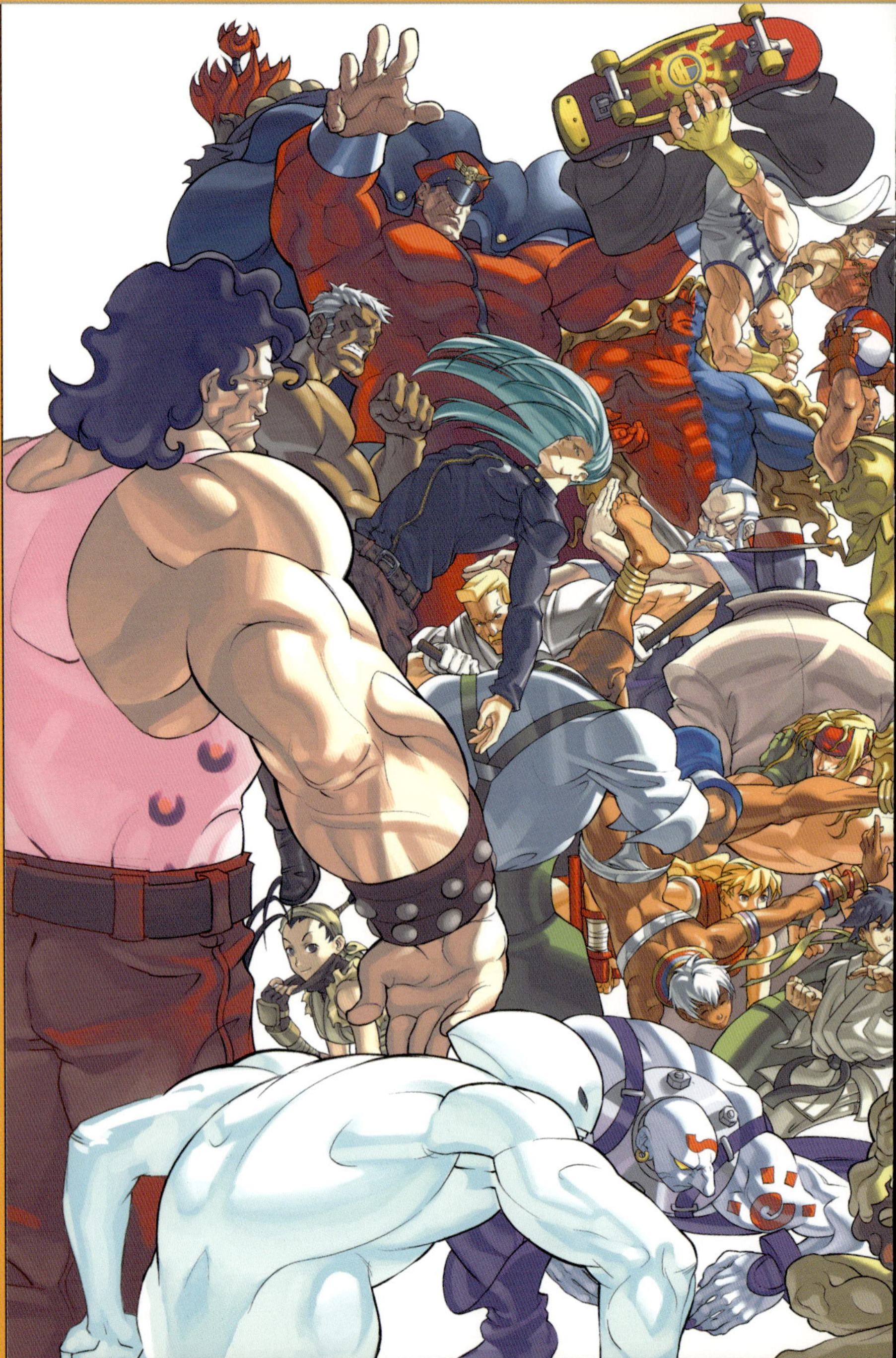

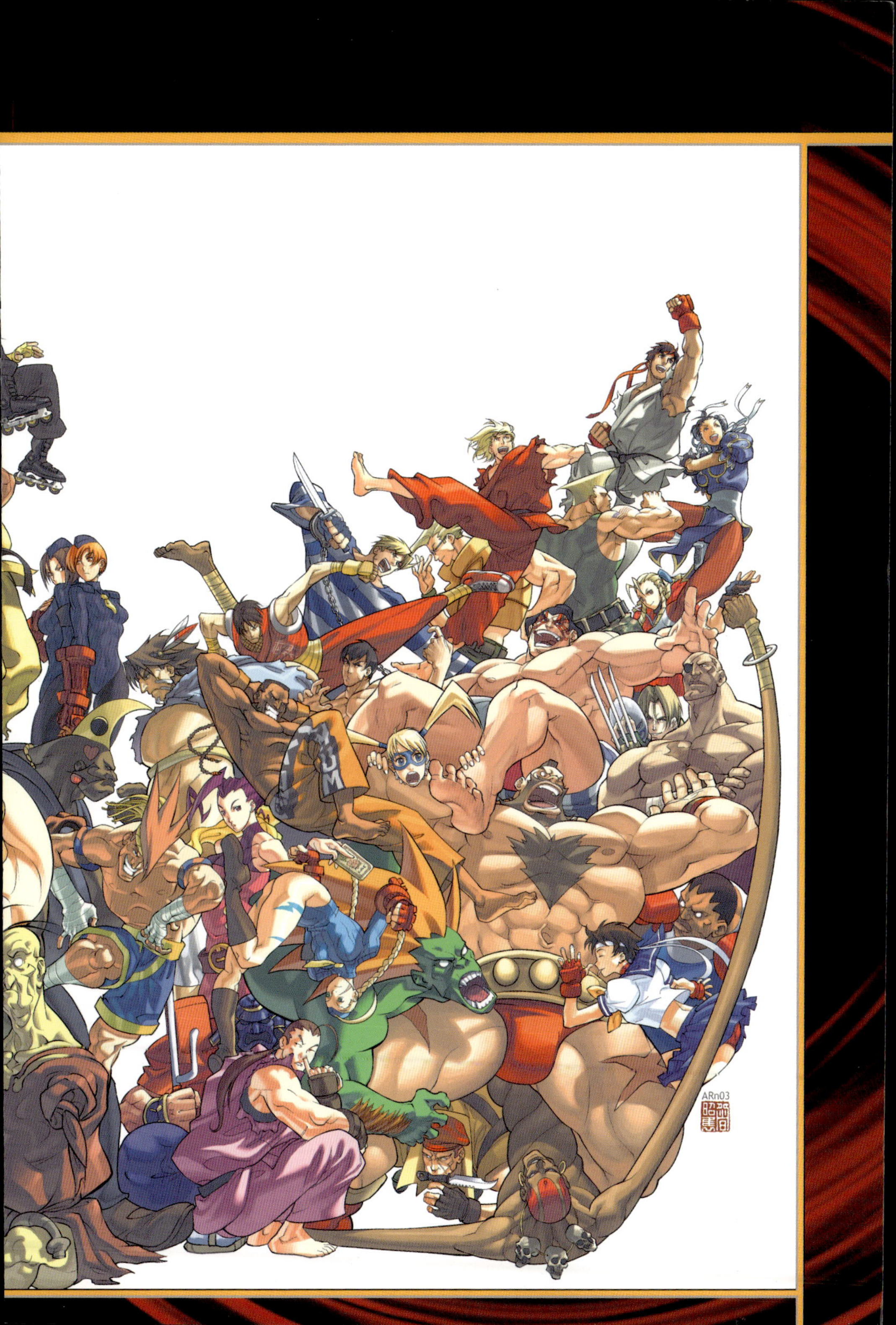
ARn03

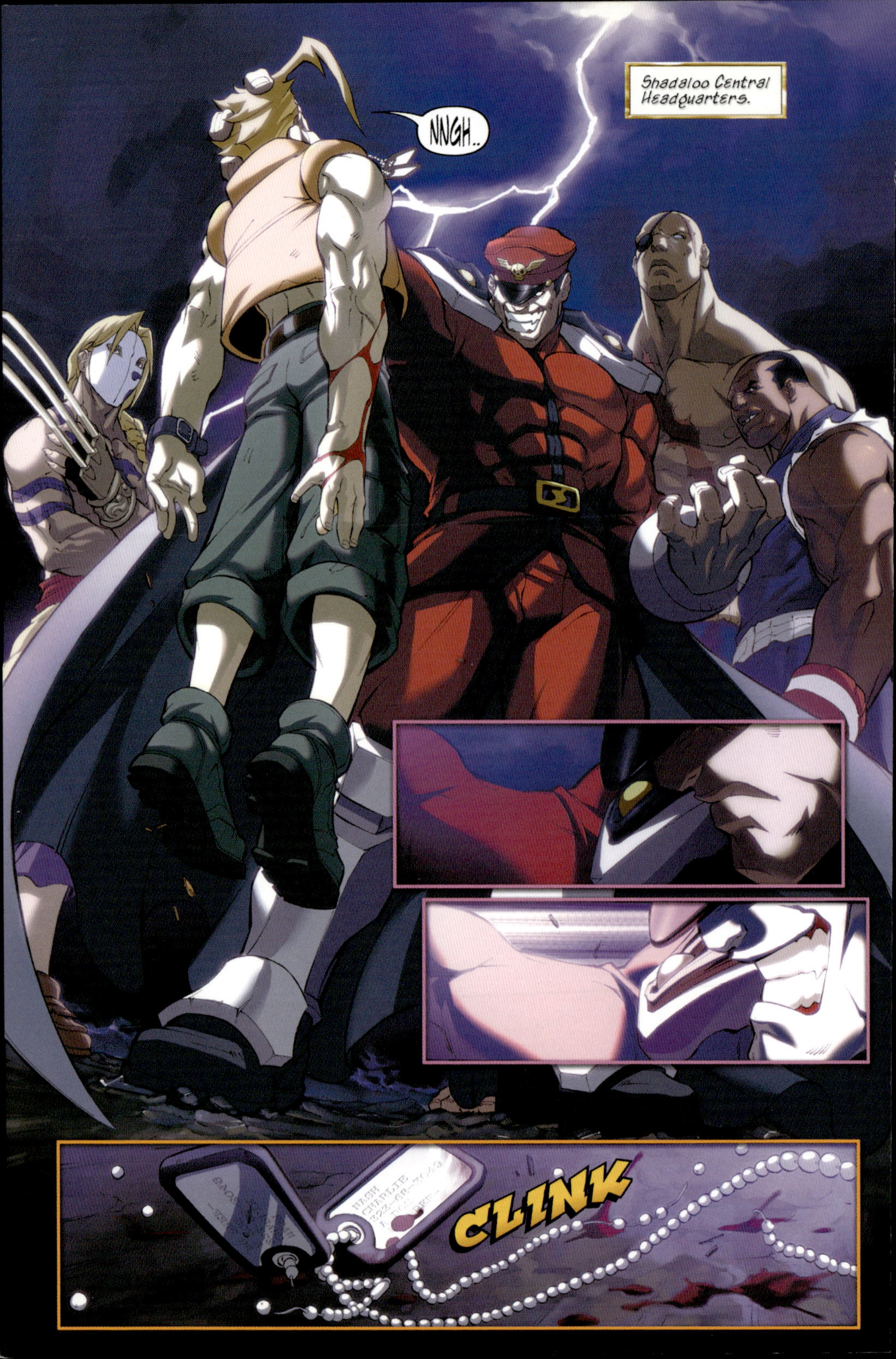
Shadaloo Central Headquarters.
NNGH..
NASH
CHARLIE
CLINK

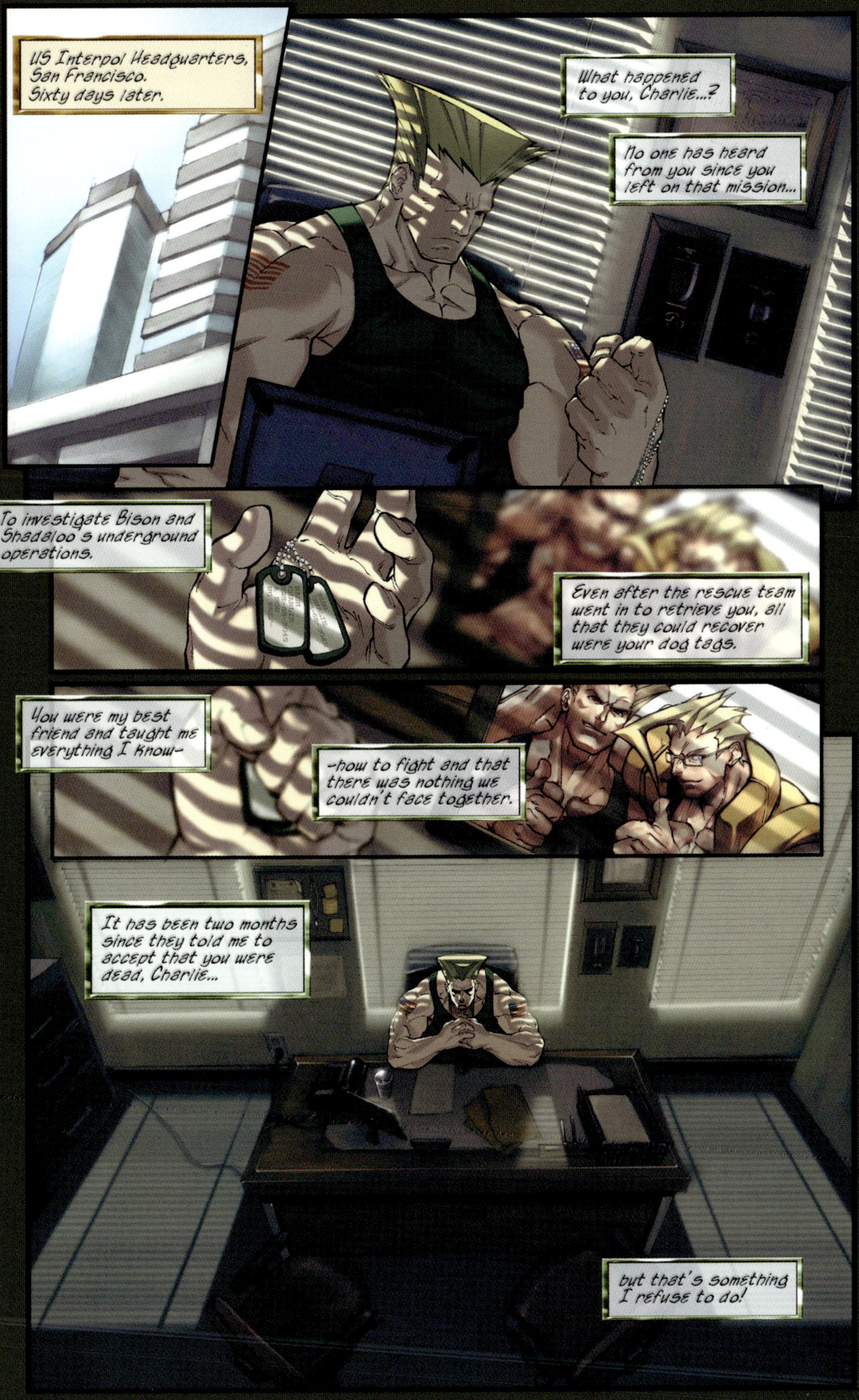
US Interpol Headquarters, San Francisco. Sixty days later.
What happened to you, Charlie...?
No one has heard from you since you left on that mission...
To investigate Bison and Shadaloo's underground operations.
Even after the rescue team went in to retrieve you, all that they could recover were your dog tags.
You were my best friend and taught me everything I know-
-how to fight and that there was nothing we couldn't face together.
It has been two months since they told me to accept that you were dead, Charlie...
but that's something I refuse to do!

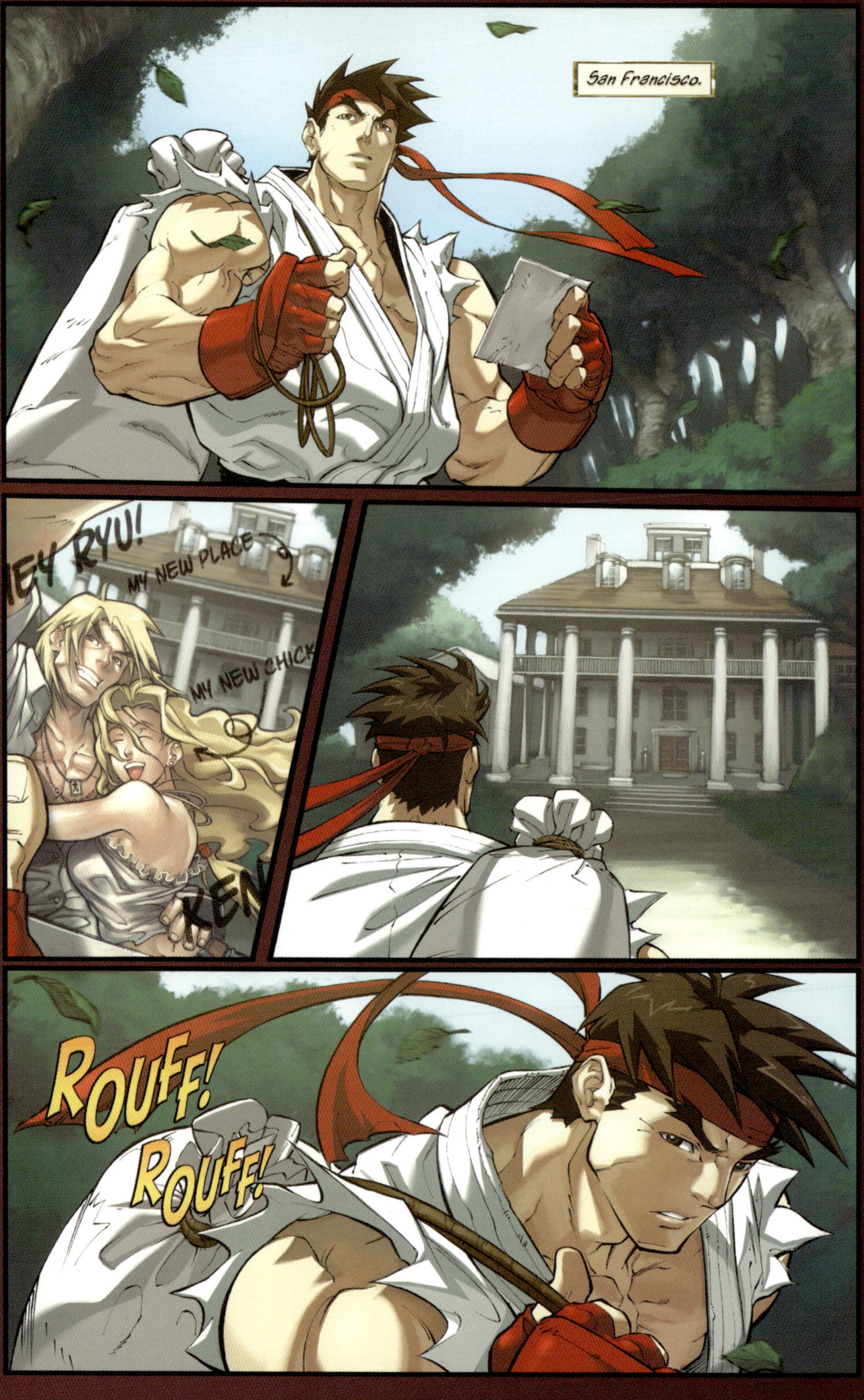
San Francisco.
HEY RYU!
MY NEW PLACE
MY NEW CHICK
KEN
ROUFF!
ROUFF!

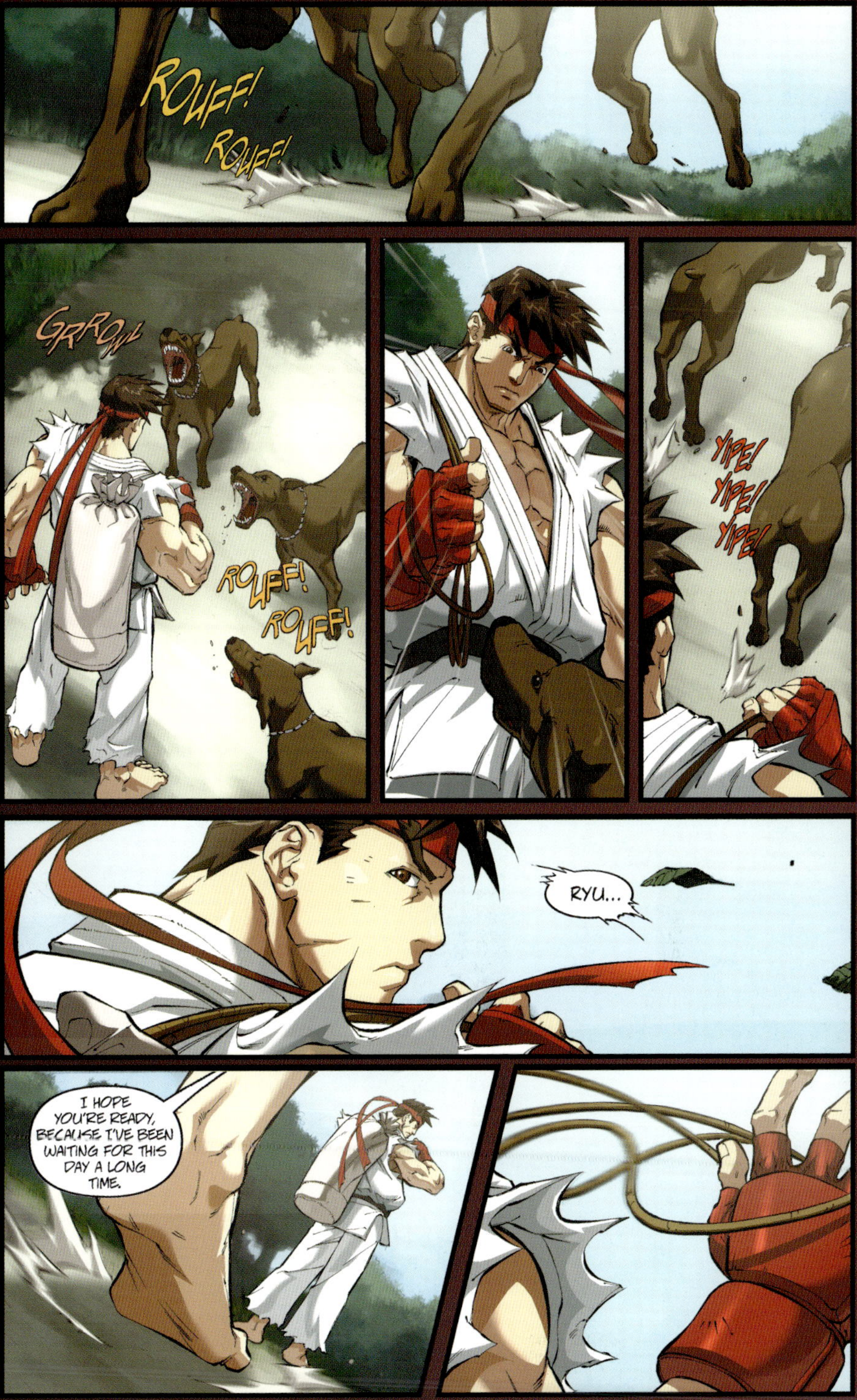
ROUFF!
ROUFF!
GRROWL
ROUFF!
ROUFF!
YIPE!
YIPE!
YIPE!
RYU...
I HOPE YOU'RE READY, BECAUSE I'VE BEEN WAITING FOR THIS DAY A LONG TIME.

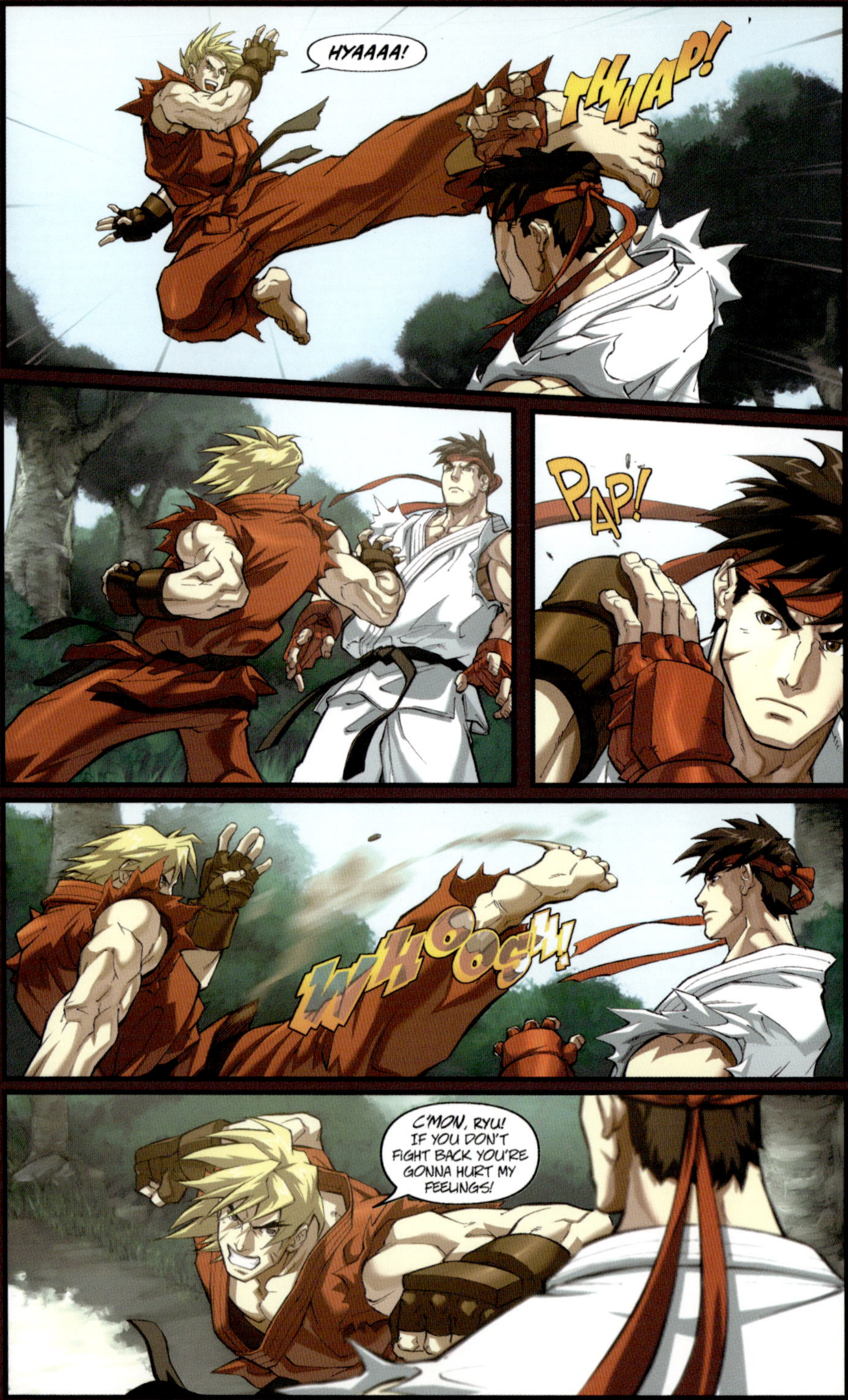
HYAAAA!
THWAP!
PAP!
WHOOSH!
C'MON, RYU! IF YOU DON'T FIGHT BACK YOU'RE GONNA HURT MY FEELINGS!

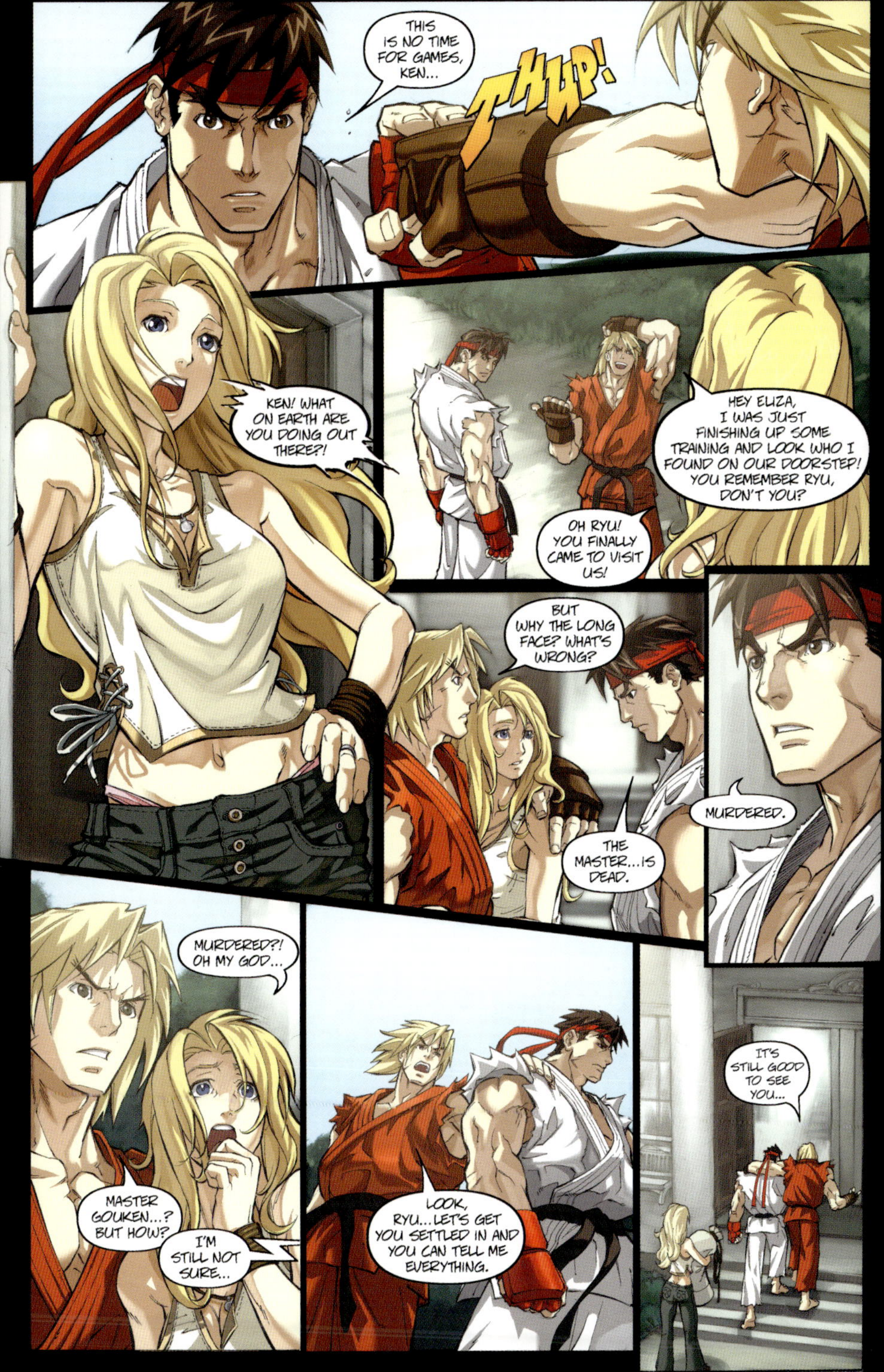
THIS IS NO TIME FOR GAMES, KEN...
THUP!
KEN! WHAT ON EARTH ARE YOU DOING OUT THERE?!
HEY ELIZA, I WAS JUST FINISHING UP SOME TRAINING AND LOOK WHO I FOUND ON OUR DOORSTEP! YOU REMEMBER RYU, DON'T YOU?
OH RYU! YOU FINALLY CAME TO VISIT US!
BUT WHY THE LONG FACE? WHAT'S WRONG?
THE MASTER...IS DEAD.
MURDERED.
MURDERED?! OH MY GOD...
MASTER GOUKEN...? BUT HOW?
I'M STILL NOT SURE...
LOOK, RYU...LET'S GET YOU SETTLED IN AND YOU CAN TELL ME EVERYTHING.
IT'S STILL GOOD TO SEE YOU...

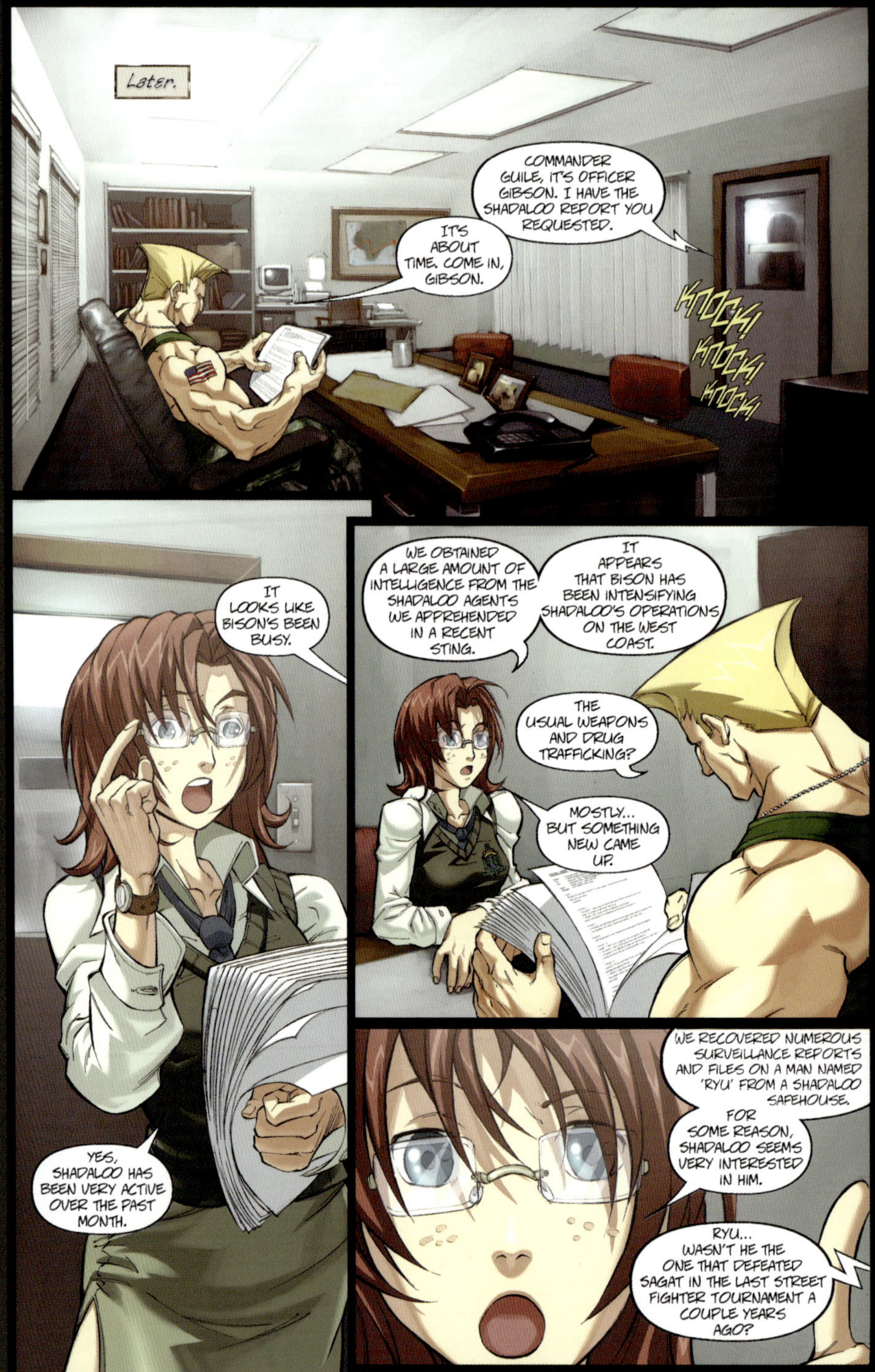
Later.
COMMANDER GUILE, IT'S OFFICER GIBSON. I HAVE THE SHADALOO REPORT YOU REQUESTED.
IT'S ABOUT TIME. COME IN, GIBSON.
KNOCK! KNOCK! KNOCK!
IT LOOKS LIKE BISON'S BEEN BUSY.
YES, SHADALOO HAS BEEN VERY ACTIVE OVER THE PAST MONTH.
WE OBTAINED A LARGE AMOUNT OF INTELLIGENCE FROM THE SHADALOO AGENTS WE APPREHENDED IN A RECENT STING.
IT APPEARS THAT BISON HAS BEEN INTENSIFYING SHADALOO'S OPERATIONS ON THE WEST COAST.
THE USUAL WEAPONS AND DRUG TRAFFICKING?
MOSTLY... BUT SOMETHING NEW CAME UP.
WE RECOVERED NUMEROUS SURVEILLANCE REPORTS AND FILES ON A MAN NAMED 'RYU' FROM A SHADALOO SAFEHOUSE.
FOR SOME REASON, SHADALOO SEEMS VERY INTERESTED IN HIM.
RYU... WASN'T HE THE ONE THAT DEFEATED SAGAT IN THE LAST STREET FIGHTER TOURNAMENT A COUPLE YEARS AGO?

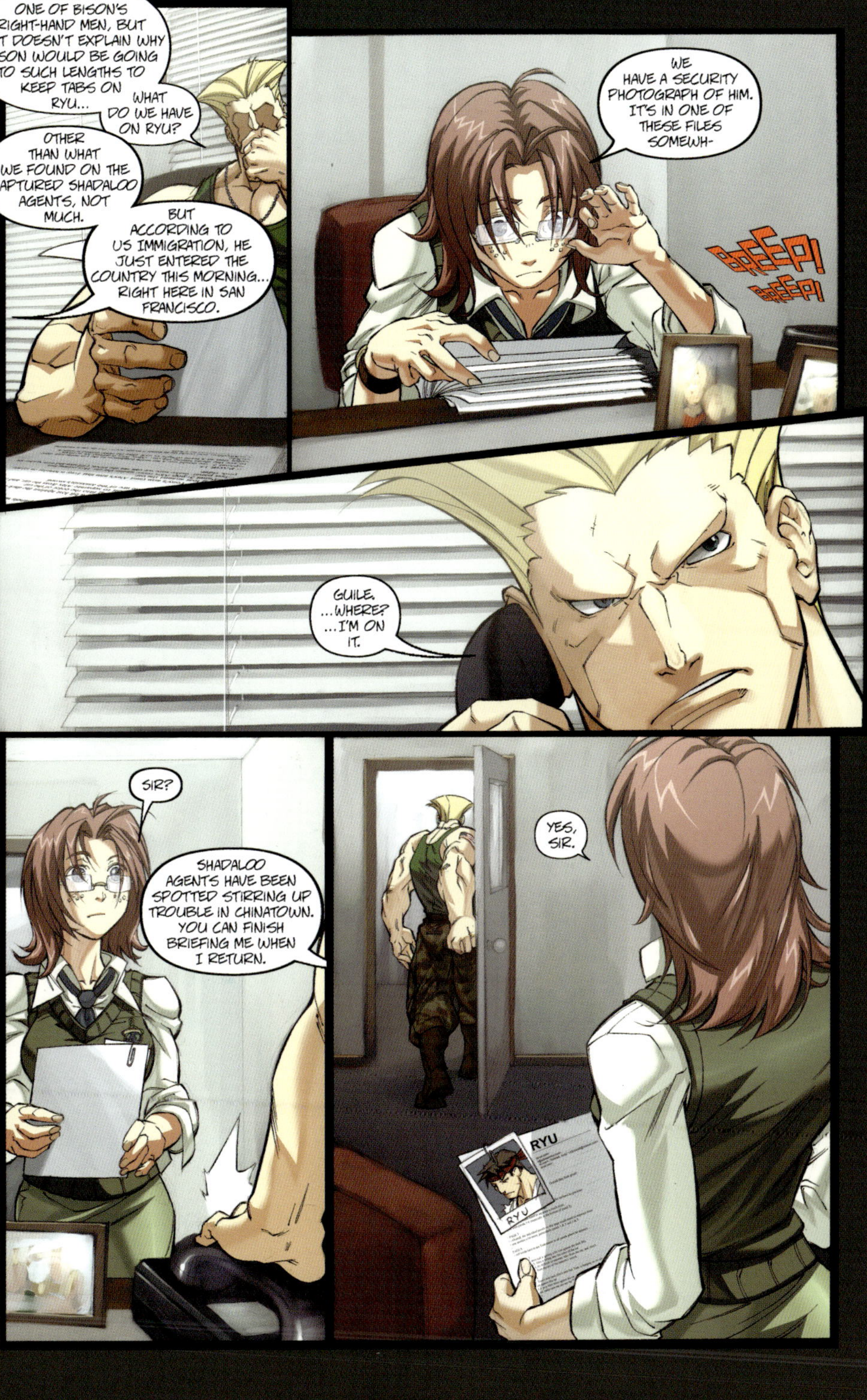
SAGAT IS ONE OF BISON'S RIGHT-HAND MEN, BUT THAT DOESN'T EXPLAIN WHY BISON WOULD BE GOING TO SUCH LENGTHS TO KEEP TABS ON RYU...
WHAT DO WE HAVE ON RYU?
OTHER THAN WHAT WE FOUND ON THE CAPTURED SHADALOO AGENTS, NOT MUCH.
BUT ACCORDING TO US IMMIGRATION, HE JUST ENTERED THE COUNTRY THIS MORNING... RIGHT HERE IN SAN FRANCISCO.
WE HAVE A SECURITY PHOTOGRAPH OF HIM. IT'S IN ONE OF THESE FILES SOMEWH-
BREEP! BREEP!
GUILE. ...WHERE? ...I'M ON IT.
SIR?
SHADALOO AGENTS HAVE BEEN SPOTTED STIRRING UP TROUBLE IN CHINATOWN. YOU CAN FINISH BRIEFING ME WHEN I RETURN.
YES, SIR.
RYU
RYU

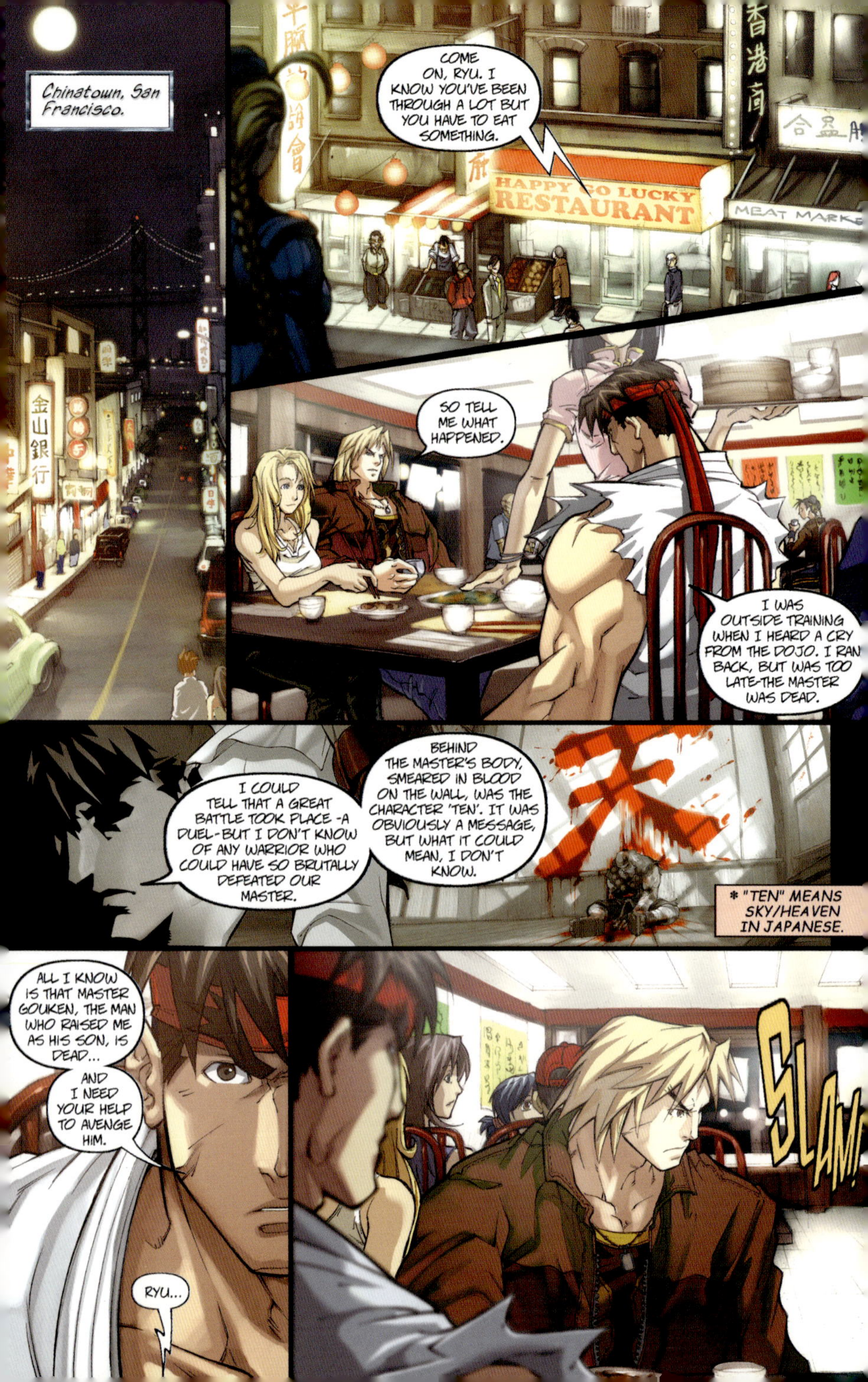
Chinatown, San Francisco.
COME ON, RYU. I KNOW YOU'VE BEEN THROUGH A LOT BUT YOU HAVE TO EAT SOMETHING.
HAPPY GO LUCKY RESTAURANT
MEAT MARKE
SO TELL ME WHAT HAPPENED.
I WAS OUTSIDE TRAINING WHEN I HEARD A CRY FROM THE DOJO. I RAN BACK, BUT WAS TOO LATE-THE MASTER WAS DEAD.
I COULD TELL THAT A GREAT BATTLE TOOK PLACE -A DUEL- BUT I DON'T KNOW OF ANY WARRIOR WHO COULD HAVE SO BRUTALLY DEFEATED OUR MASTER.
BEHIND THE MASTER'S BODY, SMEARED IN BLOOD ON THE WALL, WAS THE CHARACTER 'TEN'. IT WAS OBVIOUSLY A MESSAGE, BUT WHAT IT COULD MEAN, I DON'T KNOW.
* "TEN" MEANS SKY/HEAVEN IN JAPANESE.
ALL I KNOW IS THAT MASTER GOUKEN, THE MAN WHO RAISED ME AS HIS SON, IS DEAD...
AND I NEED YOUR HELP TO AVENGE HIM.
RYU...
SLAM!

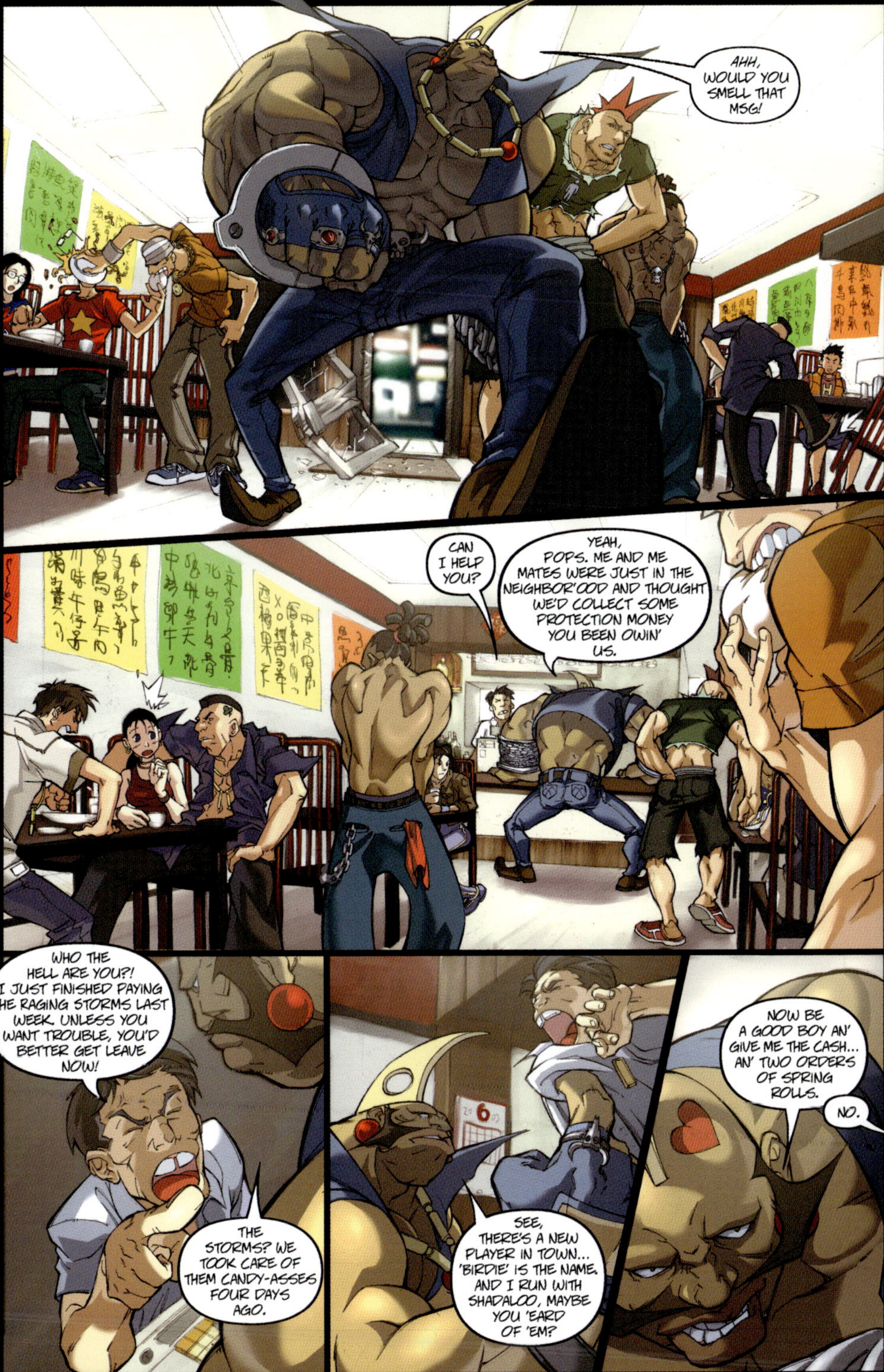
AHH, WOULD YOU SMELL THAT MSG!
CAN I HELP YOU?
YEAH, POPS. ME AND ME MATES WERE JUST IN THE NEIGHBOR'OOD AND THOUGHT WE'D COLLECT SOME PROTECTION MONEY YOU BEEN OWIN' US.
WHO THE HELL ARE YOU?! I JUST FINISHED PAYING THE RAGING STORMS LAST WEEK. UNLESS YOU WANT TROUBLE, YOU'D BETTER GET LEAVE NOW!
THE STORMS? WE TOOK CARE OF THEM CANDY-ASSES FOUR DAYS AGO.
SEE, THERE'S A NEW PLAYER IN TOWN... 'BIRDIE' IS THE NAME. AND I RUN WITH SHADALOO, MAYBE YOU 'EARD OF 'EM?
NOW BE A GOOD BOY AN' GIVE ME THE CASH... AN' TWO ORDERS OF SPRING ROLLS.
NO.

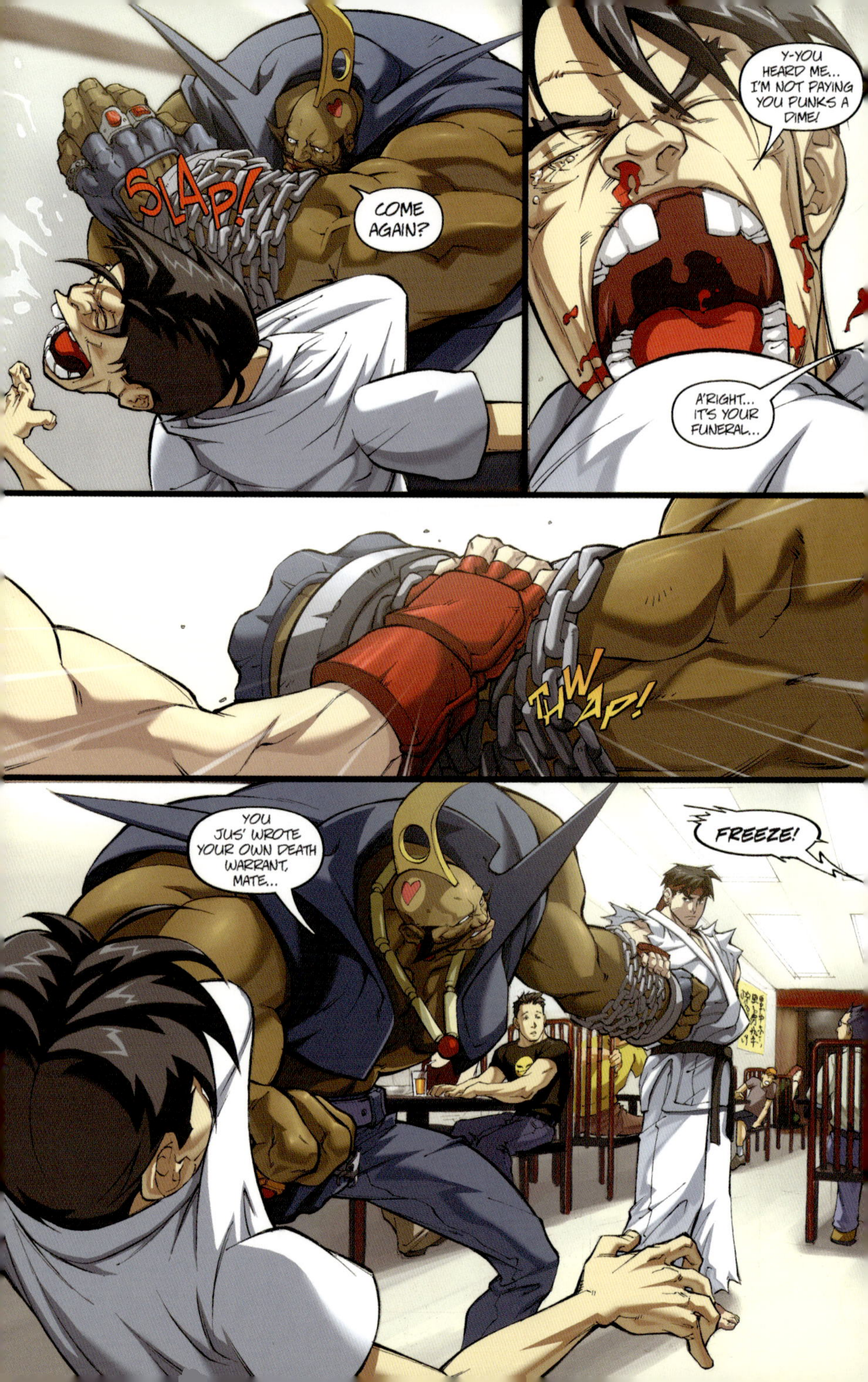
SLAP!
COME AGAIN?
Y-YOU HEARD ME... I'M NOT PAYING YOU PUNKS A DIME!
A'RIGHT... IT'S YOUR FUNERAL...
THWAP!
YOU JUS' WROTE YOUR OWN DEATH WARRANT, MATE...
FREEZE!

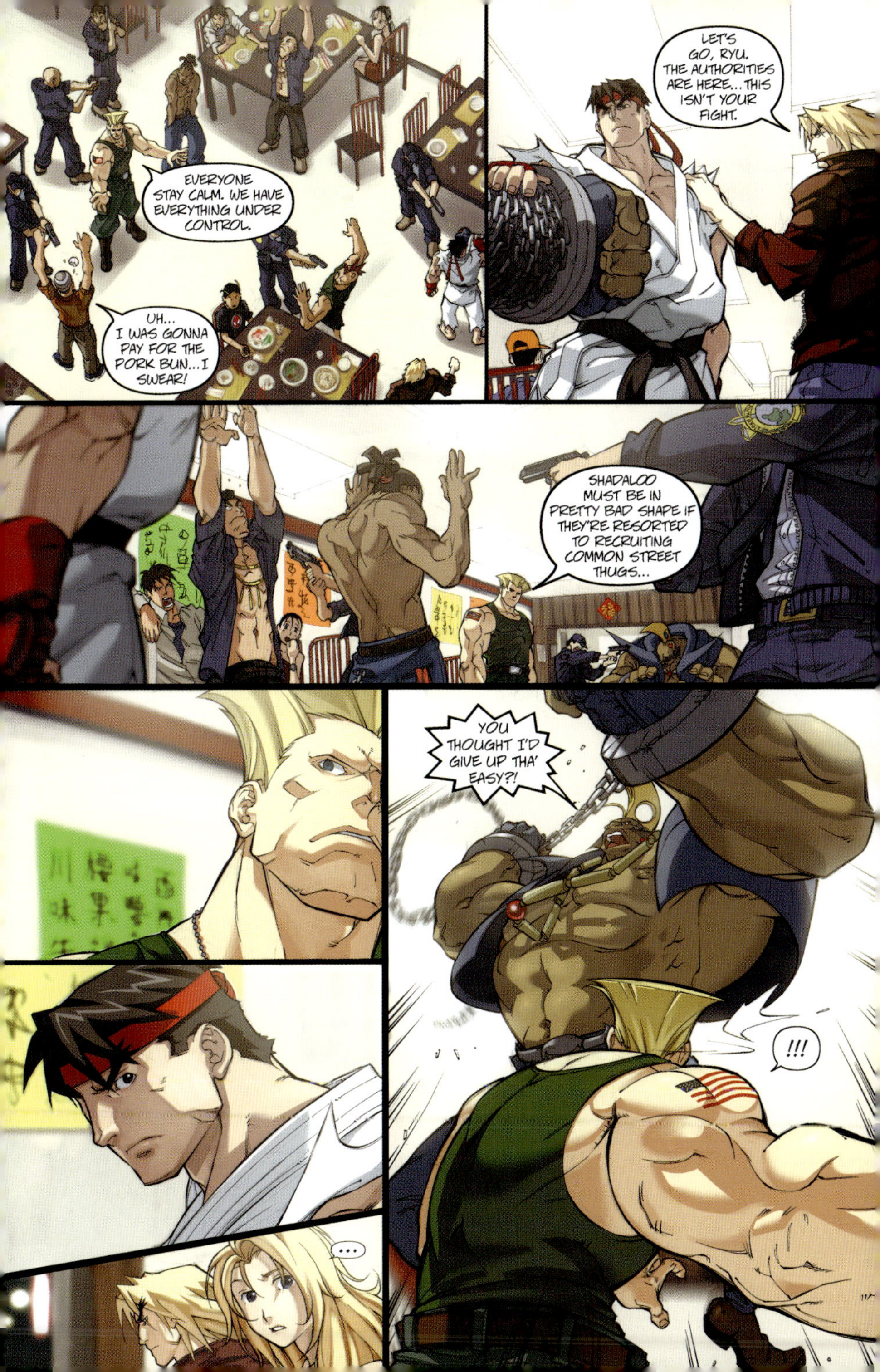
EVERYONE STAY CALM. WE HAVE EVERYTHING UNDER CONTROL.
UH... I WAS GONNA PAY FOR THE PORK BUN... I SWEAR!
LET'S GO, RYU. THE AUTHORITIES ARE HERE... THIS ISN'T YOUR FIGHT.
SHADALOO MUST BE IN PRETTY BAD SHAPE IF THEY'RE RESORTED TO RECRUITING COMMON STREET THUGS...
YOU THOUGHT I'D GIVE UP THA' EASY?!
!!!
...

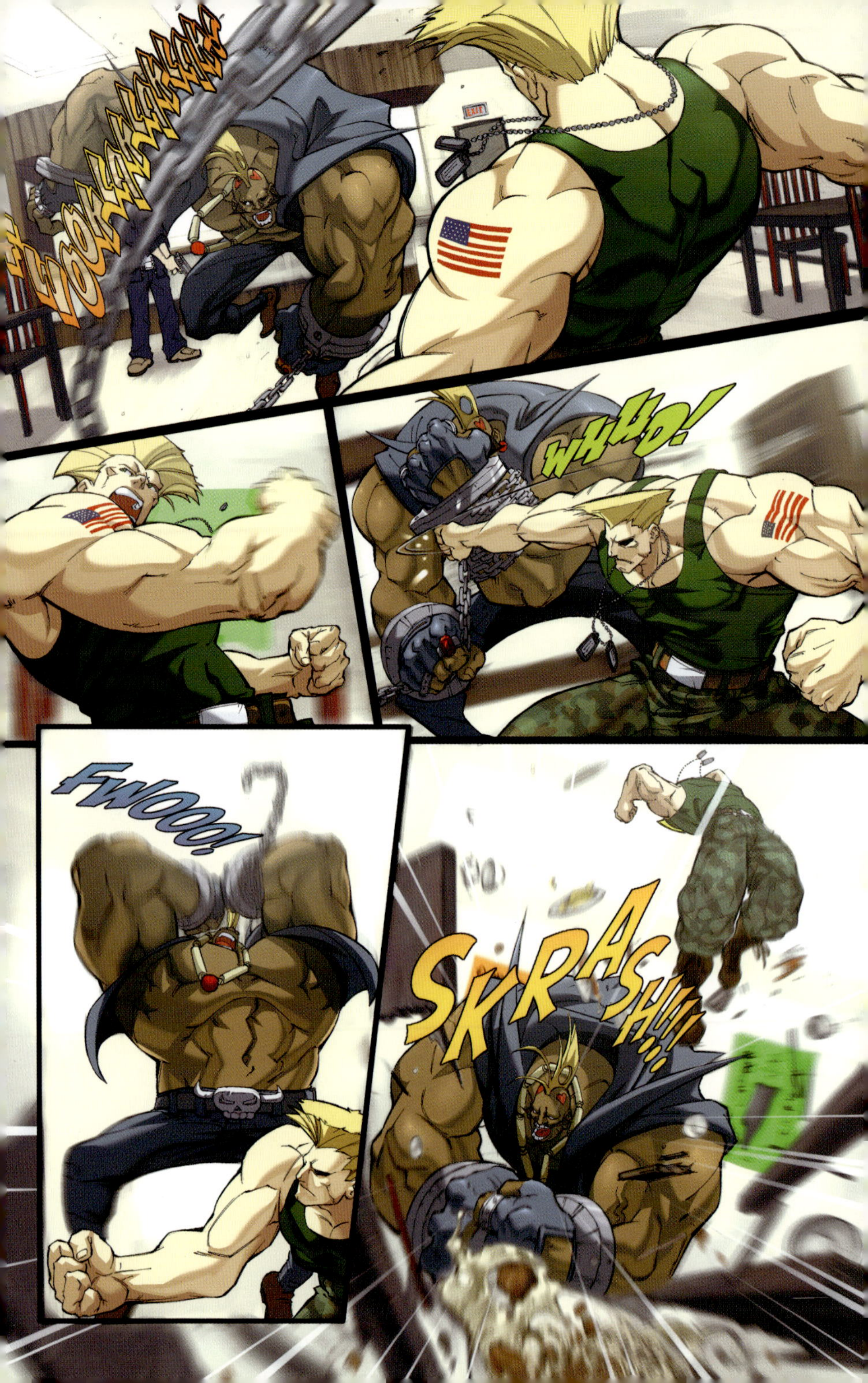
EXIT
WHUD!
FWOOOO!
SKRASH!!!

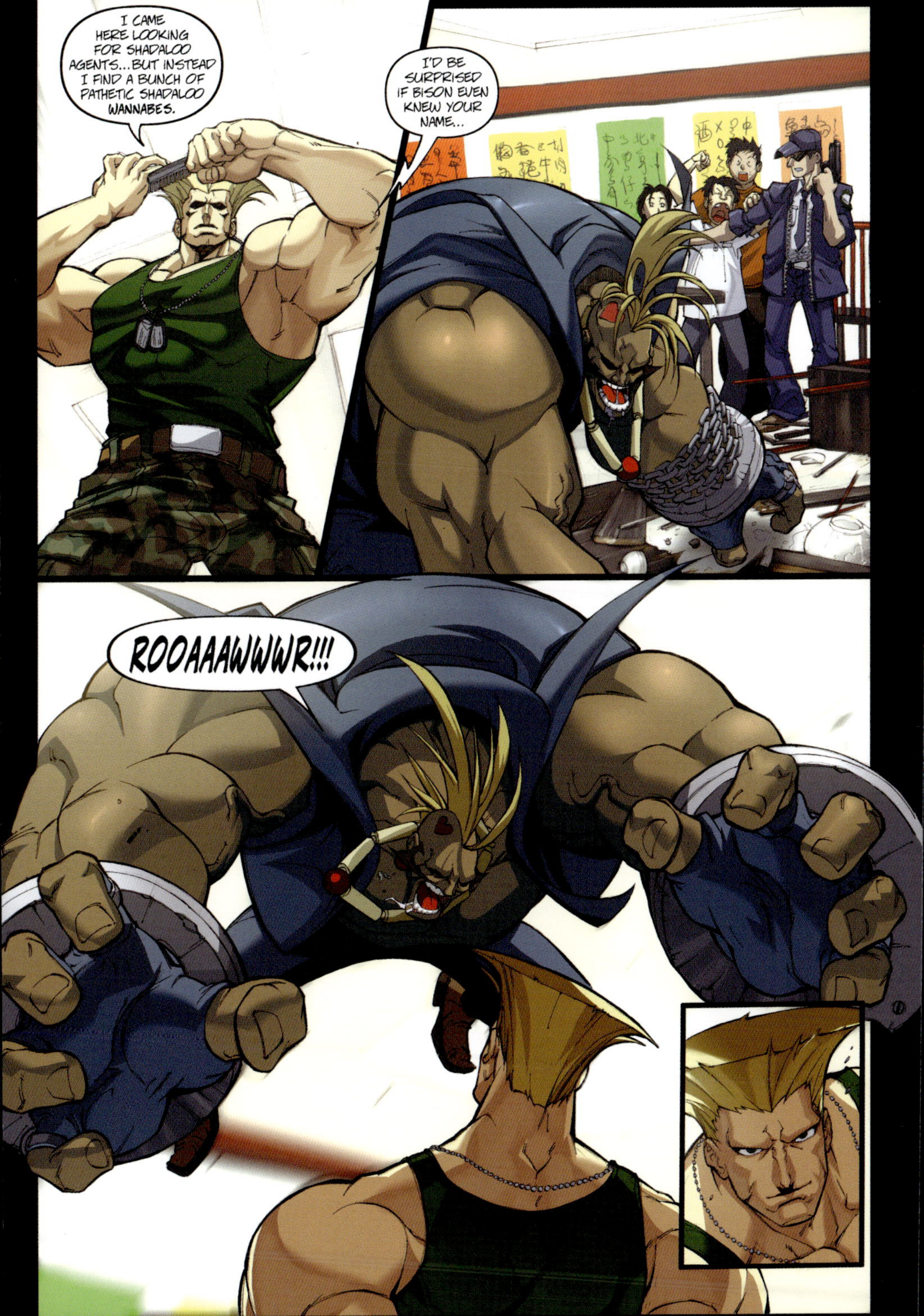
I CAME HERE LOOKING FOR SHADALOO AGENTS...BUT INSTEAD I FIND A BUNCH OF PATHETIC SHADALOO WANNABES.
I'D BE SURPRISED IF BISON EVEN KNEW YOUR NAME...
ROOAAAWWWR!!!

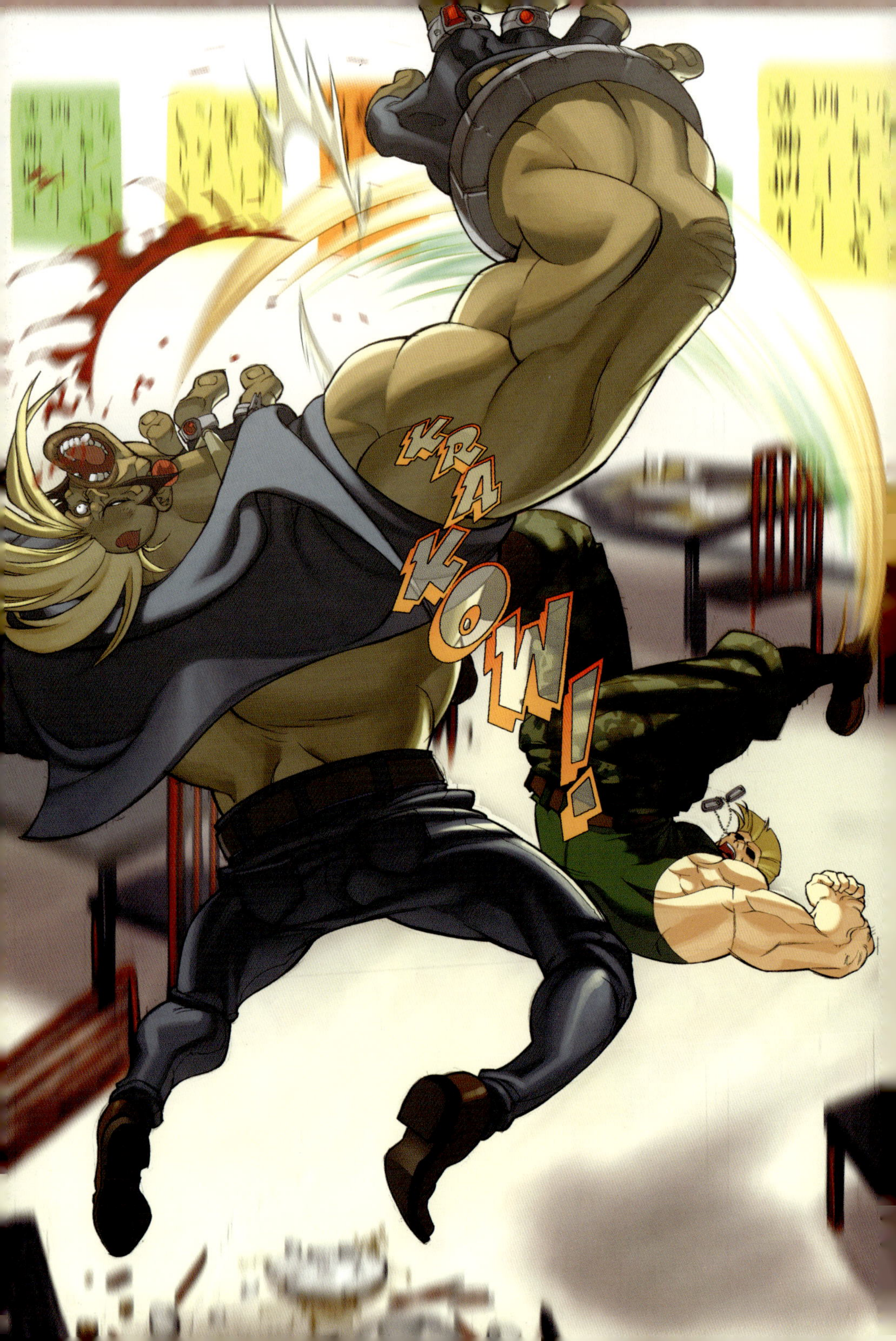
KRAKOW!

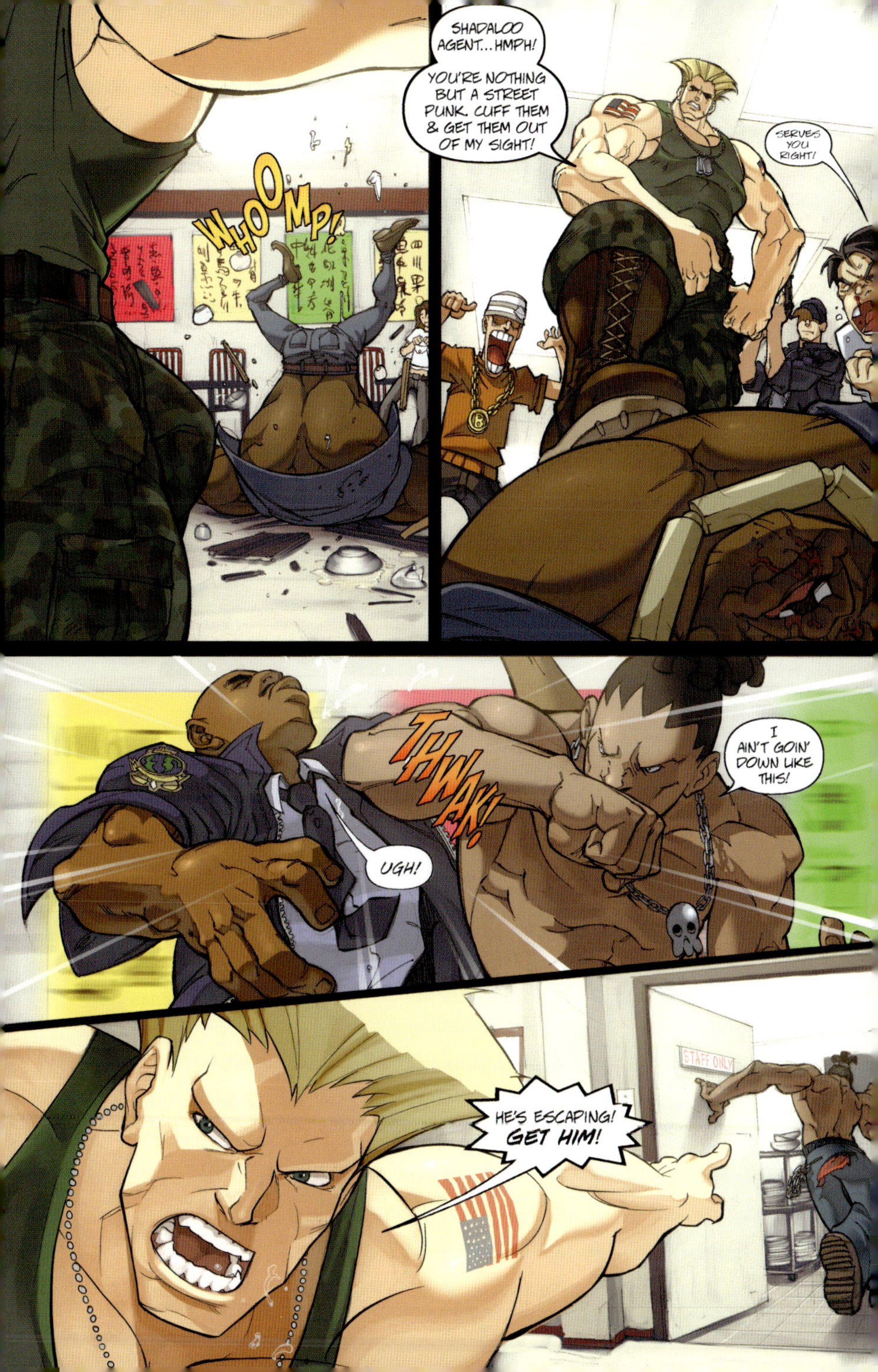
WHOOMP!
SHADALOO AGENT...HMPH!
YOU'RE NOTHING BUT A STREET PUNK. CUFF THEM & GET THEM OUT OF MY SIGHT!
SERVES YOU RIGHT!
THWAK!
I AIN'T GOIN' DOWN LIKE THIS!
UGH!
STAFF ONLY
HE'S ESCAPING! GET HIM!

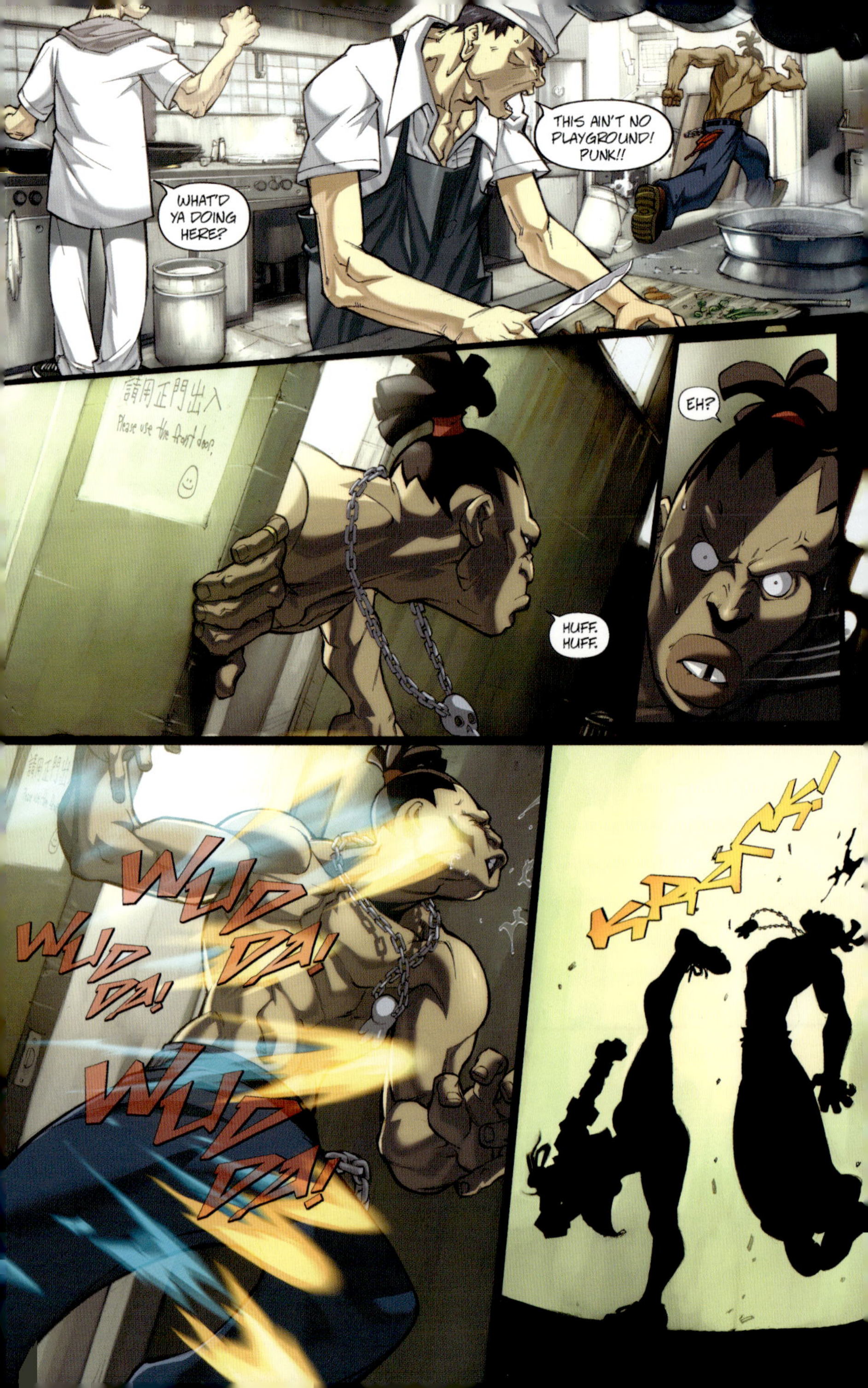
WHAT'D YA DOING HERE?
THIS AIN'T NO PLAYGROUND! PUNK!!
請用正門出入
Please use the front door.
HUFF. HUFF.
EH?
WUD DA!
WUD DA!
WUD DA!
KRAK!

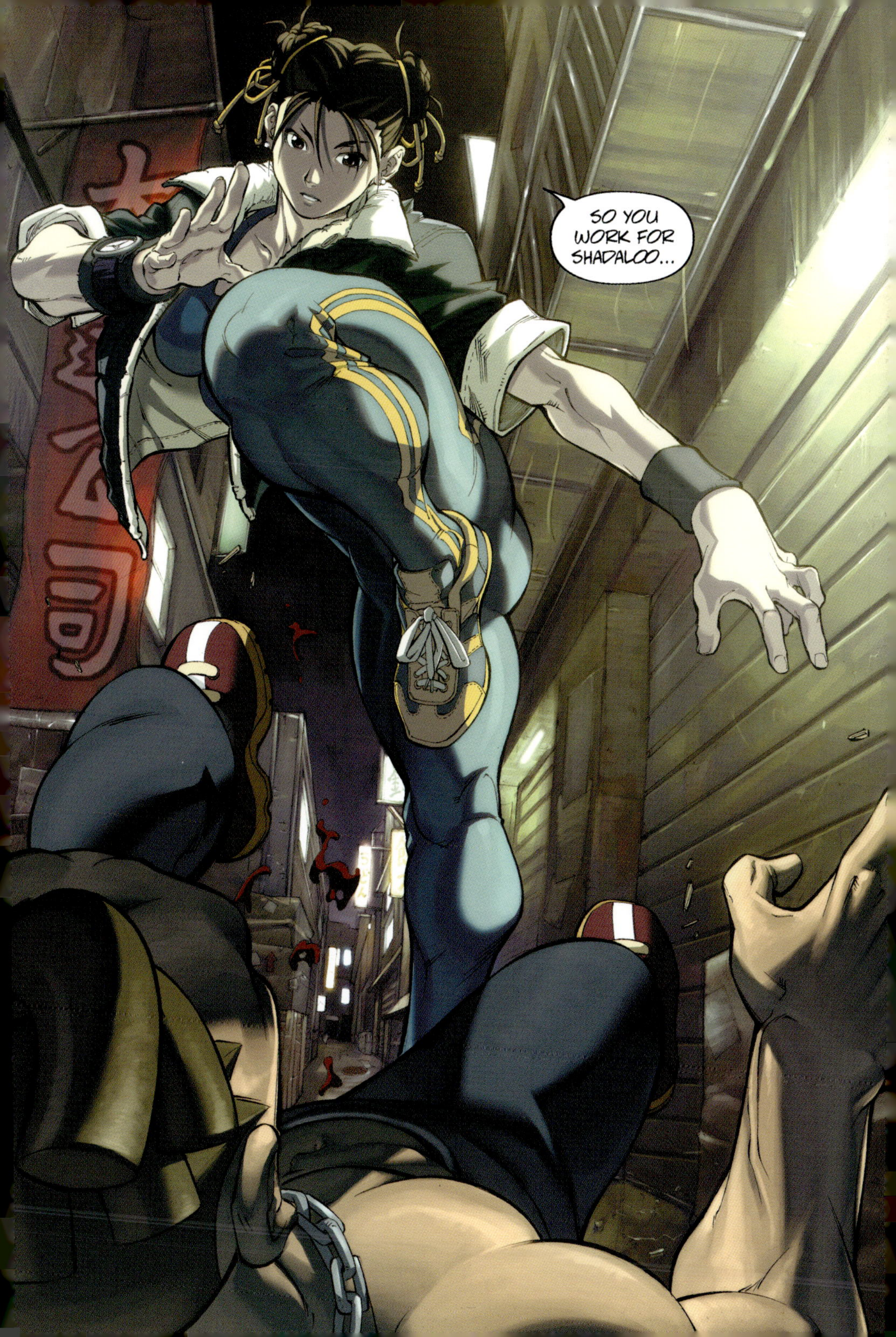
SO YOU WORK FOR SHADALOO...

Cover Art by: Arnold Tsang

Chapter 02: JAPAN

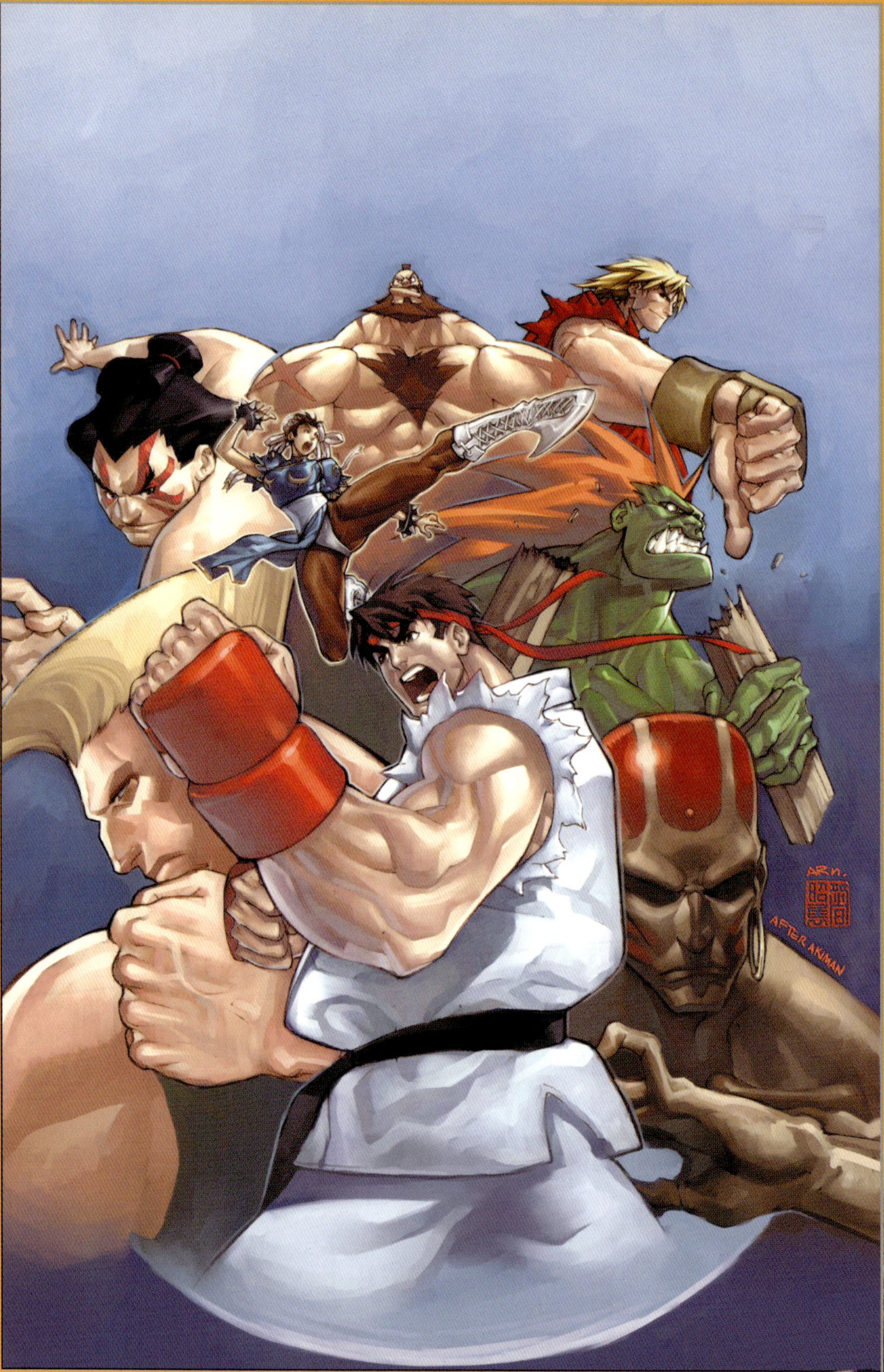
ARn.
AFTER AKIMAN

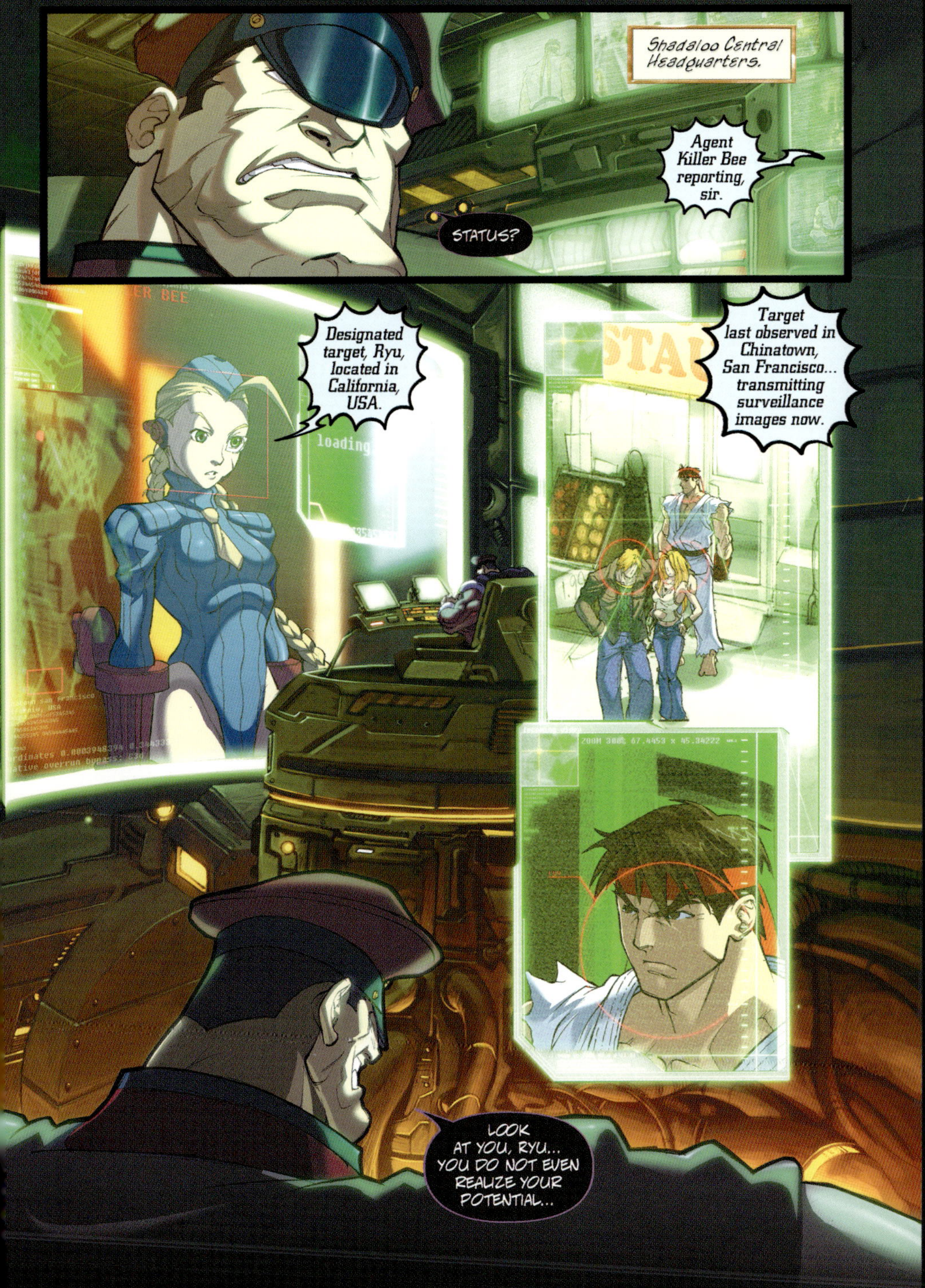
Shadaloo Central Headquarters.
Agent Killer Bee reporting, sir.
STATUS?
Designated target, Ryu, located in California, USA.
Target last observed in Chinatown, San Francisco... transmitting surveillance images now.
LOOK AT YOU, RYU... YOU DO NOT EVEN REALIZE YOUR POTENTIAL...

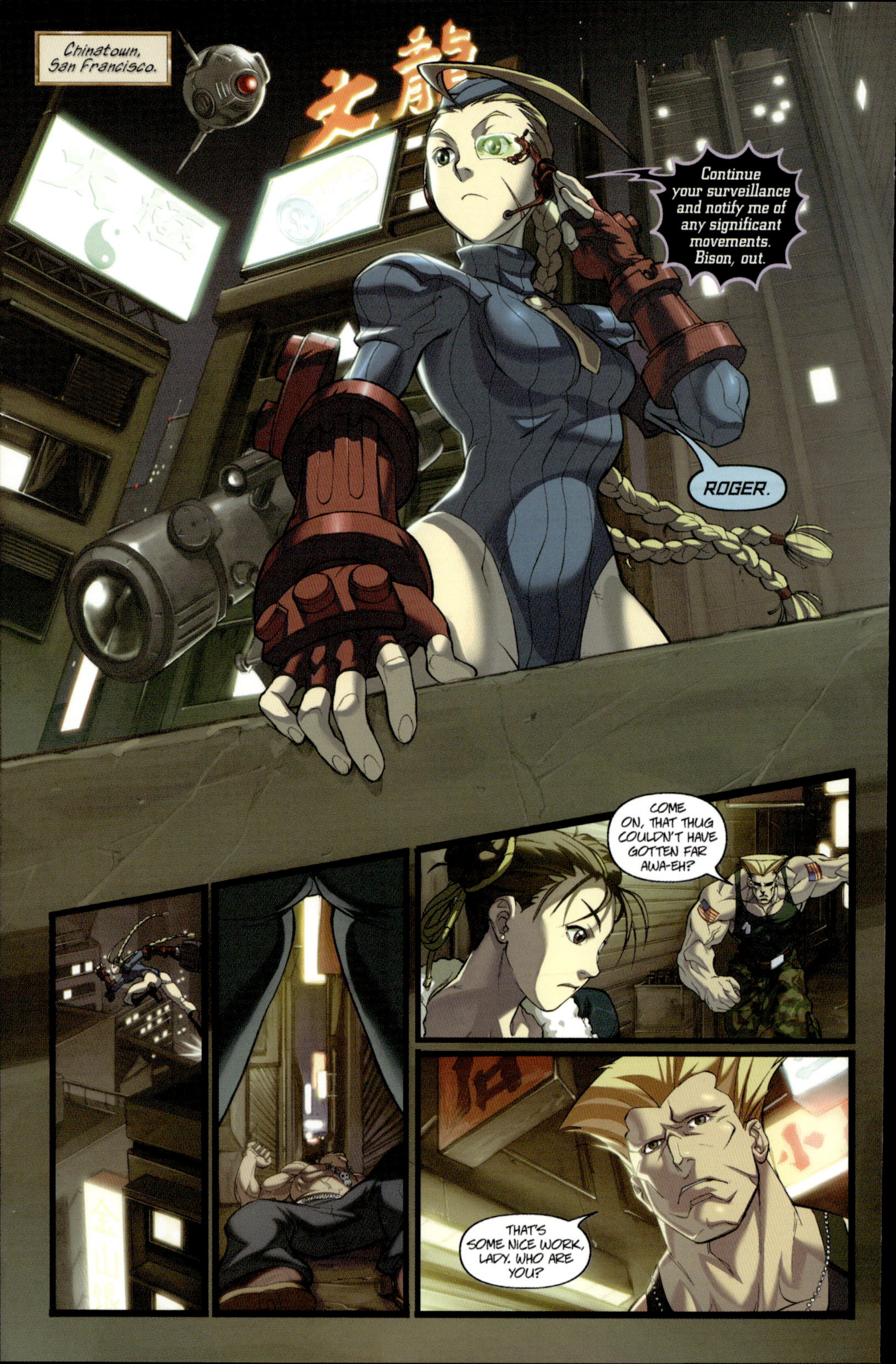
Chinatown, San Francisco.
Continue your surveillance and notify me of any significant movements. Bison, out.
ROGER.
COME ON, THAT THUG COULDN'T HAVE GOTTEN FAR AWA-EH?
THAT'S SOME NICE WORK, LADY. WHO ARE YOU?

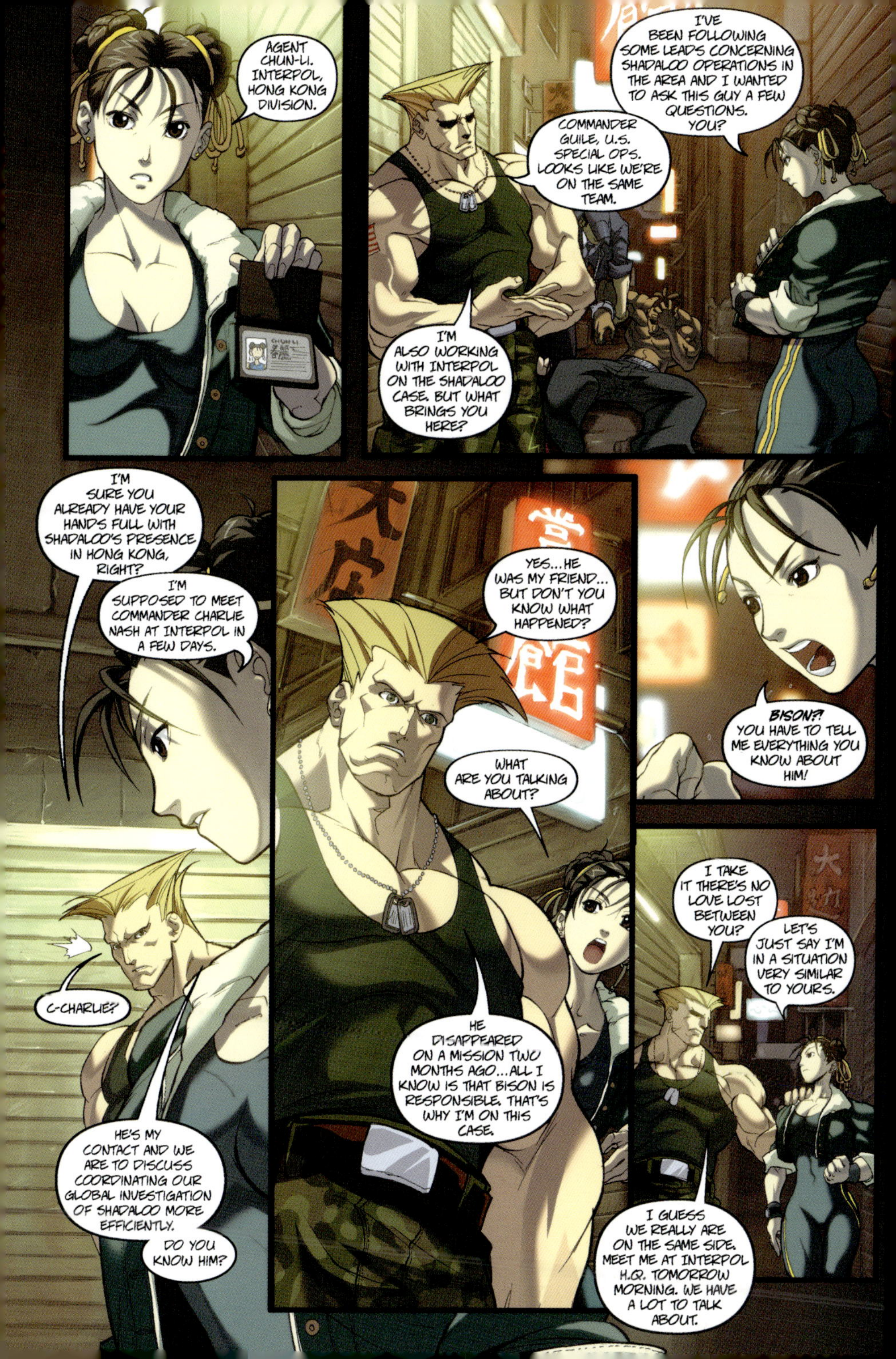

AGENT CHUN-LI. INTERPOL, HONG KONG DIVISION.
COMMANDER GUILE, U.S. SPECIAL OPS. LOOKS LIKE WE'RE ON THE SAME TEAM.
I'VE BEEN FOLLOWING SOME LEADS CONCERNING SHADALOO OPERATIONS IN THE AREA AND I WANTED TO ASK THIS GUY A FEW QUESTIONS. YOU?
I'M ALSO WORKING WITH INTERPOL ON THE SHADALOO CASE. BUT WHAT BRINGS YOU HERE?
I'M SURE YOU ALREADY HAVE YOUR HANDS FULL WITH SHADALOO'S PRESENCE IN HONG KONG, RIGHT?
I'M SUPPOSED TO MEET COMMANDER CHARLIE NASH AT INTERPOL IN A FEW DAYS.
C-CHARLIE?
HE'S MY CONTACT AND WE ARE TO DISCUSS COORDINATING OUR GLOBAL INVESTIGATION OF SHADALOO MORE EFFICIENTLY.
DO YOU KNOW HIM?
YES...HE WAS MY FRIEND... BUT DON'T YOU KNOW WHAT HAPPENED?
WHAT ARE YOU TALKING ABOUT?
HE DISAPPEARED ON A MISSION TWO MONTHS AGO...ALL I KNOW IS THAT BISON IS RESPONSIBLE. THAT'S WHY I'M ON THIS CASE.
BISON?! YOU HAVE TO TELL ME EVERYTHING YOU KNOW ABOUT HIM!
I TAKE IT THERE'S NO LOVE LOST BETWEEN YOU?
LET'S JUST SAY I'M IN A SITUATION VERY SIMILAR TO YOURS.
I GUESS WE REALLY ARE ON THE SAME SIDE. MEET ME AT INTERPOL H.Q. TOMORROW MORNING. WE HAVE A LOT TO TALK ABOUT.

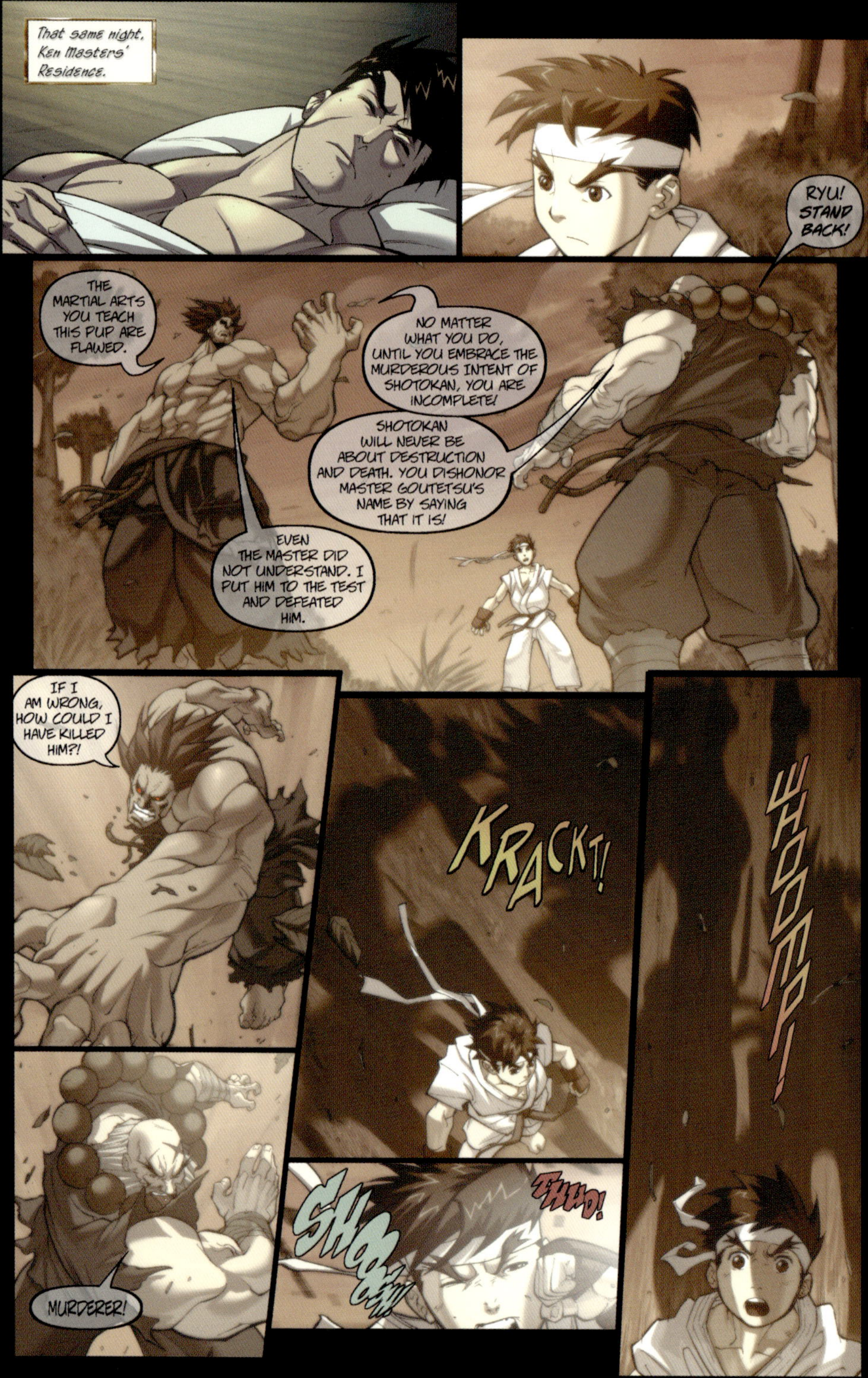
That same night. Ken Masters' Residence.
RYU! STAND BACK!
THE MARTIAL ARTS YOU TEACH THIS PUP ARE FLAWED.
NO MATTER WHAT YOU DO, UNTIL YOU EMBRACE THE MURDEROUS INTENT OF SHOTOKAN, YOU ARE INCOMPLETE!
SHOTOKAN WILL NEVER BE ABOUT DESTRUCTION AND DEATH. YOU DISHONOR MASTER GOUTETSU'S NAME BY SAYING THAT IT IS!
EVEN THE MASTER DID NOT UNDERSTAND. I PUT HIM TO THE TEST AND DEFEATED HIM.
IF I AM WRONG, HOW COULD I HAVE KILLED HIM?!
KRACKT!
WHOOMP!
MURDERER!
SHOOOM!
THUD!

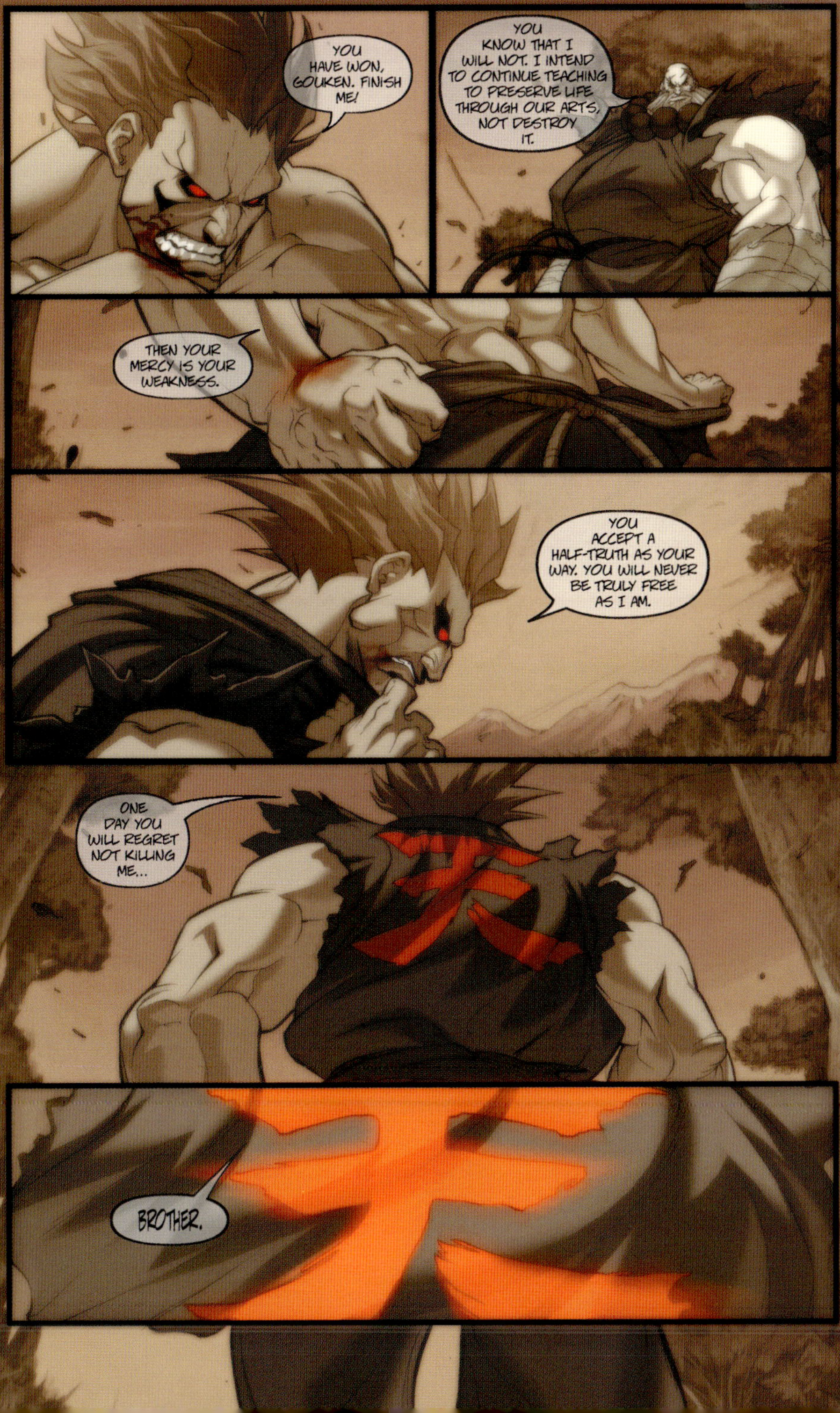
YOU HAVE WON, GOUKEN. FINISH ME!
YOU KNOW THAT I WILL NOT. I INTEND TO CONTINUE TEACHING TO PRESERVE LIFE THROUGH OUR ARTS, NOT DESTROY IT.
THEN YOUR MERCY IS YOUR WEAKNESS.
YOU ACCEPT A HALF-TRUTH AS YOUR WAY. YOU WILL NEVER BE TRULY FREE AS I AM.
ONE DAY YOU WILL REGRET NOT KILLING ME...
BROTHER.

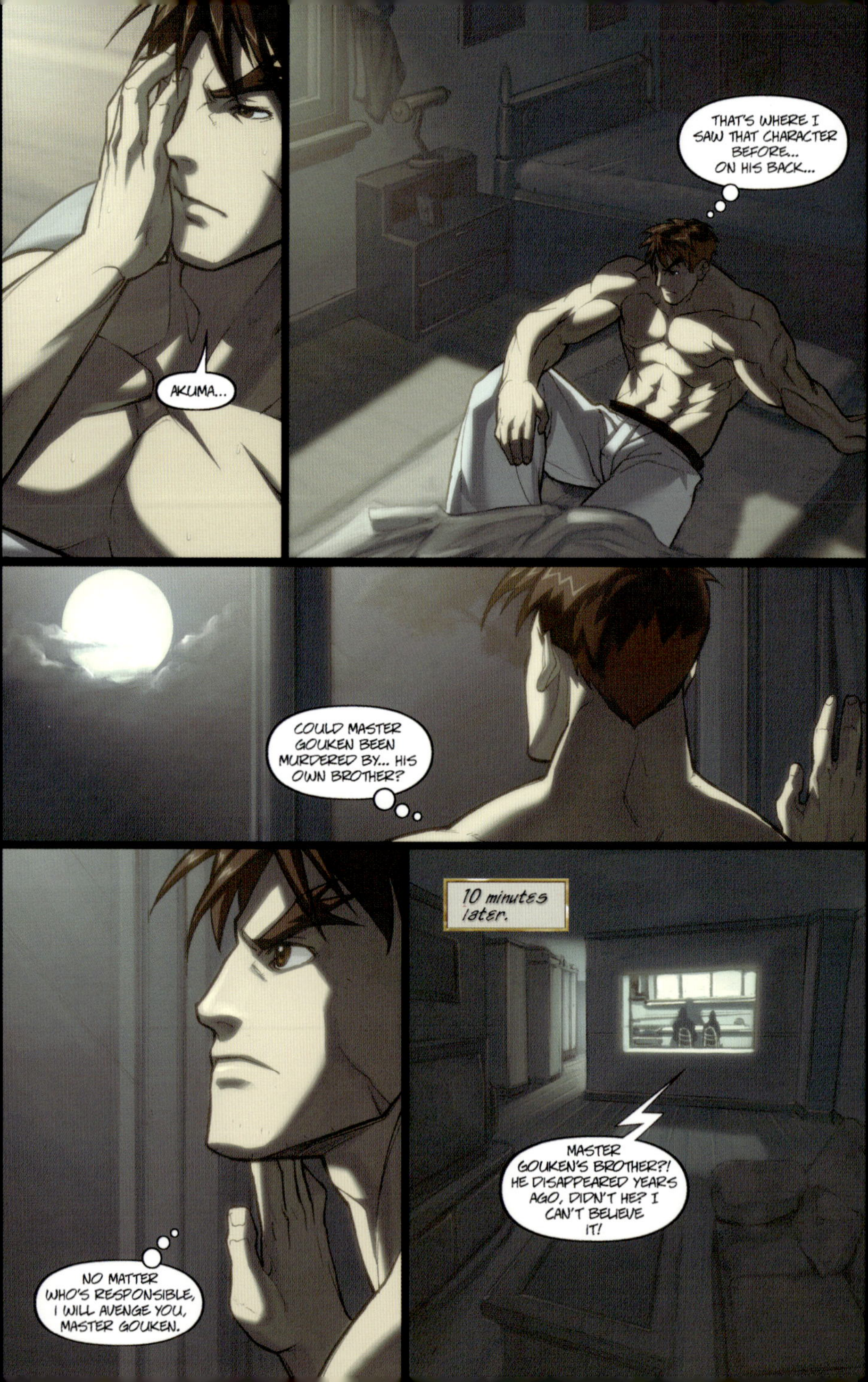
AKUMA...
THAT'S WHERE I SAW THAT CHARACTER BEFORE... ON HIS BACK...
COULD MASTER GOUKEN BEEN MURDERED BY... HIS OWN BROTHER?
NO MATTER WHO'S RESPONSIBLE, I WILL AVENGE YOU, MASTER GOUKEN.
10 minutes later.
MASTER GOUKEN'S BROTHER?! HE DISAPPEARED YEARS AGO, DIDN'T HE? I CAN'T BELIEVE IT!

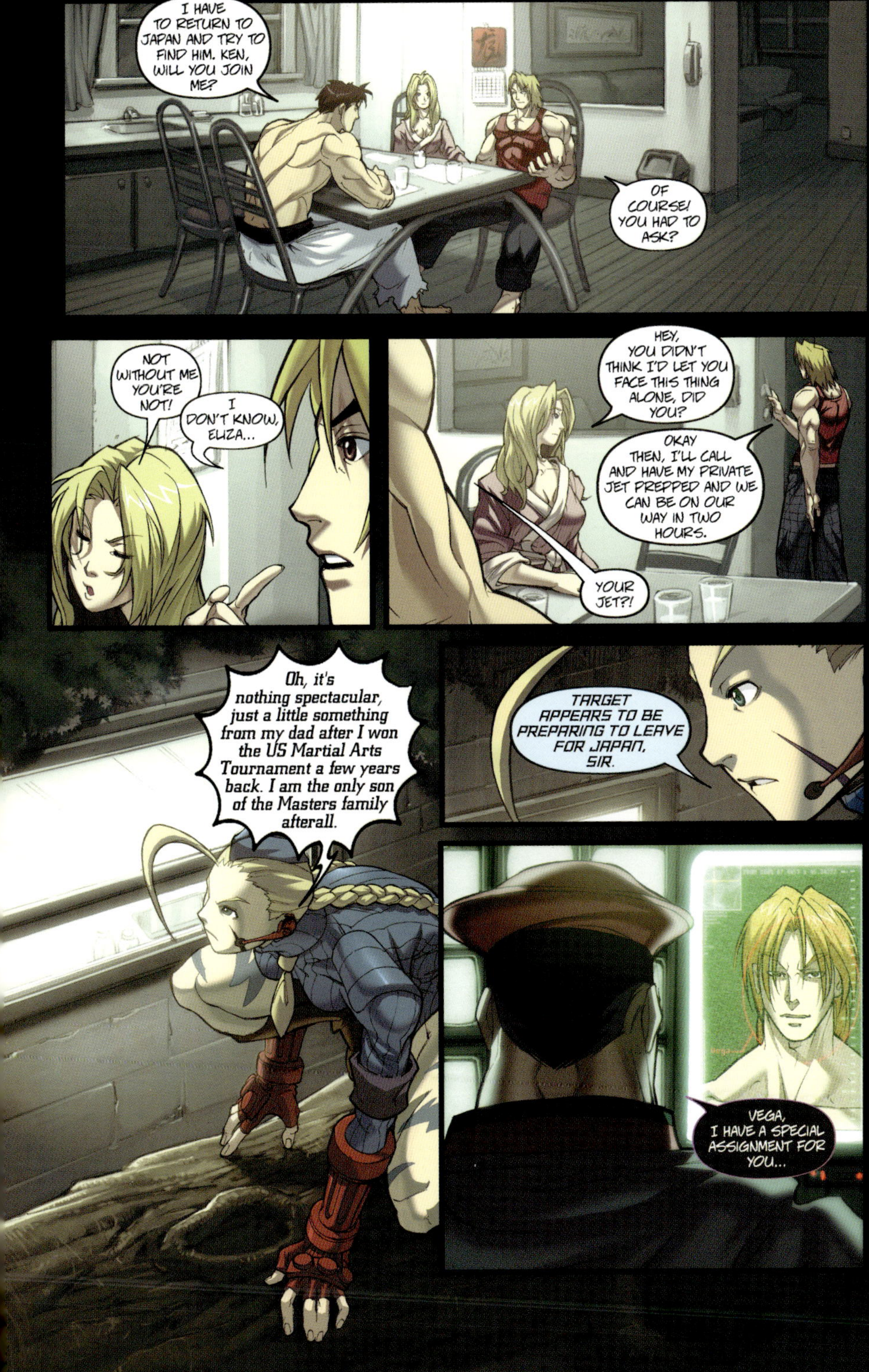
I HAVE TO RETURN TO JAPAN AND TRY TO FIND HIM. KEN, WILL YOU JOIN ME?
OF COURSE! YOU HAD TO ASK?
NOT WITHOUT ME YOU'RE NOT!
I DON'T KNOW, ELIZA...
HEY, YOU DIDN'T THINK I'D LET YOU FACE THIS THING ALONE, DID YOU?
OKAY THEN, I'LL CALL AND HAVE MY PRIVATE JET PREPPED AND WE CAN BE ON OUR WAY IN TWO HOURS.
YOUR JET?!
Oh, it's nothing spectacular, just a little something from my dad after I won the US Martial Arts Tournament a few years back. I am the only son of the Masters family afterall.
TARGET APPEARS TO BE PREPARING TO LEAVE FOR JAPAN, SIR.
VEGA, I HAVE A SPECIAL ASSIGNMENT FOR YOU...

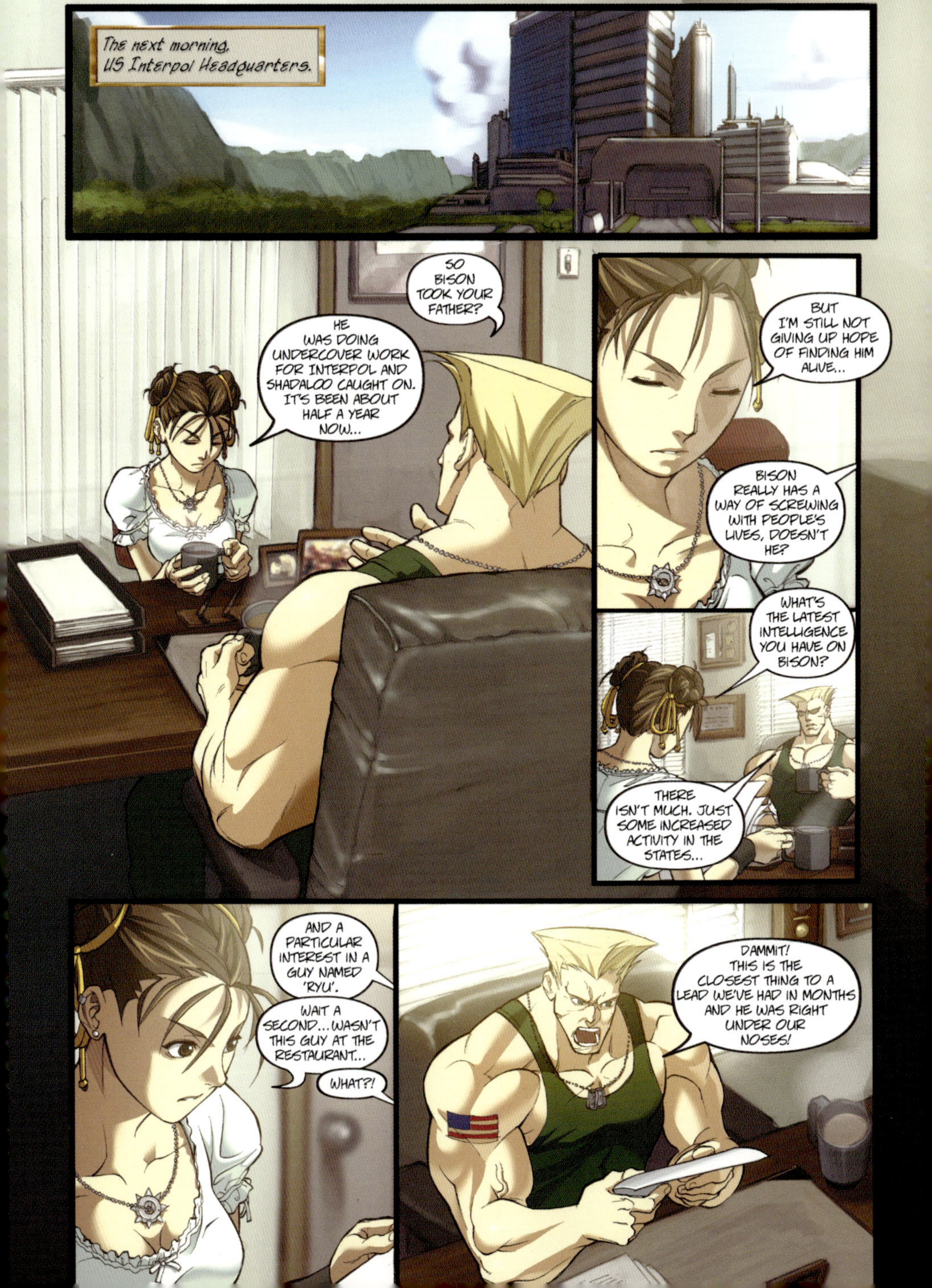
The next morning,
US Interpol Headquarters.
SO BISON TOOK YOUR FATHER?
HE WAS DOING UNDERCOVER WORK FOR INTERPOL AND SHADALOO CAUGHT ON. IT'S BEEN ABOUT HALF A YEAR NOW...
BUT I'M STILL NOT GIVING UP HOPE OF FINDING HIM ALIVE...
BISON REALLY HAS A WAY OF SCREWING WITH PEOPLE'S LIVES, DOESN'T HE?
WHAT'S THE LATEST INTELLIGENCE YOU HAVE ON BISON?
THERE ISN'T MUCH. JUST SOME INCREASED ACTIVITY IN THE STATES...
AND A PARTICULAR INTEREST IN A GUY NAMED 'RYU'.
WAIT A SECOND... WASN'T THIS GUY AT THE RESTAURANT...
WHAT?!
DAMMIT! THIS IS THE CLOSEST THING TO A LEAD WE'VE HAD IN MONTHS AND HE WAS RIGHT UNDER OUR NOSES!

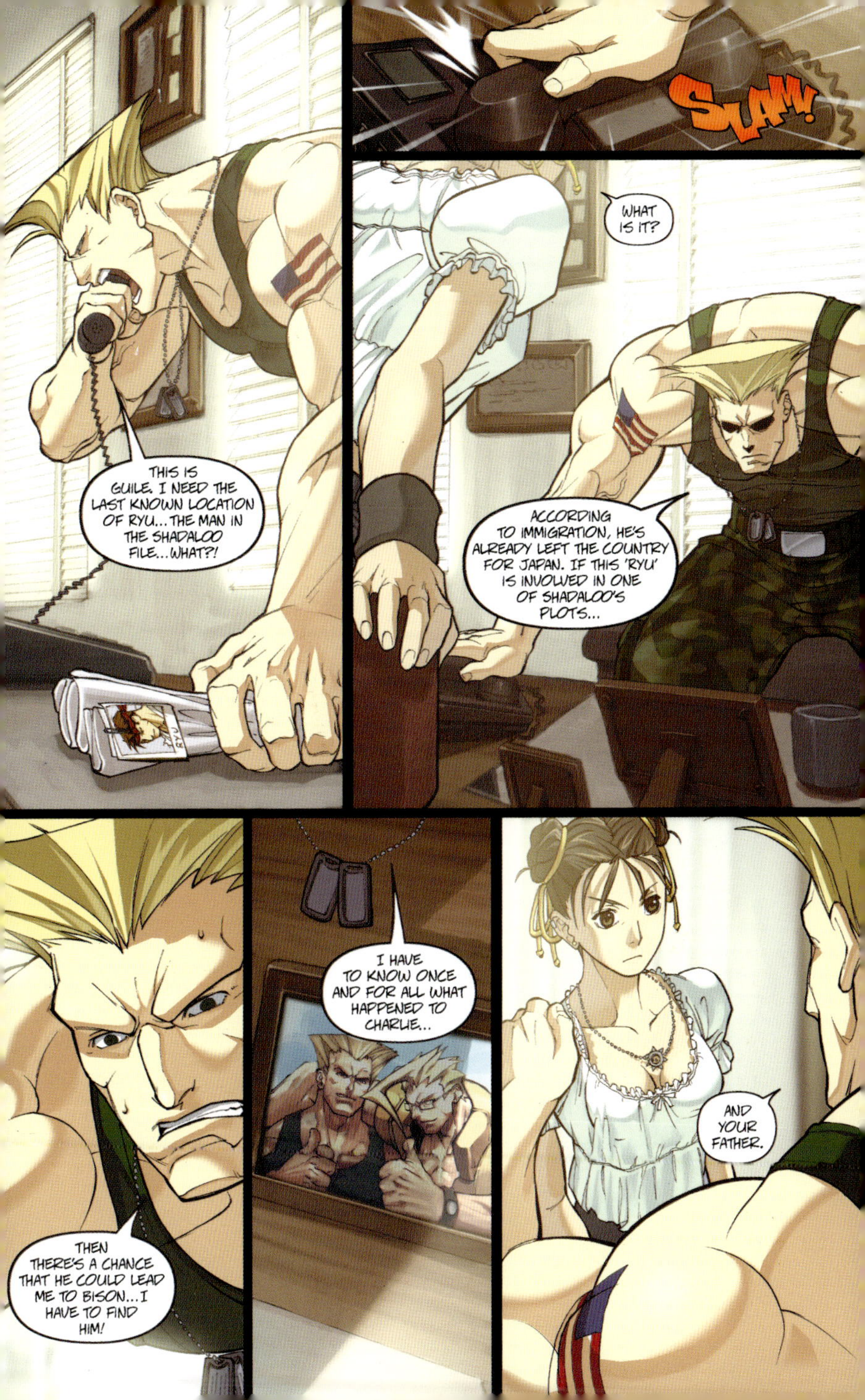
THIS IS GUILE. I NEED THE LAST KNOWN LOCATION OF RYU... THE MAN IN THE SHADALOO FILE... WHAT?!
SLAM!
WHAT IS IT?
ACCORDING TO IMMIGRATION, HE'S ALREADY LEFT THE COUNTRY FOR JAPAN. IF THIS 'RYU' IS INVOLVED IN ONE OF SHADALOO'S PLOTS...
THEN THERE'S A CHANCE THAT HE COULD LEAD ME TO BISON... I HAVE TO FIND HIM!
I HAVE TO KNOW ONCE AND FOR ALL WHAT HAPPENED TO CHARLIE...
AND YOUR FATHER.

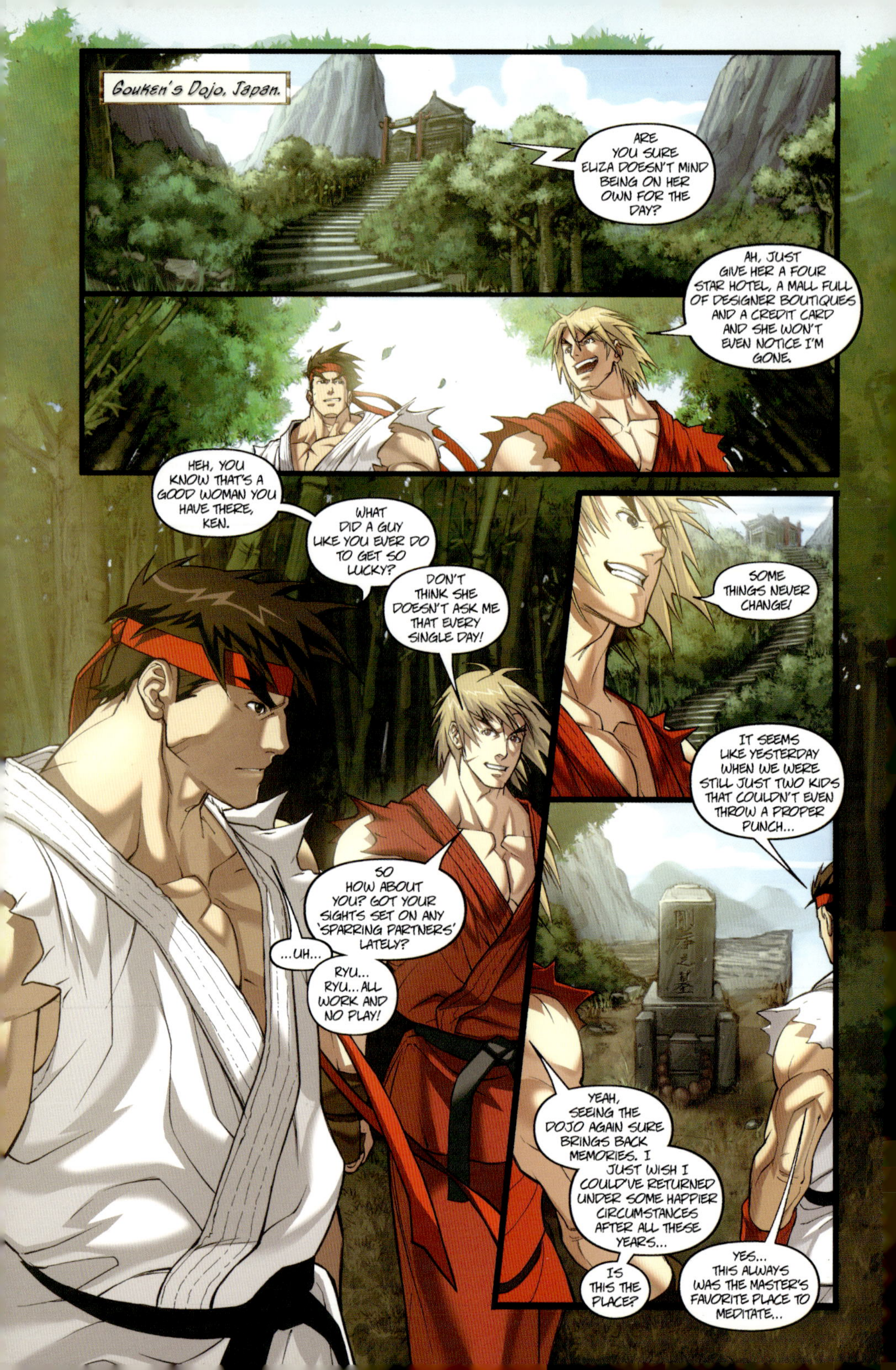

Gouken's Dojo, Japan.
ARE YOU SURE ELIZA DOESN'T MIND BEING ON HER OWN FOR THE DAY?
AH, JUST GIVE HER A FOUR STAR HOTEL, A MALL FULL OF DESIGNER BOUTIQUES AND A CREDIT CARD AND SHE WON'T EVEN NOTICE I'M GONE.
HEH, YOU KNOW THAT'S A GOOD WOMAN YOU HAVE THERE, KEN.
WHAT DID A GUY LIKE YOU EVER DO TO GET SO LUCKY?
DON'T THINK SHE DOESN'T ASK ME THAT EVERY SINGLE DAY!
SO HOW ABOUT YOU? GOT YOUR SIGHTS SET ON ANY 'SPARRING PARTNERS' LATELY?
...UH...
RYU... RYU... ALL WORK AND NO PLAY!
SOME THINGS NEVER CHANGE!
IT SEEMS LIKE YESTERDAY WHEN WE WERE STILL JUST TWO KIDS THAT COULDN'T EVEN THROW A PROPER PUNCH...
YEAH, SEEING THE DOJO AGAIN SURE BRINGS BACK MEMORIES. I JUST WISH I COULD'VE RETURNED UNDER SOME HAPPIER CIRCUMSTANCES AFTER ALL THESE YEARS...
IS THIS THE PLACE?
YES... THIS ALWAYS WAS THE MASTER'S FAVORITE PLACE TO MEDITATE...

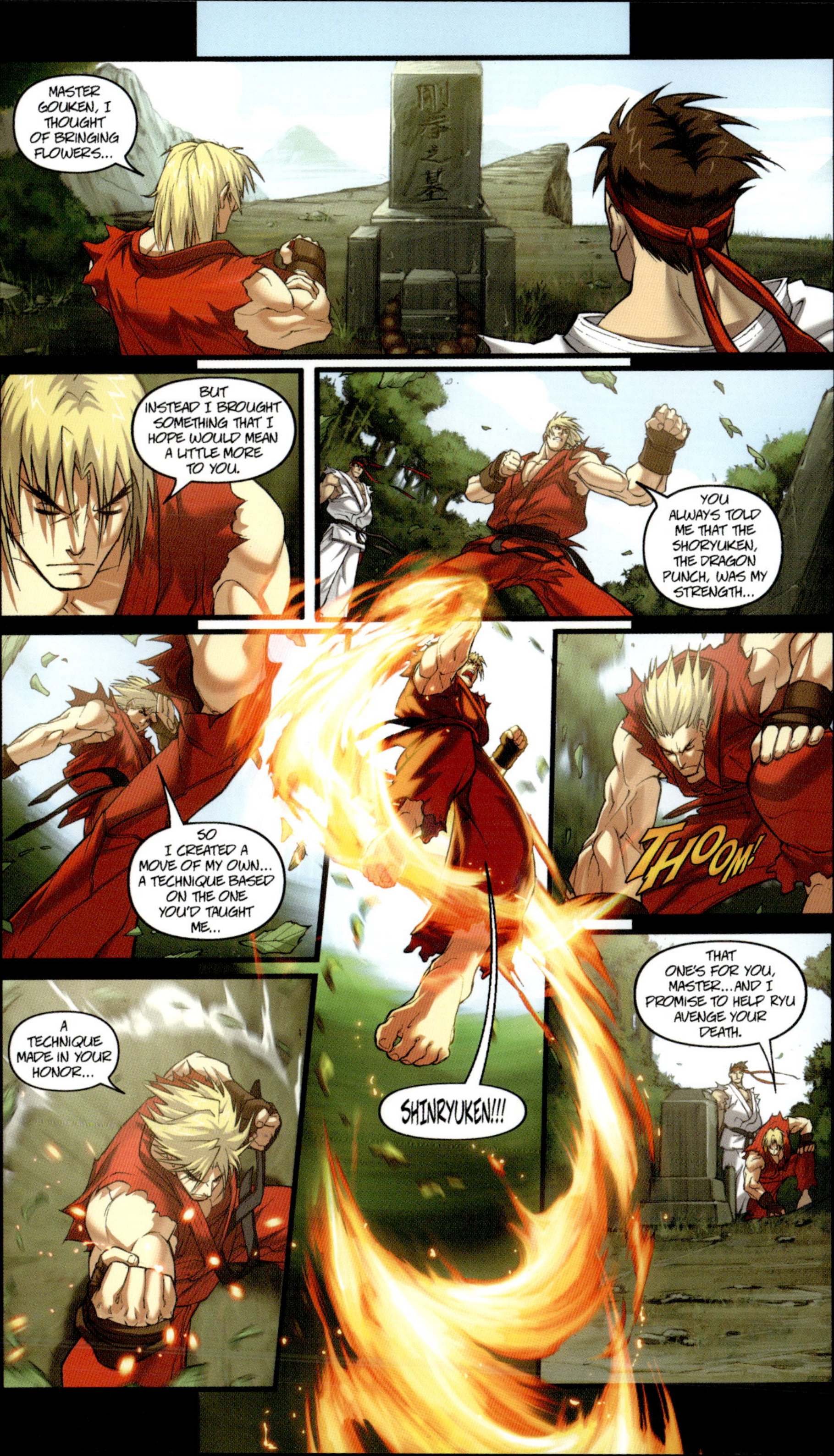

MASTER GOUKEN, I THOUGHT OF BRINGING FLOWERS...
剛拳之墓
BUT INSTEAD I BROUGHT SOMETHING THAT I HOPE WOULD MEAN A LITTLE MORE TO YOU.
YOU ALWAYS TOLD ME THAT THE SHORYUKEN, THE DRAGON PUNCH, WAS MY STRENGTH...
SO I CREATED A MOVE OF MY OWN... A TECHNIQUE BASED ON THE ONE YOU'D TAUGHT ME...
THOOM!
A TECHNIQUE MADE IN YOUR HONOR...
SHINRYUKEN!!!
THAT ONE'S FOR YOU, MASTER...AND I PROMISE TO HELP RYU AVENGE YOUR DEATH.

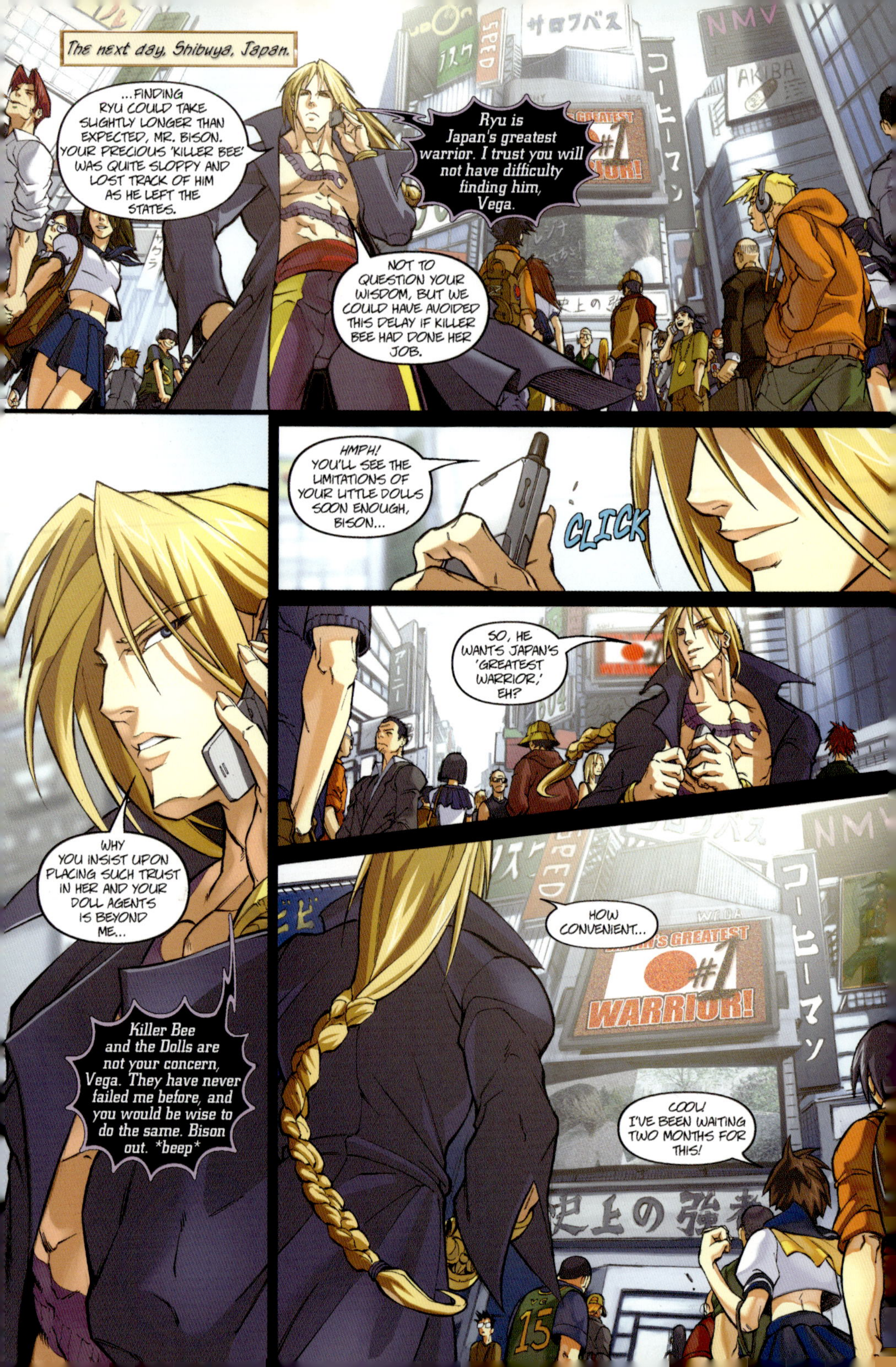

The next day, Shibuya, Japan.
...FINDING RYU COULD TAKE SLIGHTLY LONGER THAN EXPECTED, MR. BISON. YOUR PRECIOUS 'KILLER BEE' WAS QUITE SLOPPY AND LOST TRACK OF HIM AS HE LEFT THE STATES.
Ryu is Japan's greatest warrior. I trust you will not have difficulty finding him, Vega.
NOT TO QUESTION YOUR WISDOM, BUT WE COULD HAVE AVOIDED THIS DELAY IF KILLER BEE HAD DONE HER JOB.
WHY YOU INSIST UPON PLACING SUCH TRUST IN HER AND YOUR DOLL AGENTS IS BEYOND ME...
Killer Bee and the Dolls are not your concern, Vega. They have never failed me before, and you would be wise to do the same. Bison out. *beep*
HMPH! YOU'LL SEE THE LIMITATIONS OF YOUR LITTLE DOLLS SOON ENOUGH, BISON...
CLICK
SO, HE WANTS JAPAN'S 'GREATEST WARRIOR,' EH?
HOW CONVENIENT...
COOL! I'VE BEEN WAITING TWO MONTHS FOR THIS!

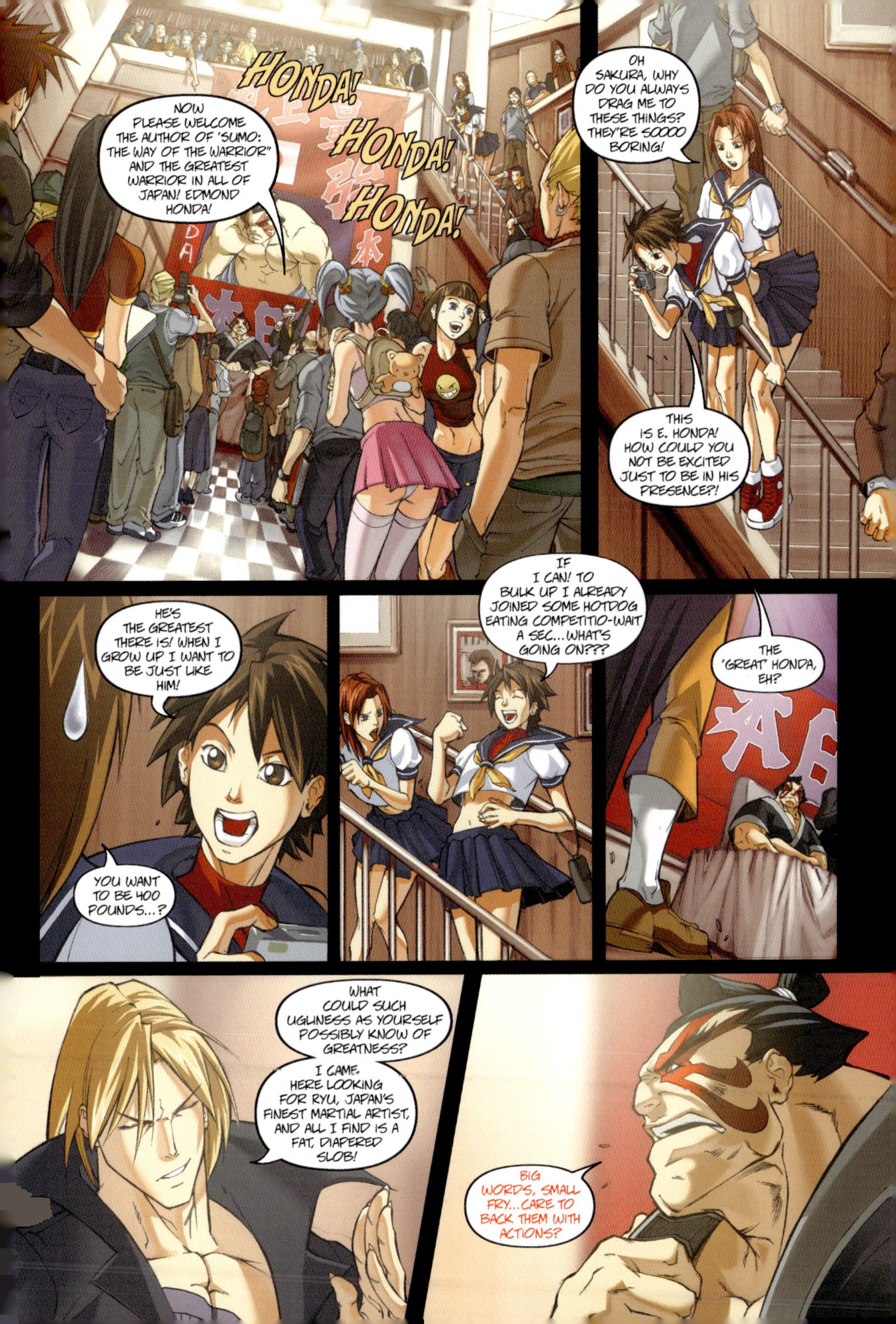
NOW PLEASE WELCOME THE AUTHOR OF 'SUMO: THE WAY OF THE WARRIOR" AND THE GREATEST WARRIOR IN ALL OF JAPAN! EDMOND HONDA!
HONDA! HONDA! HONDA!
OH SAKURA, WHY DO YOU ALWAYS DRAG ME TO THESE THINGS? THEY'RE SOOOO BORING!
THIS IS E. HONDA! HOW COULD YOU NOT BE EXCITED JUST TO BE IN HIS PRESENCE?!
HE'S THE GREATEST THERE IS! WHEN I GROW UP I WANT TO BE JUST LIKE HIM!
YOU WANT TO BE 400 POUNDS...?
IF I CAN! TO BULK UP I ALREADY JOINED SOME HOTDOG EATING COMPETITIO-WAIT A SEC...WHAT'S GOING ON???
THE 'GREAT' HONDA, EH?
WHAT COULD SUCH UGLINESS AS YOURSELF POSSIBLY KNOW OF GREATNESS?
I CAME HERE LOOKING FOR RYU, JAPAN'S FINEST MARTIAL ARTIST, AND ALL I FIND IS A FAT, DIAPERED SLOB!
BIG WORDS, SMALL FRY...CARE TO BACK THEM WITH ACTIONS?

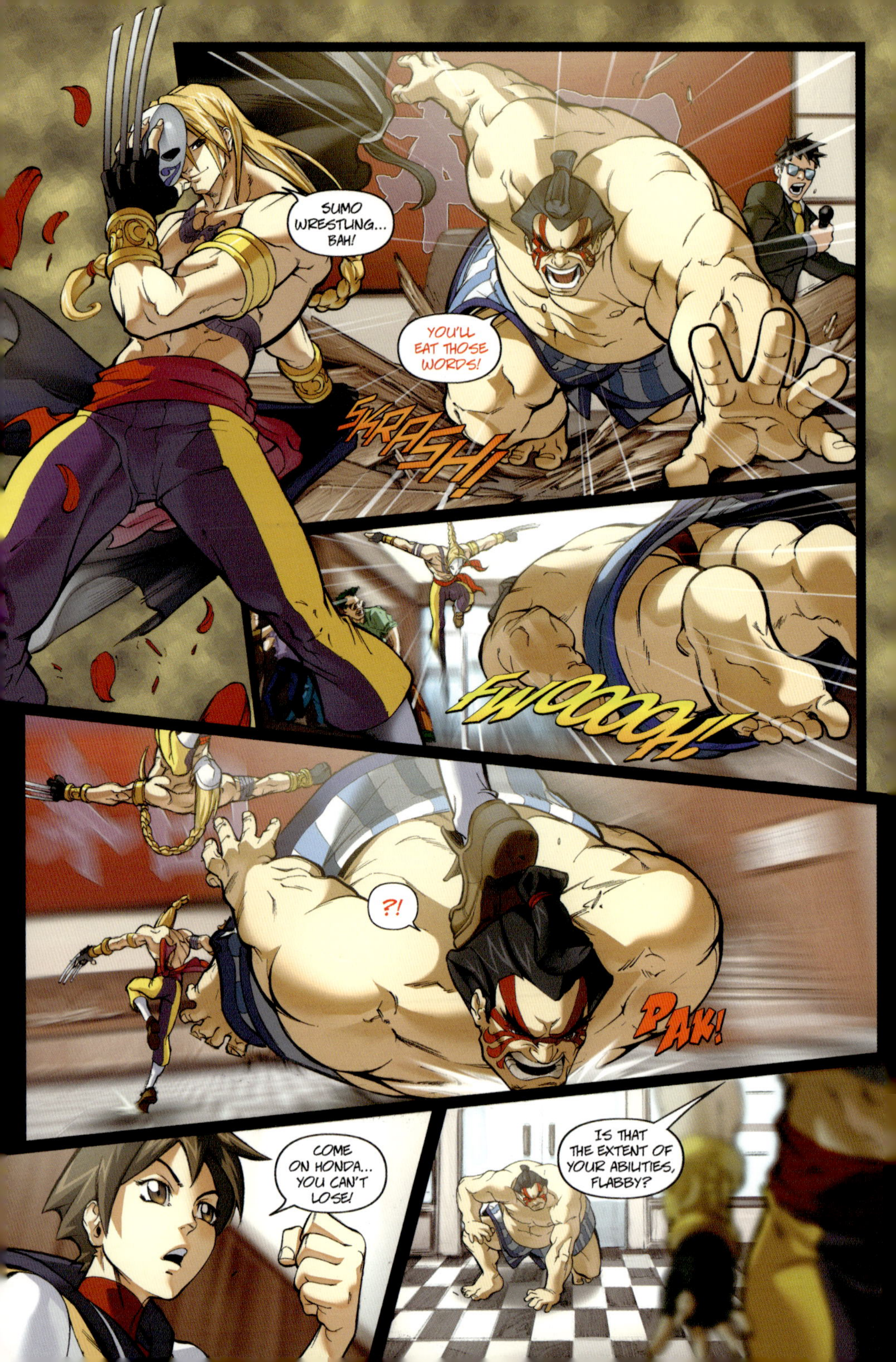
SUMO WRESTLING... BAH!
YOU'LL EAT THOSE WORDS!
SKRASH!
FWOOOOOH!
?!
PAK!
COME ON HONDA... YOU CAN'T LOSE!
IS THAT THE EXTENT OF YOUR ABILITIES, FLABBY?

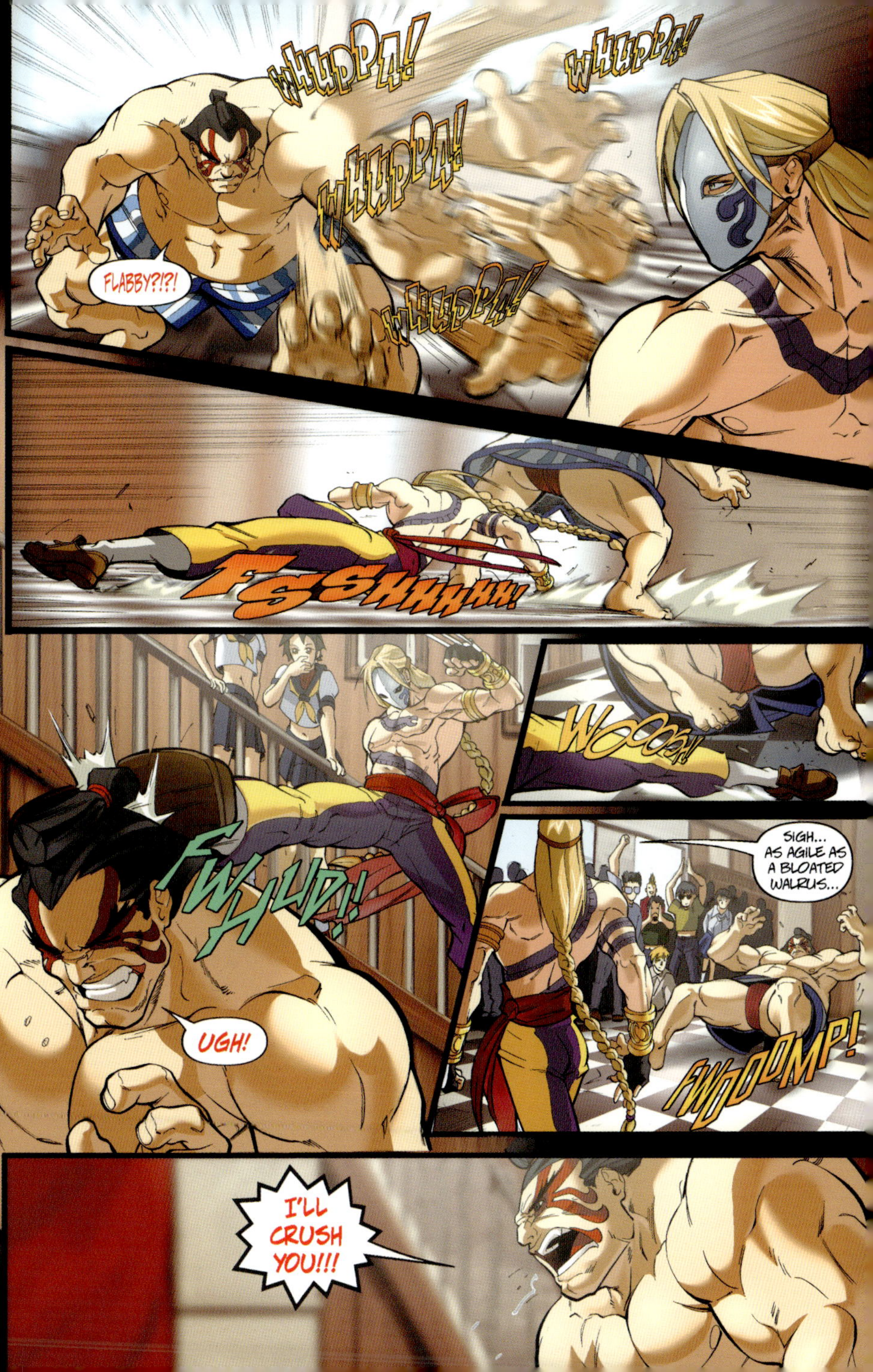
WHUPPA!
WHUPPA!
WHUPPA!
WHUPPA!
FLABBY?!?!
FSSHHHHHH!
WOOOSH!
FWUD!!
UGH!
SIGH... AS AGILE AS A BLOATED WALRUS...
FWOOOMP!
I'LL CRUSH YOU!!!

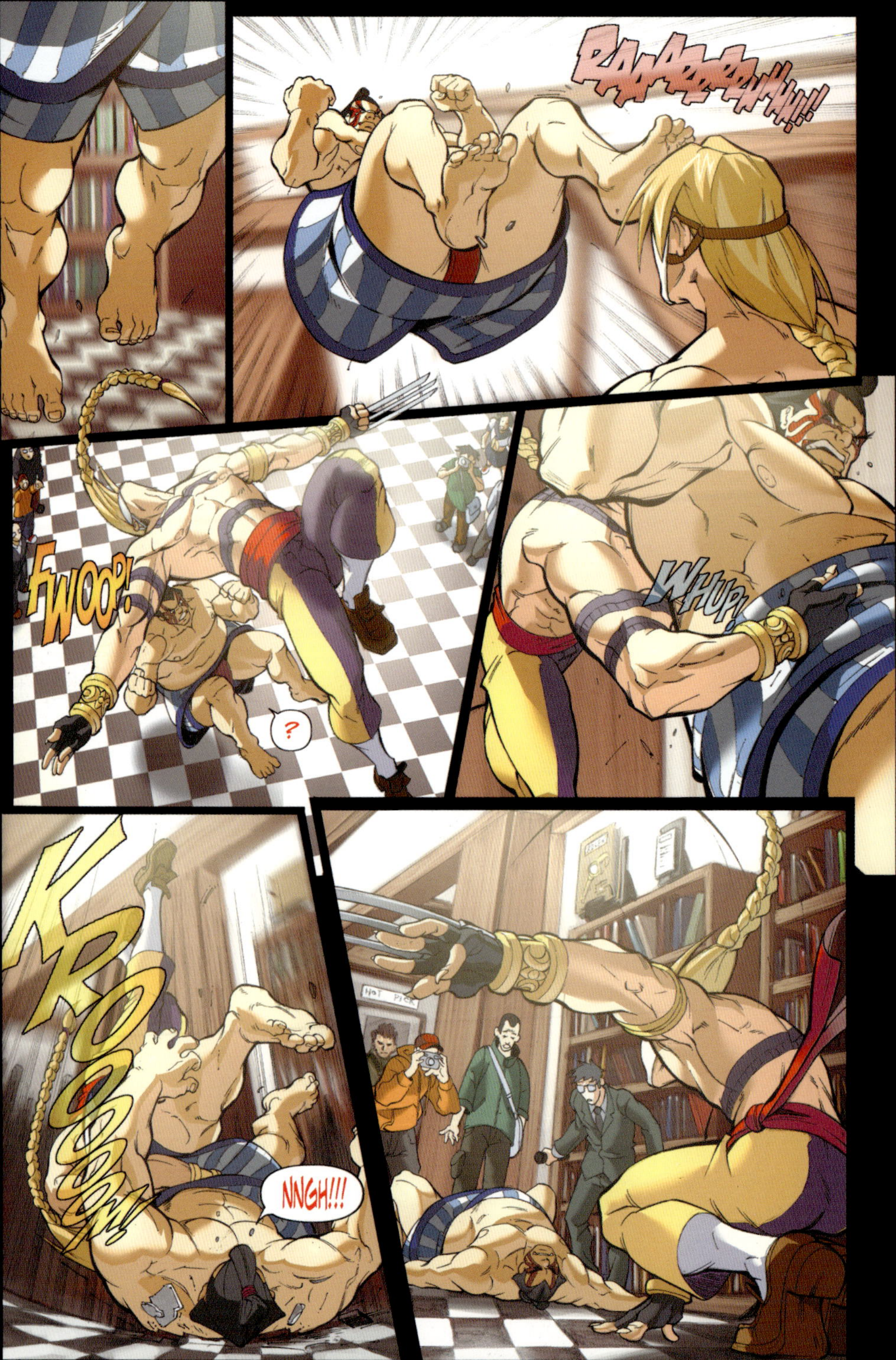
RAAARRGHHH!!!
FWOOP!
?
WHUP!
KROOOOM
NNGH!!!

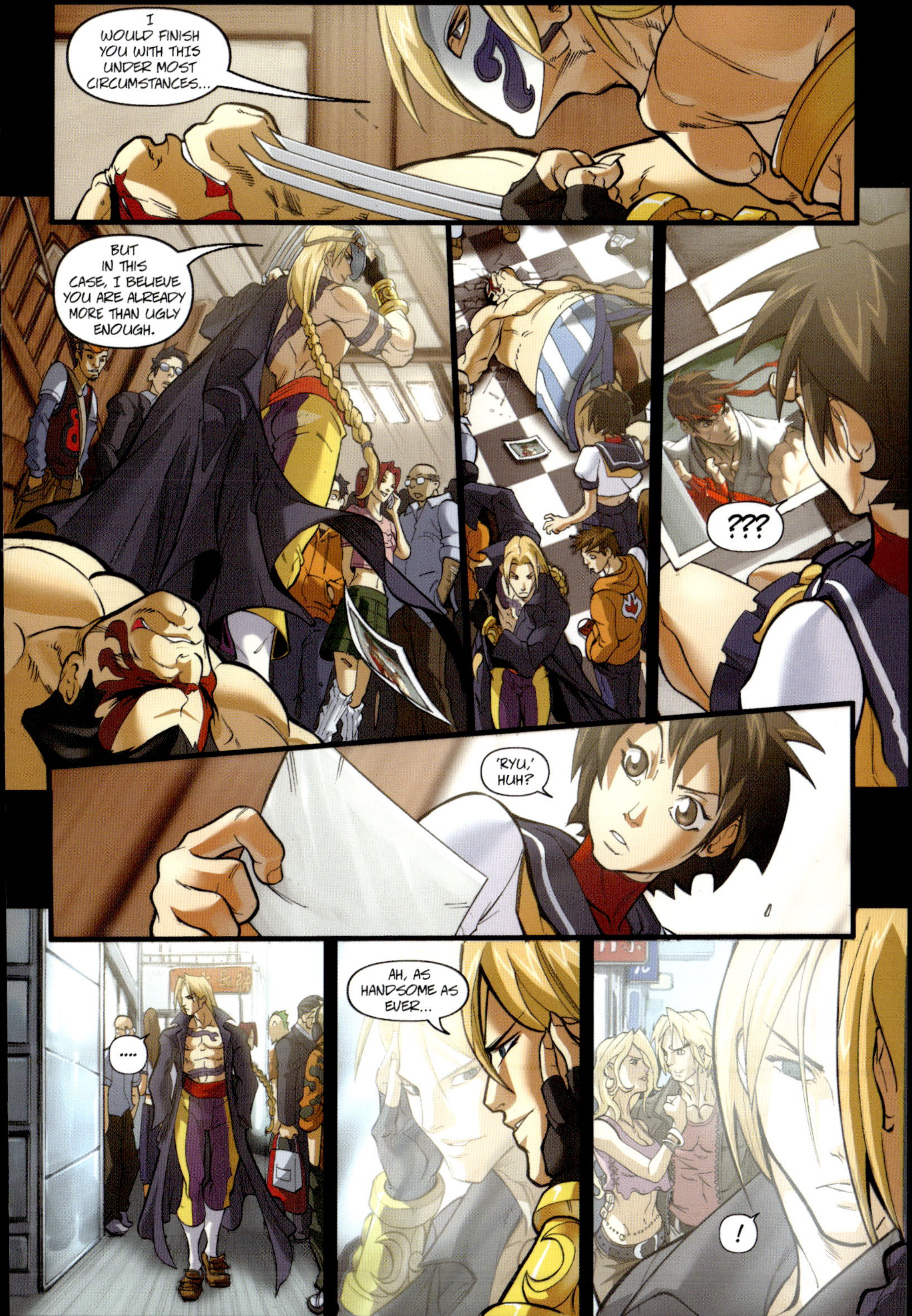
I WOULD FINISH YOU WITH THIS UNDER MOST CIRCUMSTANCES...
BUT IN THIS CASE, I BELIEVE YOU ARE ALREADY MORE THAN UGLY ENOUGH.
???
'RYU,' HUH?
....
AH, AS HANDSOME AS EVER...
!

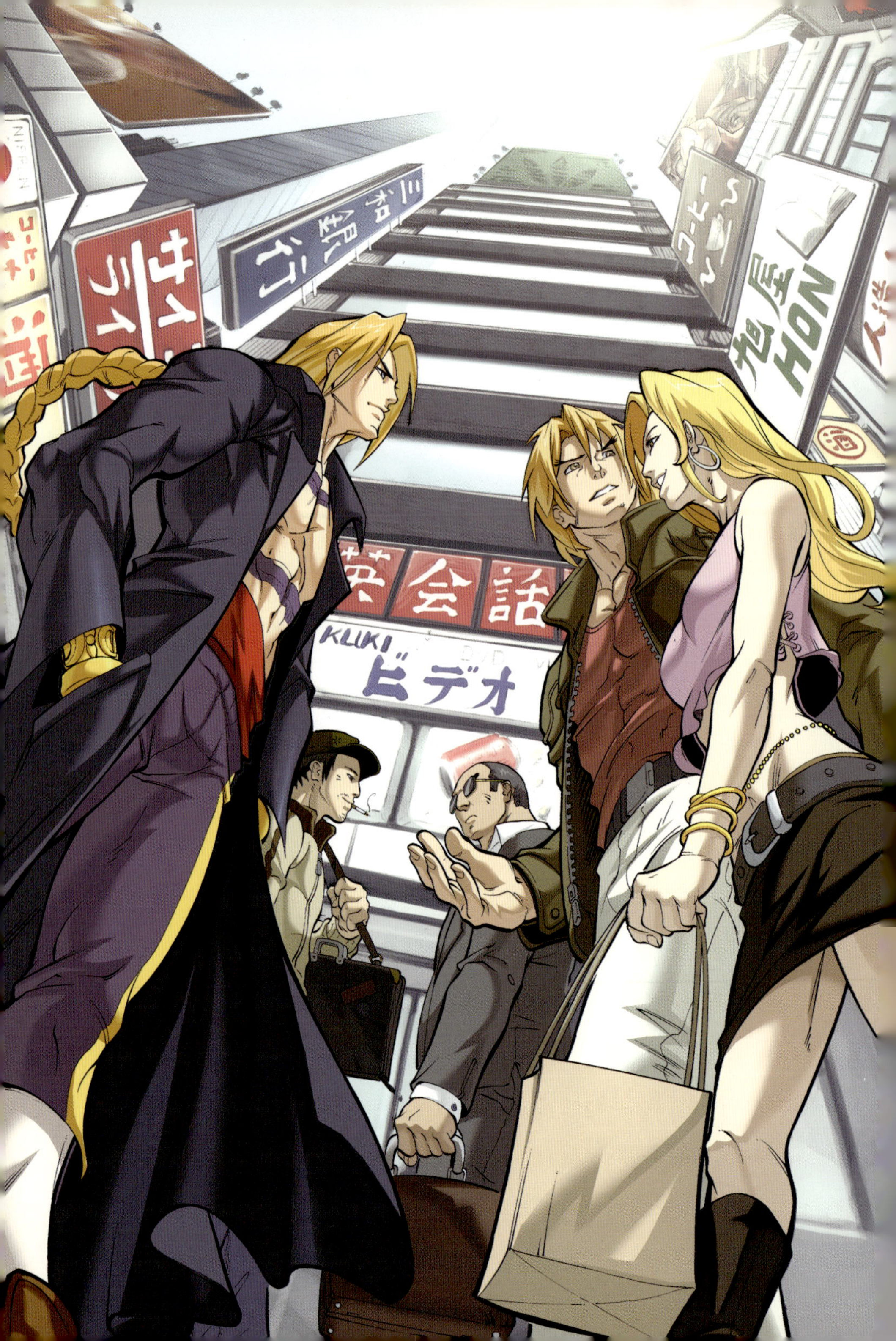

三和銀行
英会話
KUKI
ビデオ
HON

Cover Art by: Alvin Lee and Ramil Sunga

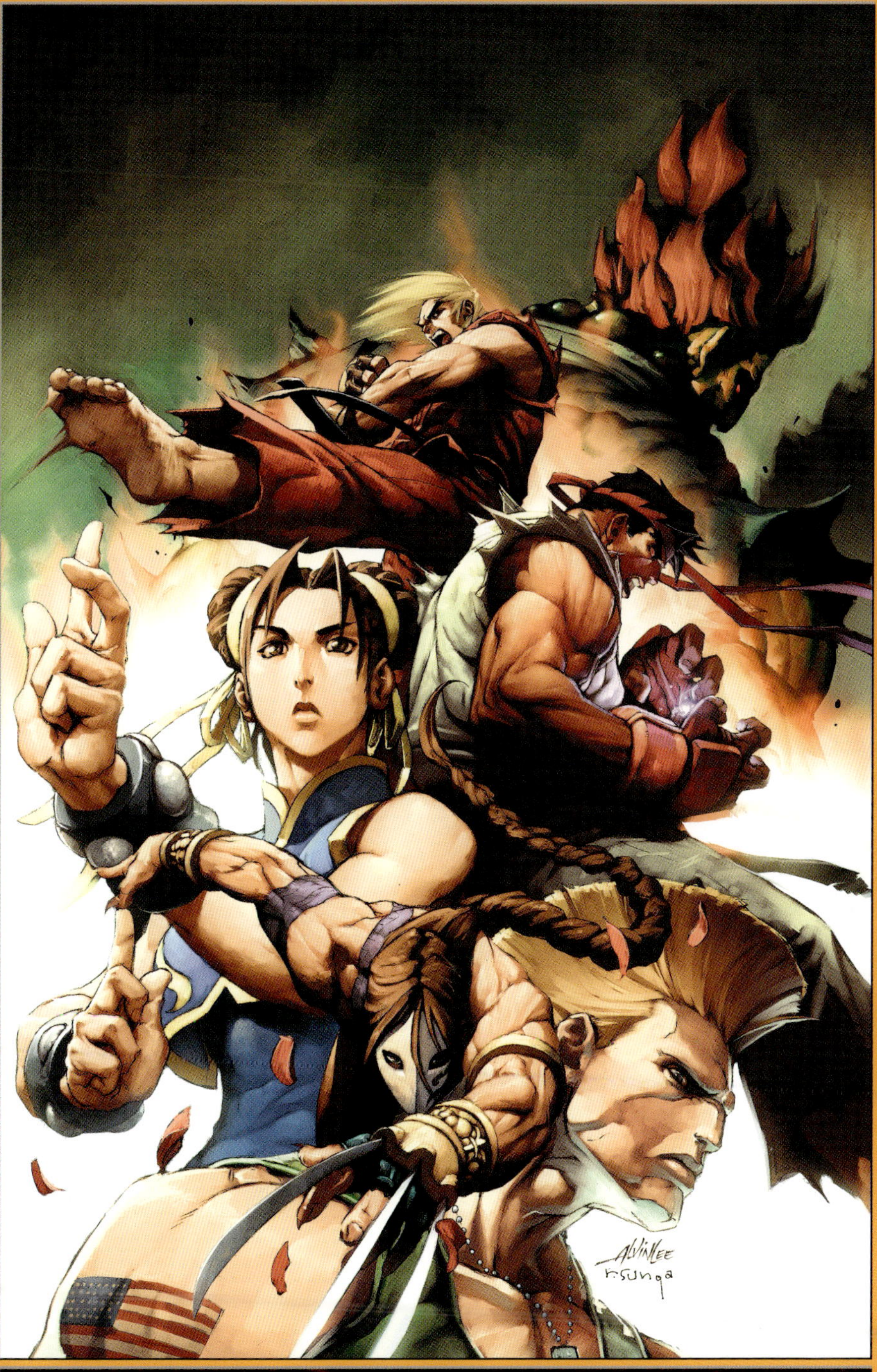
AlvinLee
r.sunga

Chapter 03: VEGA ATTACKS

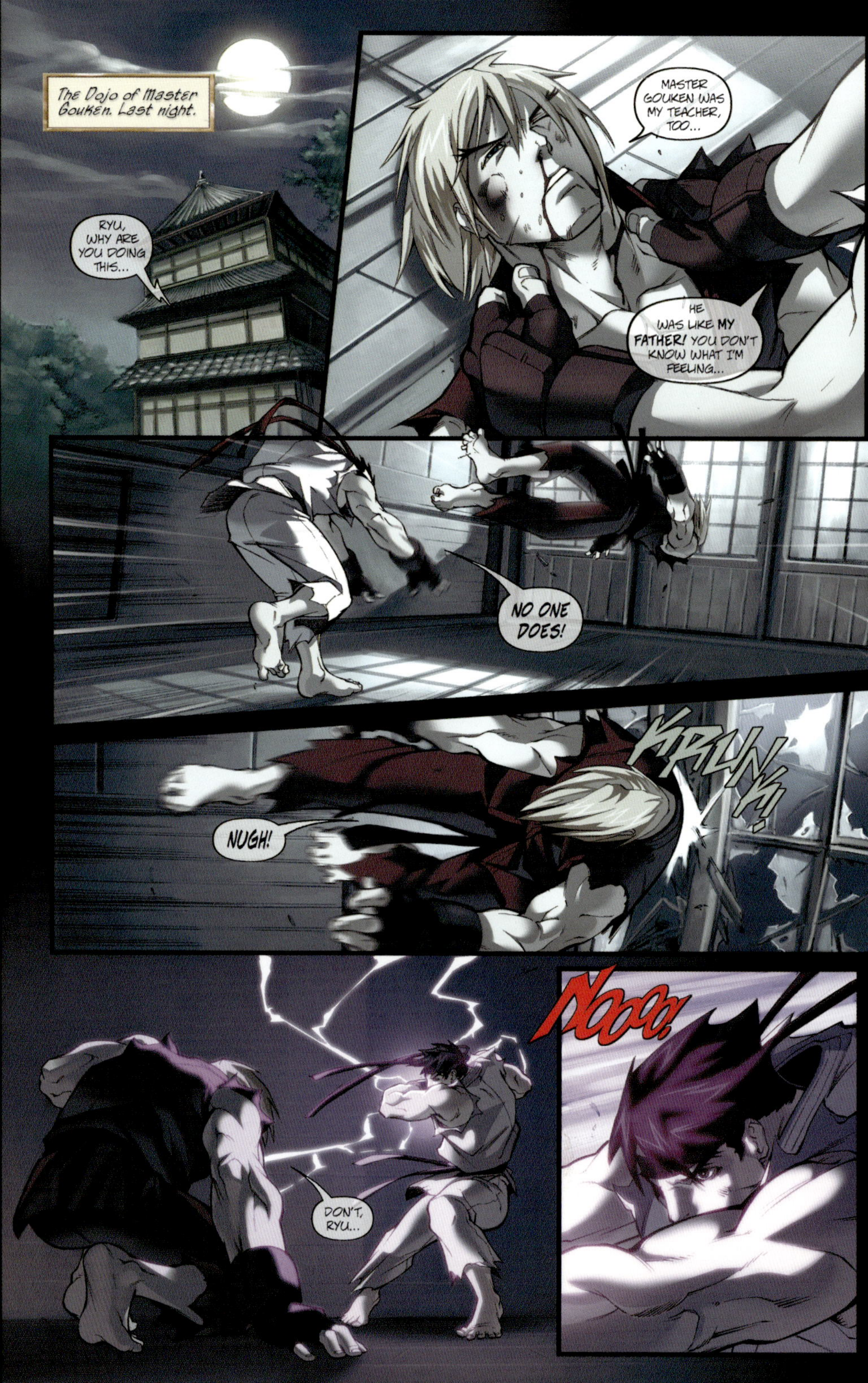
The Dojo of Master Gouken. Last night.
RYU, WHY ARE YOU DOING THIS...
MASTER GOUKEN WAS MY TEACHER, TOO...
HE WAS LIKE MY FATHER! YOU DON'T KNOW WHAT I'M FEELING...
NO ONE DOES!
KRUNK!
NUGH!
NOOOO!
DON'T, RYU...

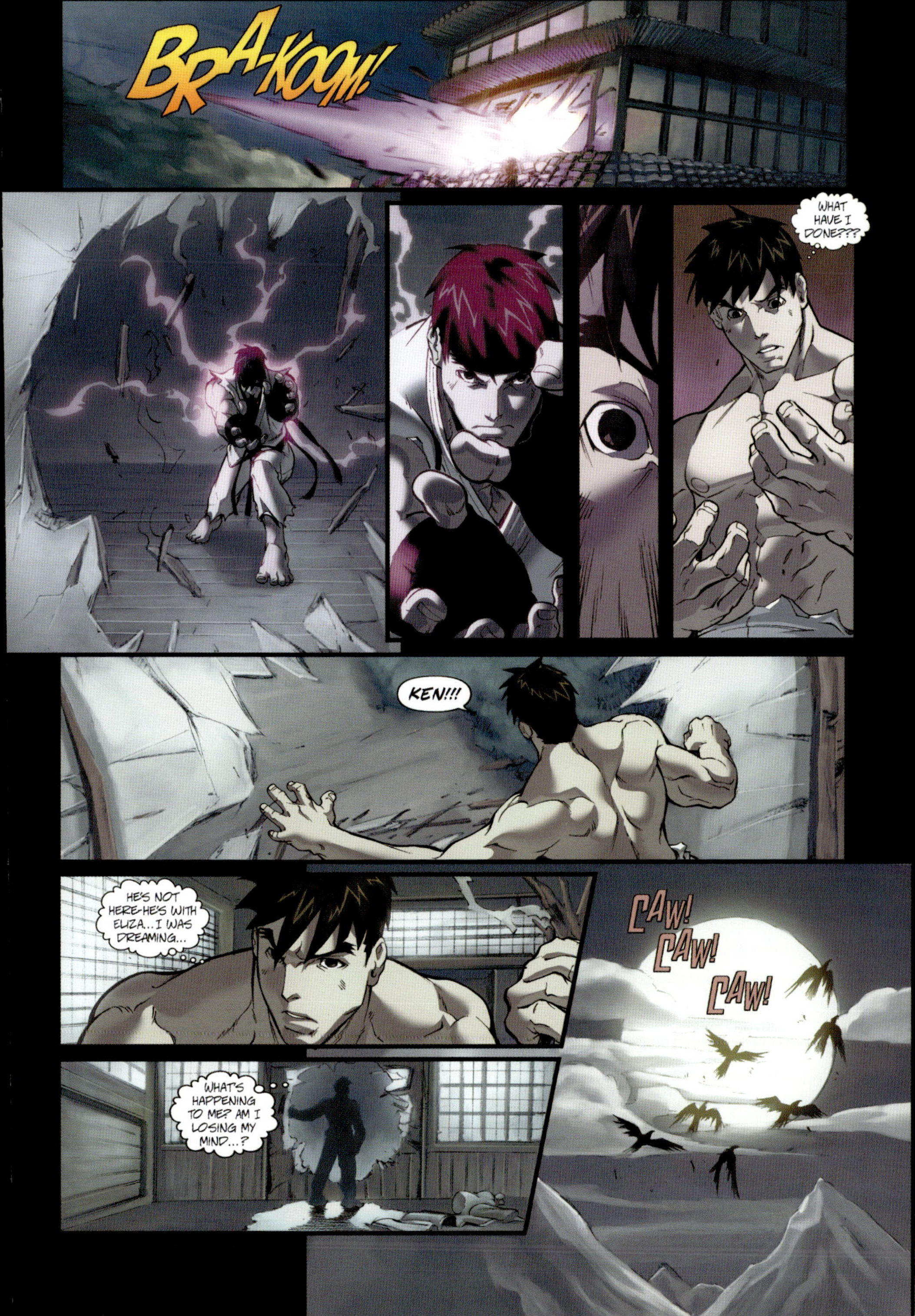
BRA-KOOM!
WHAT HAVE I DONE???
KEN!!!
HE'S NOT HERE-HE'S WITH ELIZA... I WAS DREAMING...
CAW! CAW! CAW!
WHAT'S HAPPENING TO ME? AM I LOSING MY MIND...?

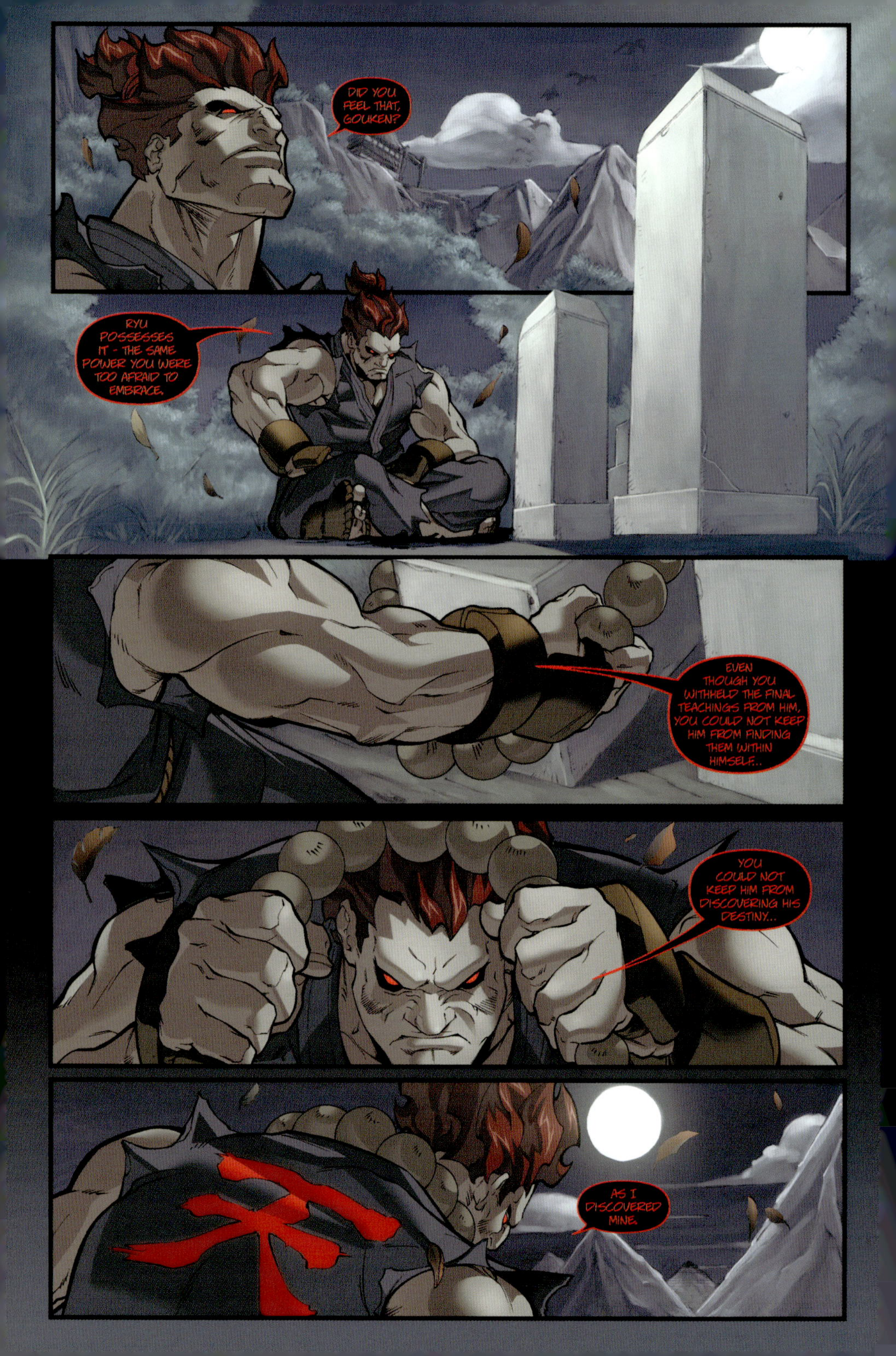
DID YOU FEEL THAT, GOUKEN?
RYU POSSESSES IT - THE SAME POWER YOU WERE TOO AFRAID TO EMBRACE.
EVEN THOUGH YOU WITHHELD THE FINAL TEACHINGS FROM HIM, YOU COULD NOT KEEP HIM FROM FINDING THEM WITHIN HIMSELF...
YOU COULD NOT KEEP HIM FROM DISCOVERING HIS DESTINY...
AS I DISCOVERED MINE.

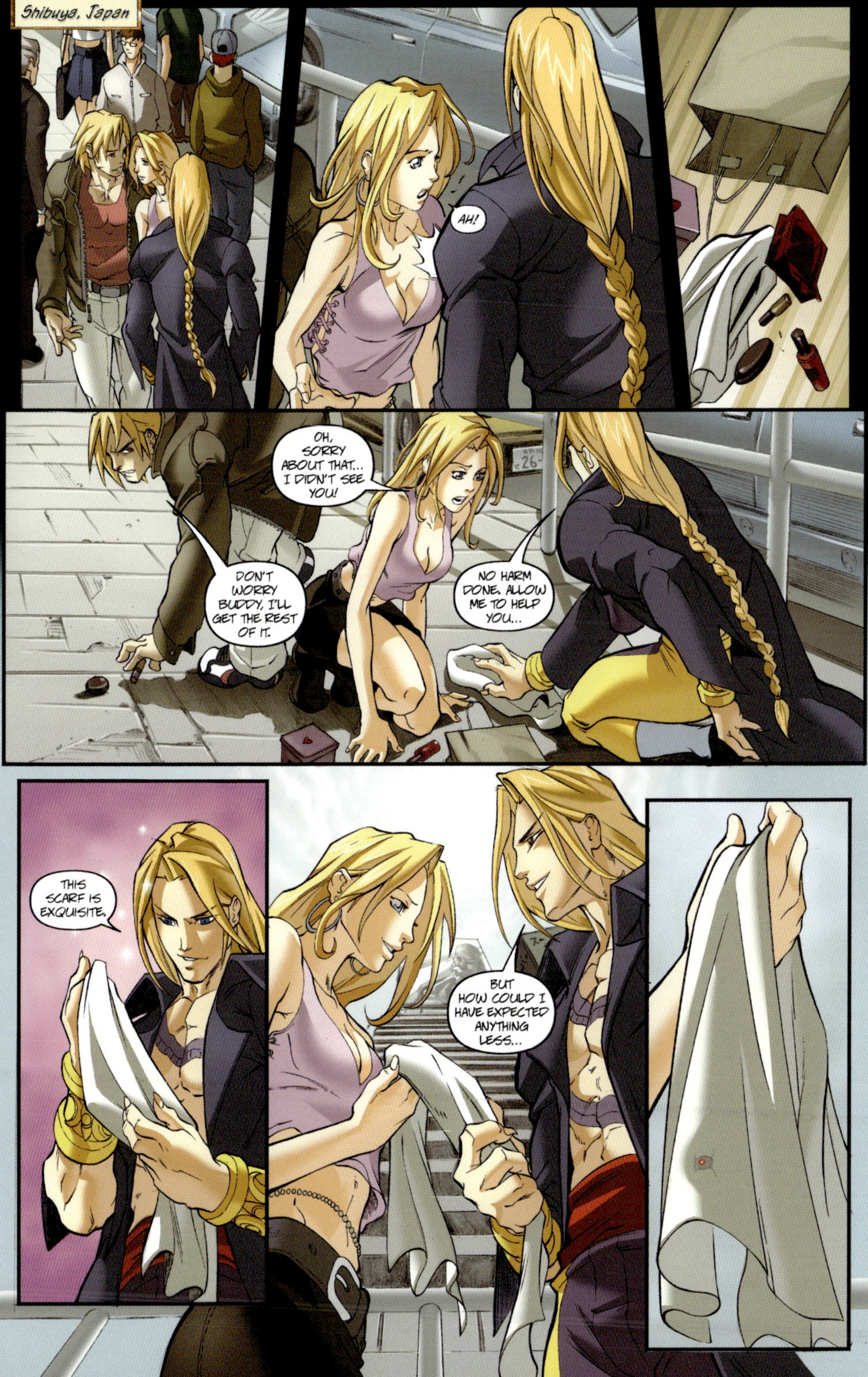
Shibuya, Japan
AH!
OH, SORRY ABOUT THAT... I DIDN'T SEE YOU!
DON'T WORRY BUDDY, I'LL GET THE REST OF IT.
NO HARM DONE. ALLOW ME TO HELP YOU...
THIS SCARF IS EXQUISITE.
BUT HOW COULD I HAVE EXPECTED ANYTHING LESS...

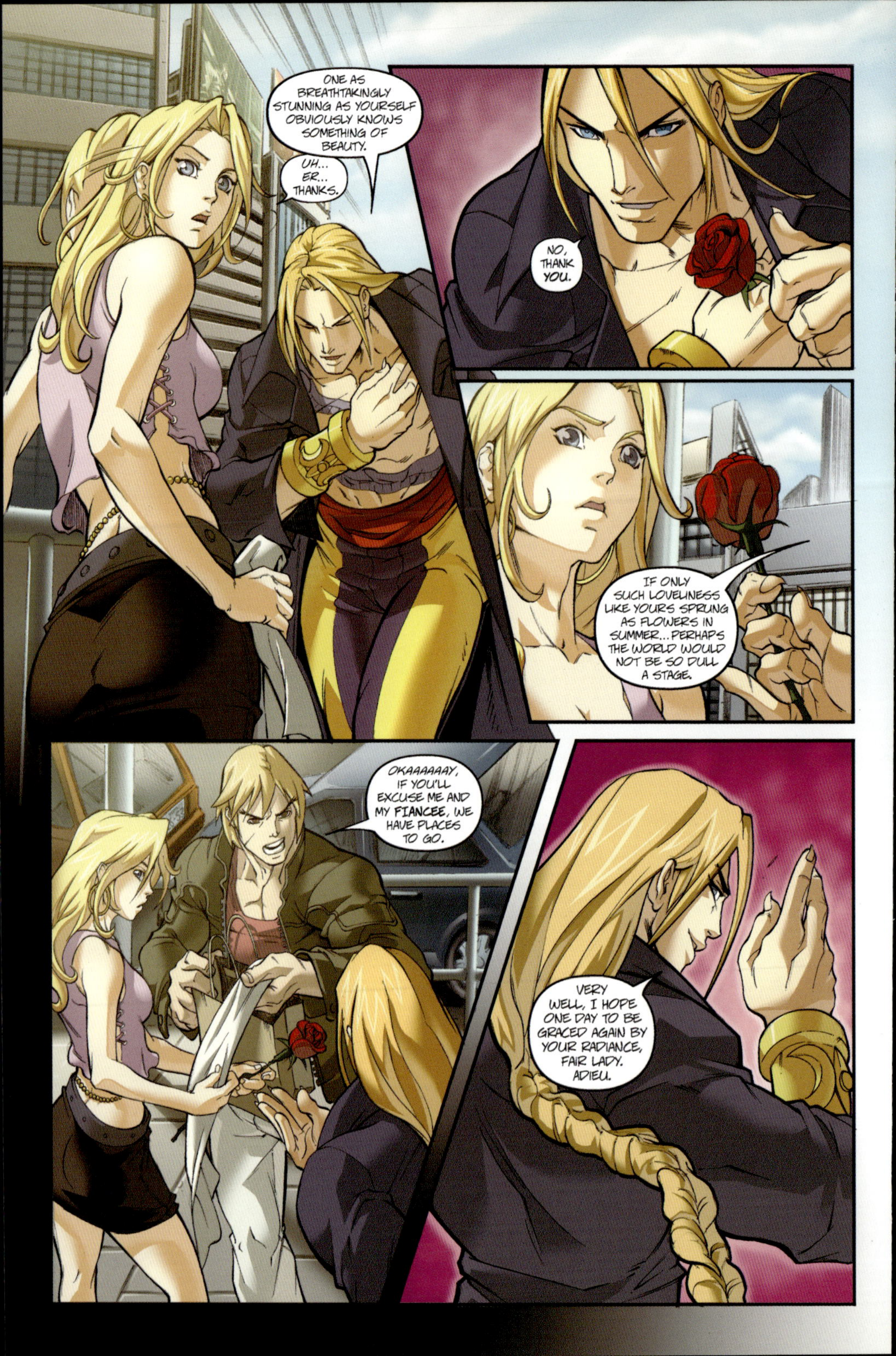
ONE AS BREATHTAKINGLY STUNNING AS YOURSELF OBVIOUSLY KNOWS SOMETHING OF BEAUTY.
UH... ER... THANKS.
NO, THANK YOU.
IF ONLY SUCH LOVELINESS LIKE YOURS SPRUNG AS FLOWERS IN SUMMER... PERHAPS THE WORLD WOULD NOT BE SO DULL A STAGE.
OKAAAAAAY, IF YOU'LL EXCUSE ME AND MY FIANCEE, WE HAVE PLACES TO GO.
VERY WELL, I HOPE ONE DAY TO BE GRACED AGAIN BY YOUR RADIANCE, FAIR LADY. ADIEU.

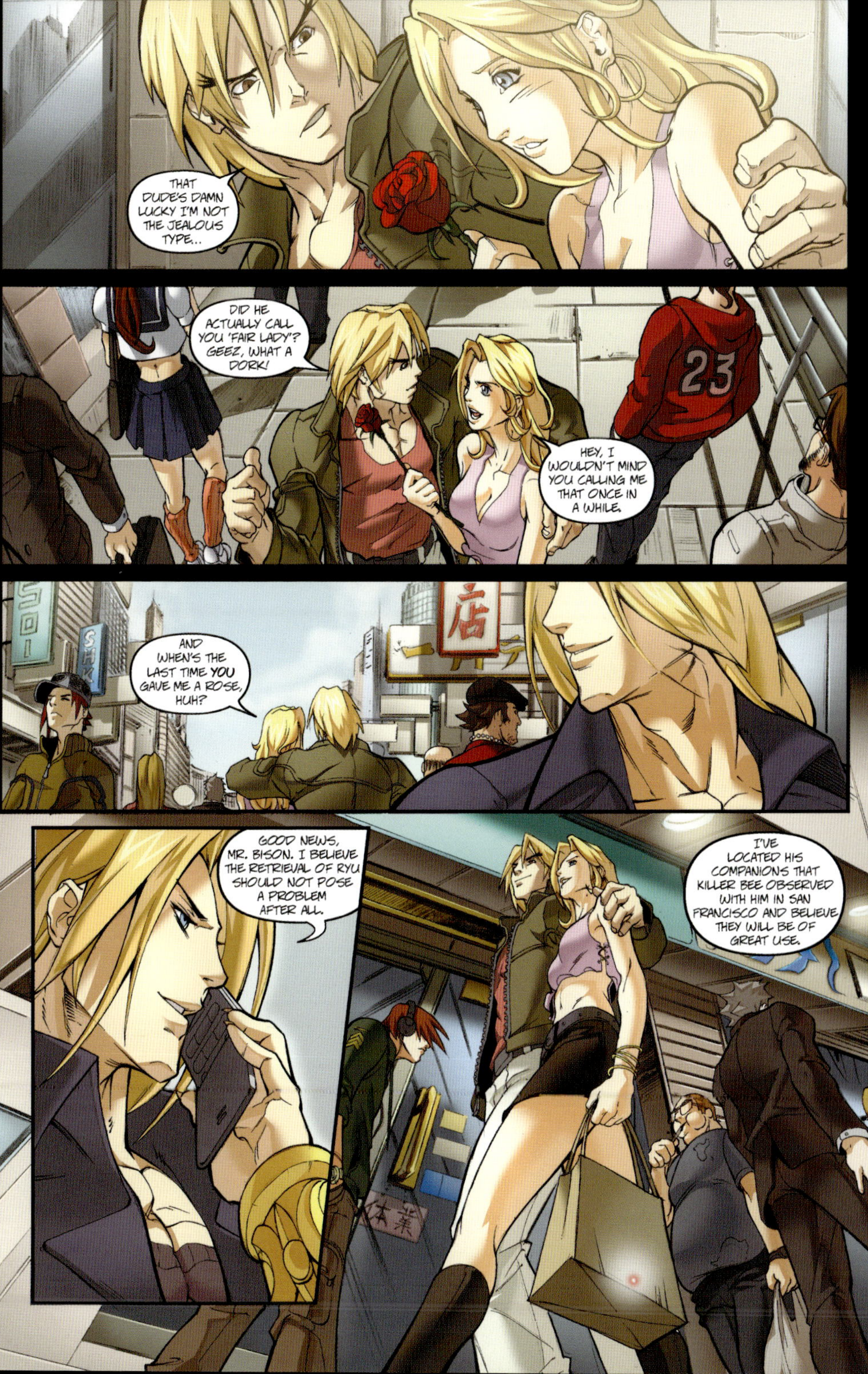
THAT DUDE'S DAMN LUCKY I'M NOT THE JEALOUS TYPE...
DID HE ACTUALLY CALL YOU 'FAIR LADY'? GEEZ, WHAT A DORK!
HEY, I WOULDN'T MIND YOU CALLING ME THAT ONCE IN A WHILE.
23
AND WHEN'S THE LAST TIME YOU GAVE ME A ROSE, HUH?
GOOD NEWS, MR. BISON. I BELIEVE THE RETRIEVAL OF RYU SHOULD NOT POSE A PROBLEM AFTER ALL.
I'VE LOCATED HIS COMPANIONS THAT KILLER BEE OBSERVED WITH HIM IN SAN FRANCISCO AND BELIEVE THEY WILL BE OF GREAT USE.

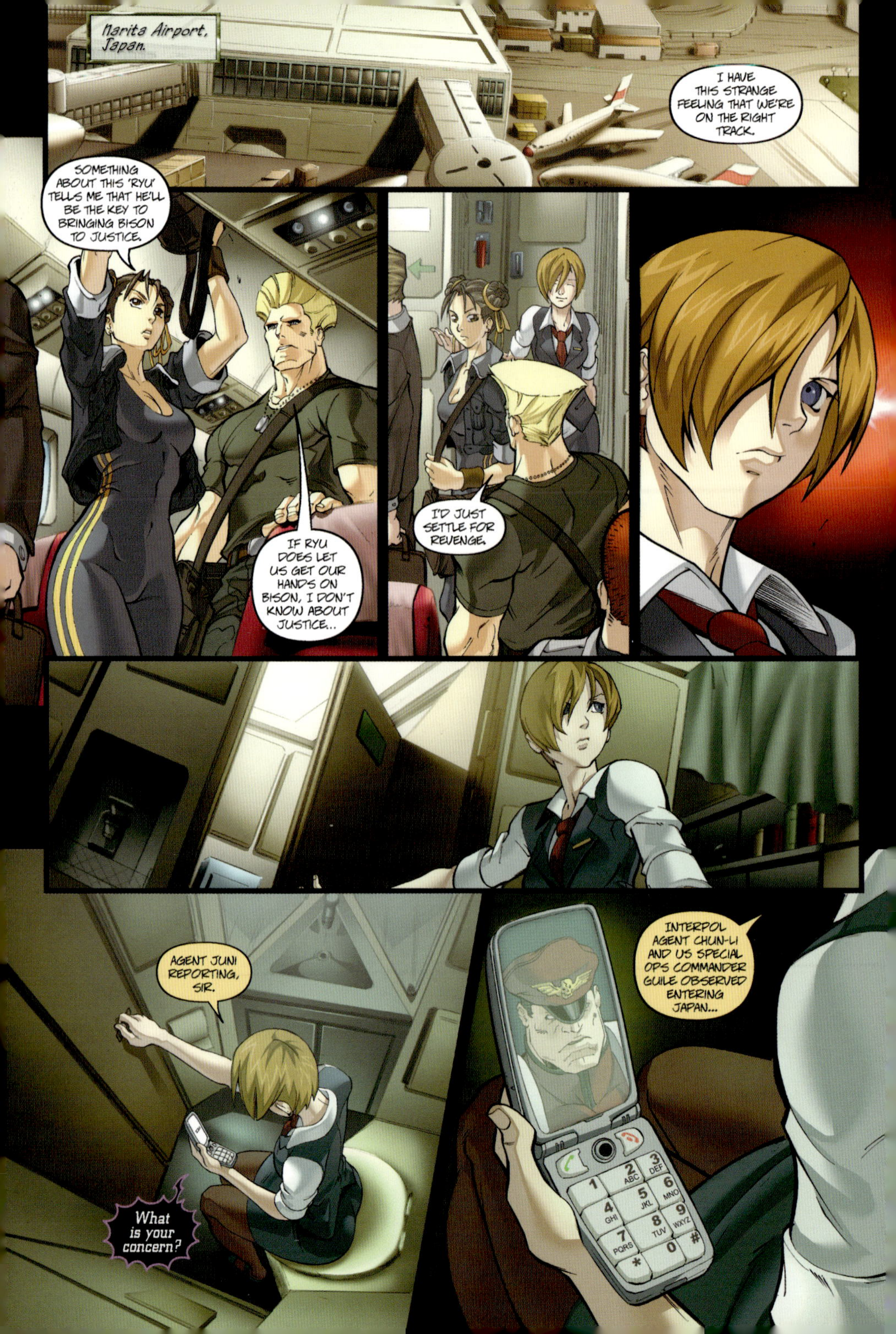
Narita Airport, Japan.
I HAVE THIS STRANGE FEELING THAT WE'RE ON THE RIGHT TRACK.
SOMETHING ABOUT THIS 'RYU' TELLS ME THAT HE'LL BE THE KEY TO BRINGING BISON TO JUSTICE.
IF RYU DOES LET US GET OUR HANDS ON BISON, I DON'T KNOW ABOUT JUSTICE...
I'D JUST SETTLE FOR REVENGE.
AGENT JUNI REPORTING, SIR.
What is your concern?
INTERPOL AGENT CHUN-LI AND US SPECIAL OPS COMMANDER GUILE OBSERVED ENTERING JAPAN...

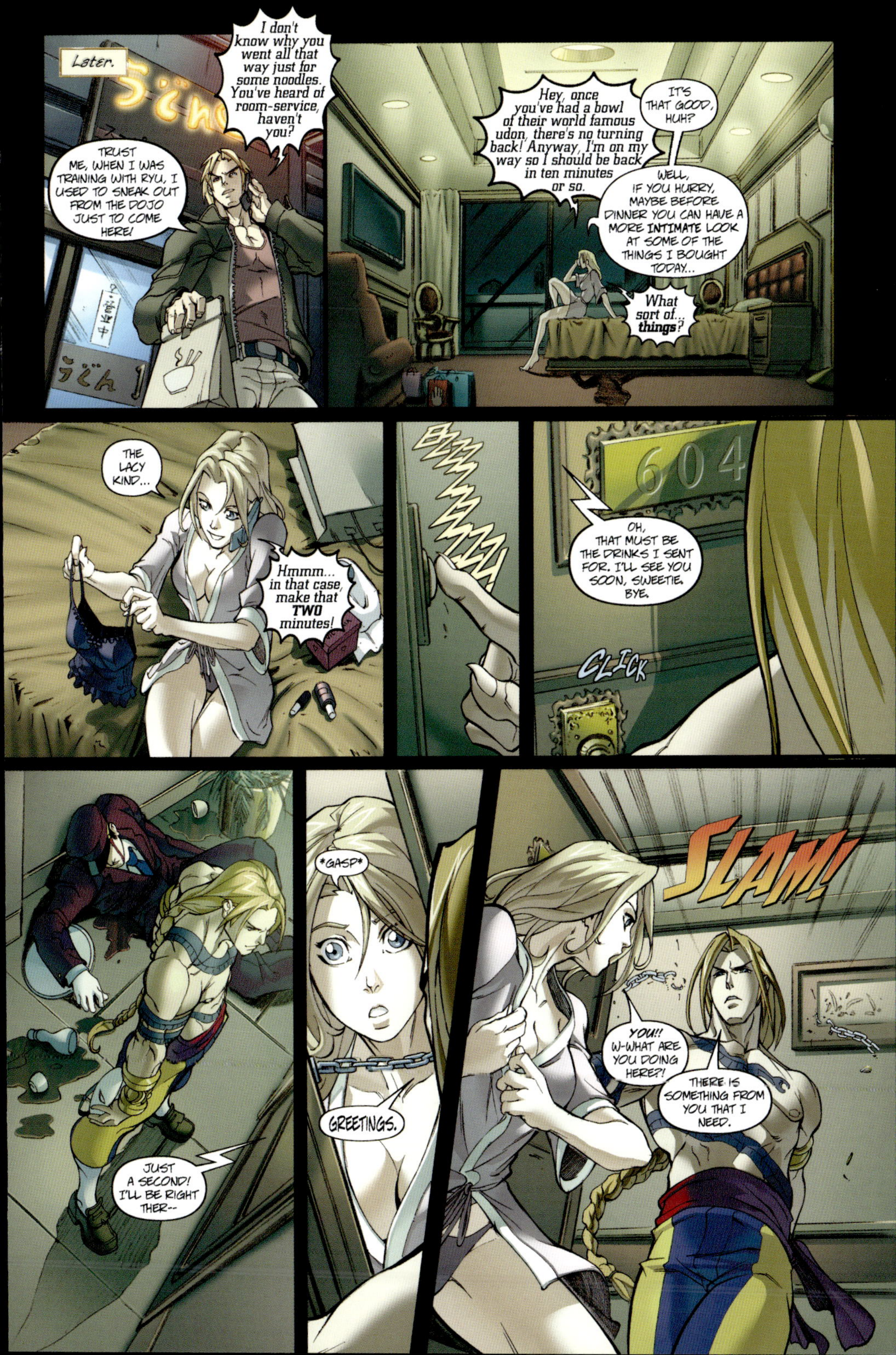
Later.
I don't know why you went all that way just for some noodles. You've heard of room-service, haven't you?
TRUST ME, WHEN I WAS TRAINING WITH RYU, I USED TO SNEAK OUT FROM THE DOJO JUST TO COME HERE!
Hey, once you've had a bowl of their world famous udon, there's no turning back! Anyway, I'm on my way so I should be back in ten minutes or so.
IT'S THAT GOOD, HUH?
WELL, IF YOU HURRY, MAYBE BEFORE DINNER YOU CAN HAVE A MORE INTIMATE LOOK AT SOME OF THE THINGS I BOUGHT TODAY...
What sort of... things?
THE LACY KIND...
Hmmm... in that case, make that TWO minutes!
604
OH, THAT MUST BE THE DRINKS I SENT FOR. I'LL SEE YOU SOON, SWEETIE. BYE.
CLICK
JUST A SECOND! I'LL BE RIGHT THER--
GASP
GREETINGS.
SLAM!
YOU!! W-WHAT ARE YOU DOING HERE?!
THERE IS SOMETHING FROM YOU THAT I NEED.

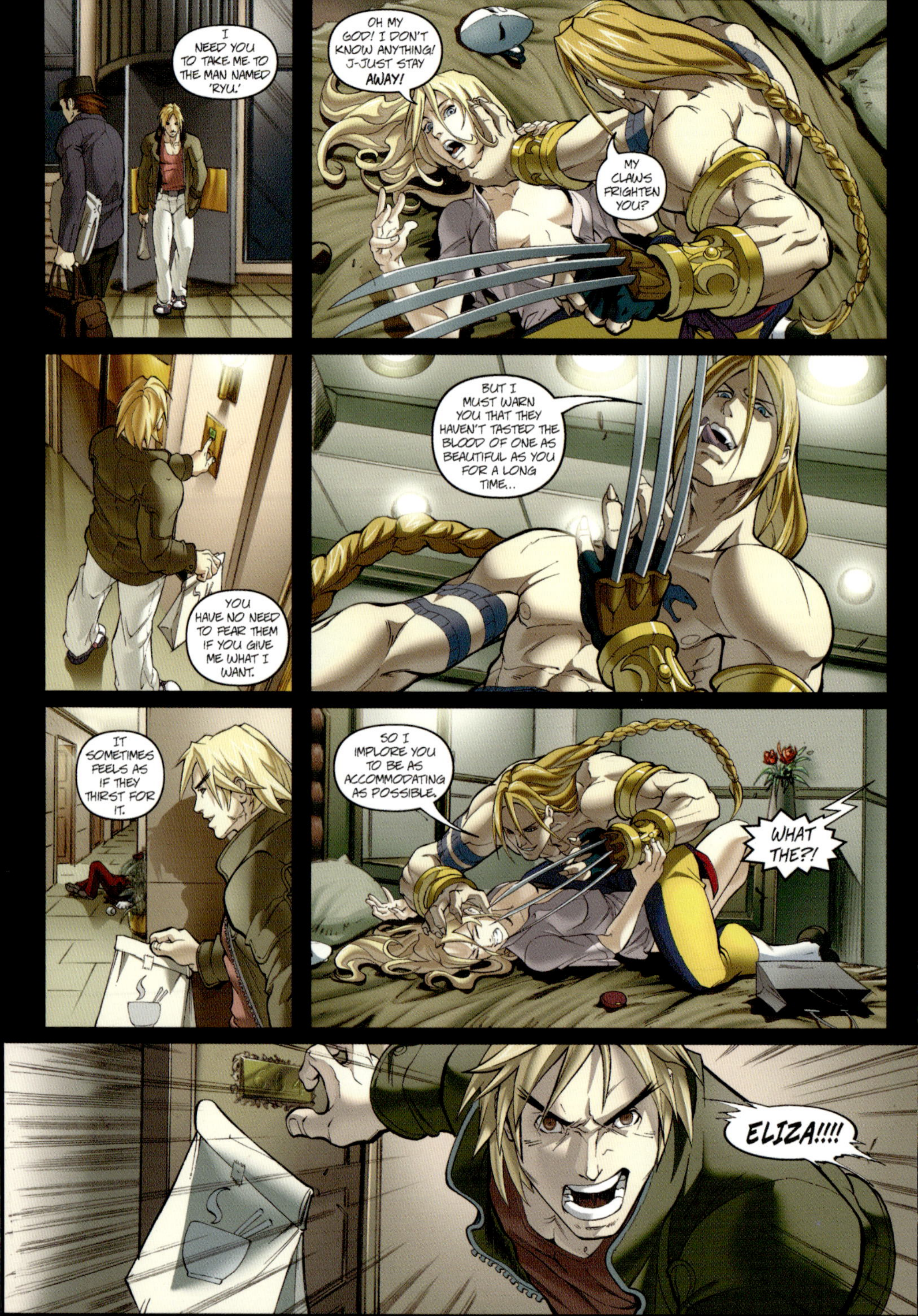

I NEED YOU TO TAKE ME TO THE MAN NAMED 'RYU.'
OH MY GOD! I DON'T KNOW ANYTHING! J-JUST STAY AWAY!
MY CLAWS FRIGHTEN YOU?
BUT I MUST WARN YOU THAT THEY HAVEN'T TASTED THE BLOOD OF ONE AS BEAUTIFUL AS YOU FOR A LONG TIME...
YOU HAVE NO NEED TO FEAR THEM IF YOU GIVE ME WHAT I WANT.
IT SOMETIMES FEELS AS IF THEY THIRST FOR IT.
SO I IMPLORE YOU TO BE AS ACCOMMODATING AS POSSIBLE.
WHAT THE?!
ELIZA!!!!

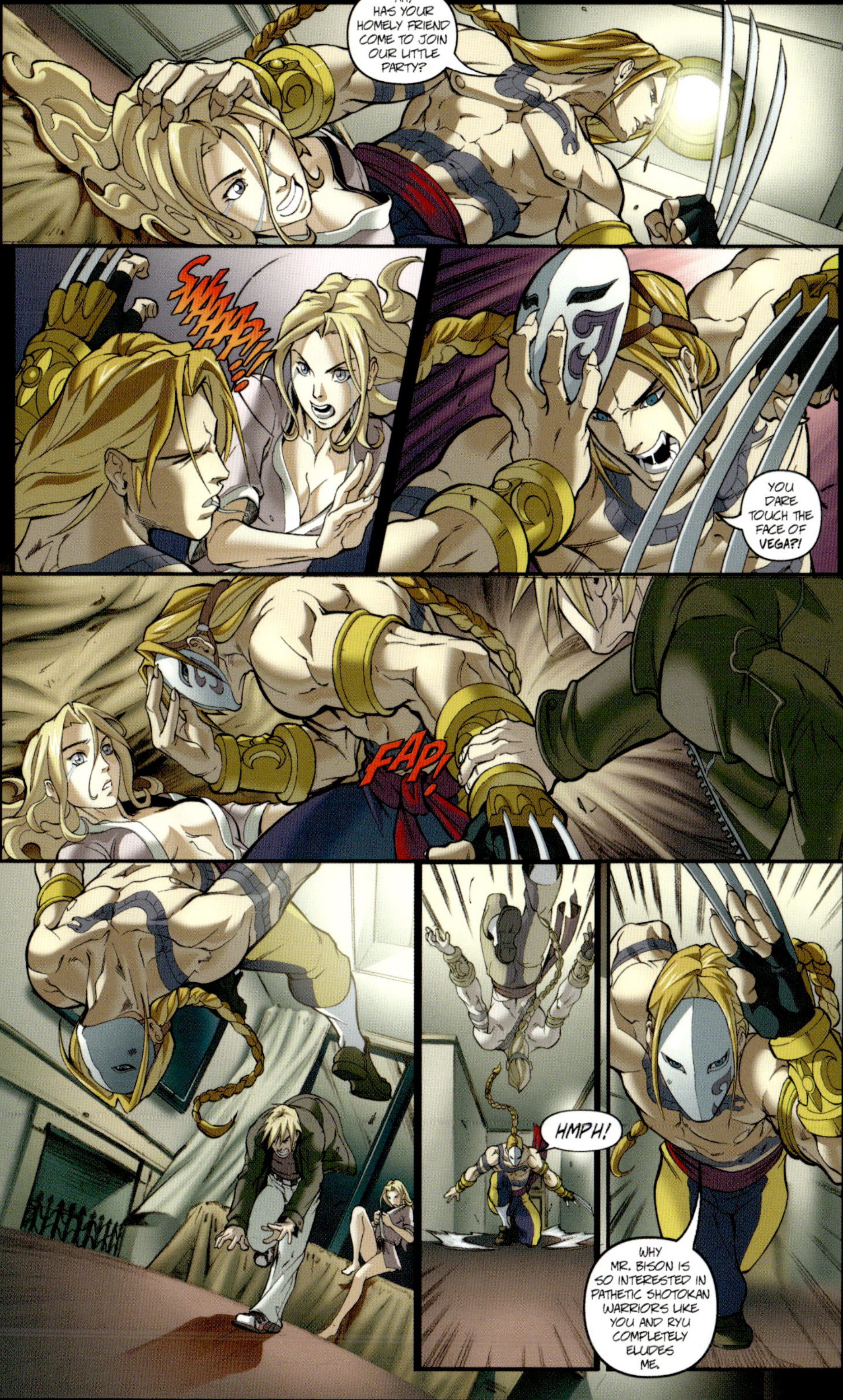
AH, HAS YOUR HOMELY FRIEND COME TO JOIN OUR LITTLE PARTY?
SWAAAP!!!
YOU DARE TOUCH THE FACE OF VEGA?!
FAP!
HMPH!
WHY MR. BISON IS SO INTERESTED IN PATHETIC SHOTOKAN WARRIORS LIKE YOU AND RYU COMPLETELY ELUDES ME.

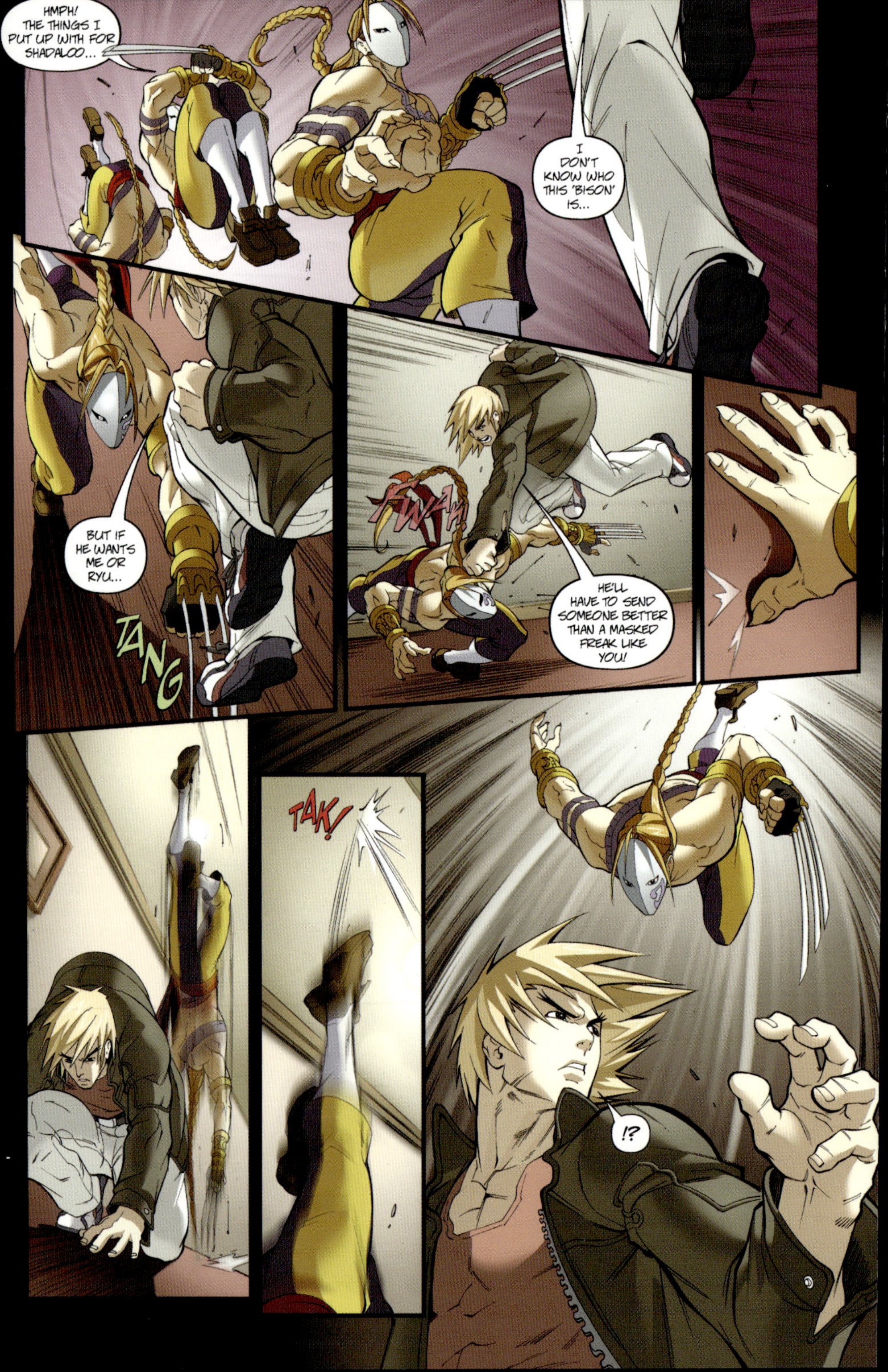
HMPH! THE THINGS I PUT UP WITH FOR SHADALOO...
I DON'T KNOW WHO THIS 'BISON' IS...
BUT IF HE WANTS ME OR RYU...
TANG
FWAH
HE'LL HAVE TO SEND SOMEONE BETTER THAN A MASKED FREAK LIKE YOU!
TAK!
!?

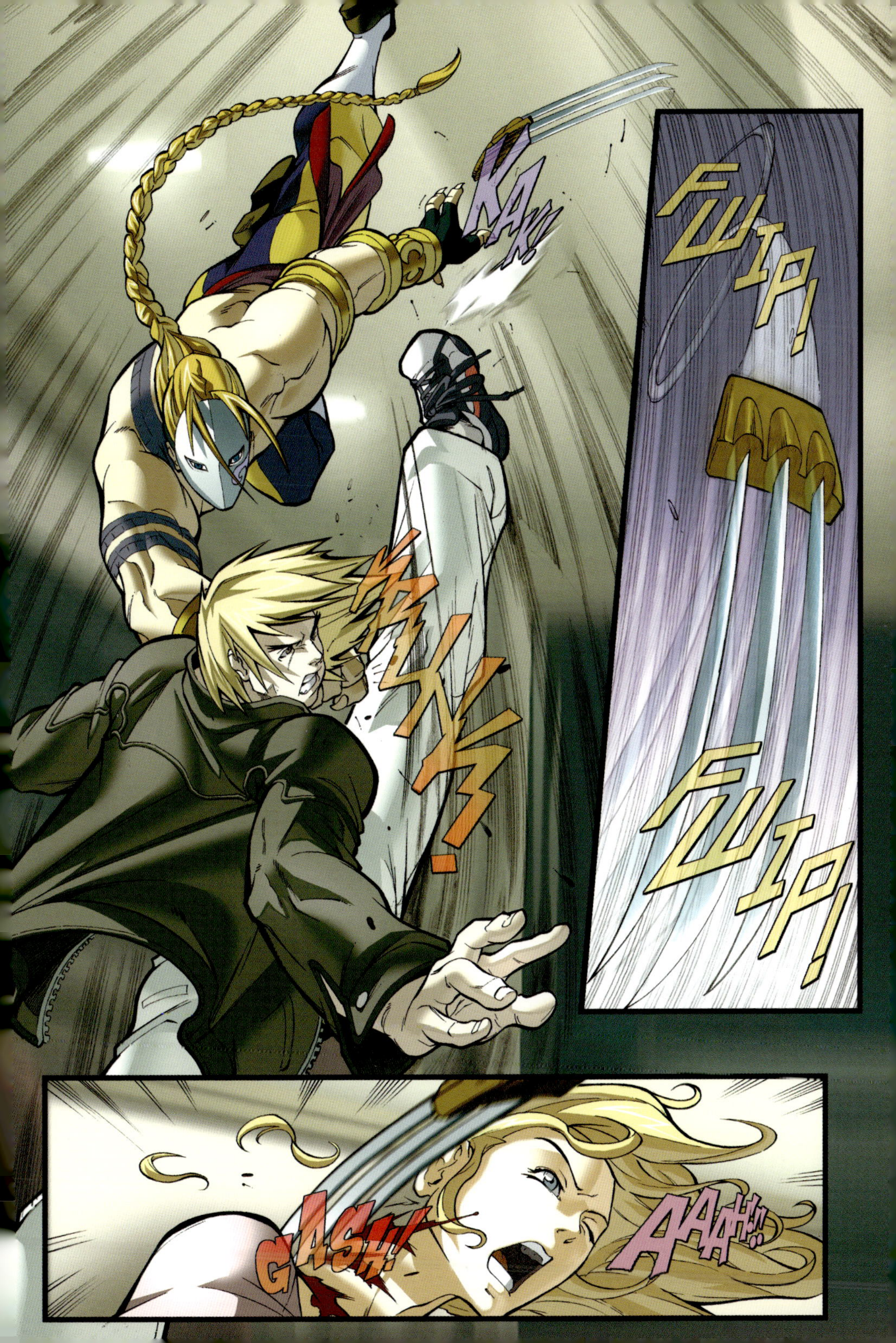
KAK!
FWIP!
FWIP!
GASH!
AAAH!!!

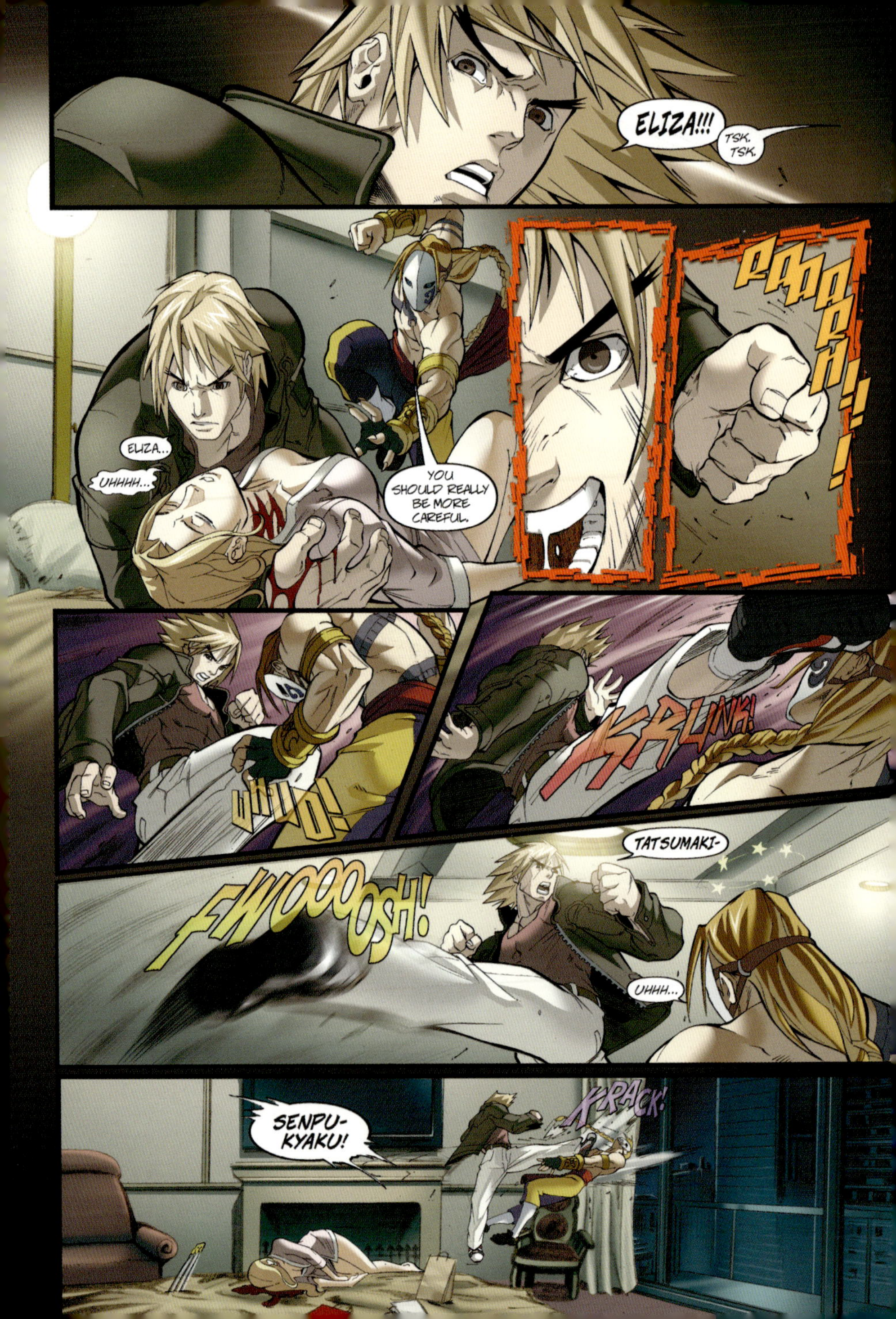
ELIZA!!!
TSK. TSK.
ELIZA...
UHHHH...
YOU SHOULD REALLY BE MORE CAREFUL.
RAAAAH!!!
WHUD!
KRUNK!
FWOOOOOSH!
TATSUMAKI-
UHHH...
SENPU-KYAKU!
K-RACK!

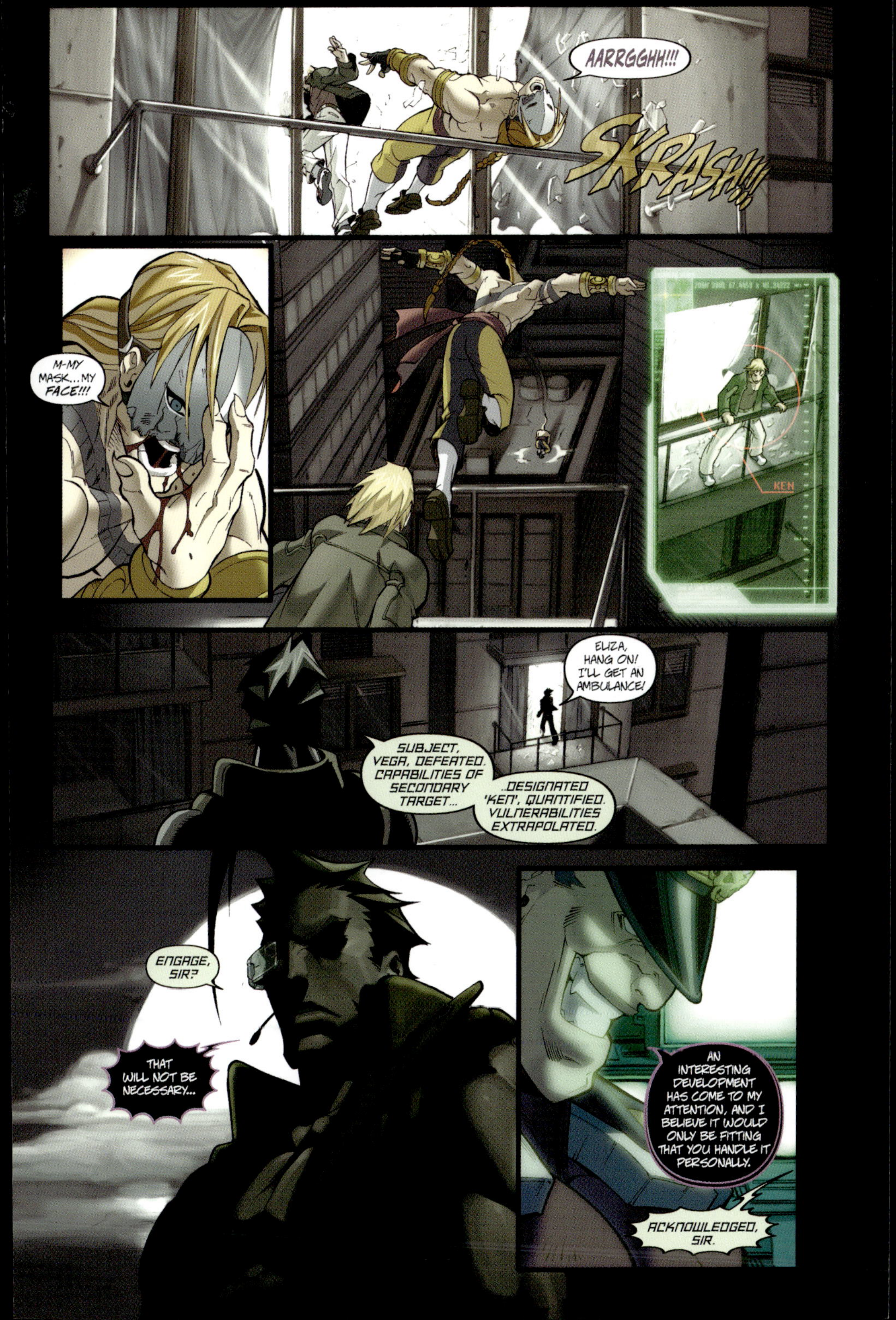
AARRGGHH!!!
SKRASH!!!
M-MY MASK...MY FACE!!!
KEN
ELIZA, HANG ON! I'LL GET AN AMBULANCE!
SUBJECT, VEGA, DEFEATED. CAPABILITIES OF SECONDARY TARGET...
..DESIGNATED 'KEN', QUANTIFIED. VULNERABILITIES EXTRAPOLATED.
ENGAGE, SIR?
THAT WILL NOT BE NECESSARY...
AN INTERESTING DEVELOPMENT HAS COME TO MY ATTENTION, AND I BELIEVE IT WOULD ONLY BE FITTING THAT YOU HANDLE IT PERSONALLY.
ACKNOWLEDGED, SIR.

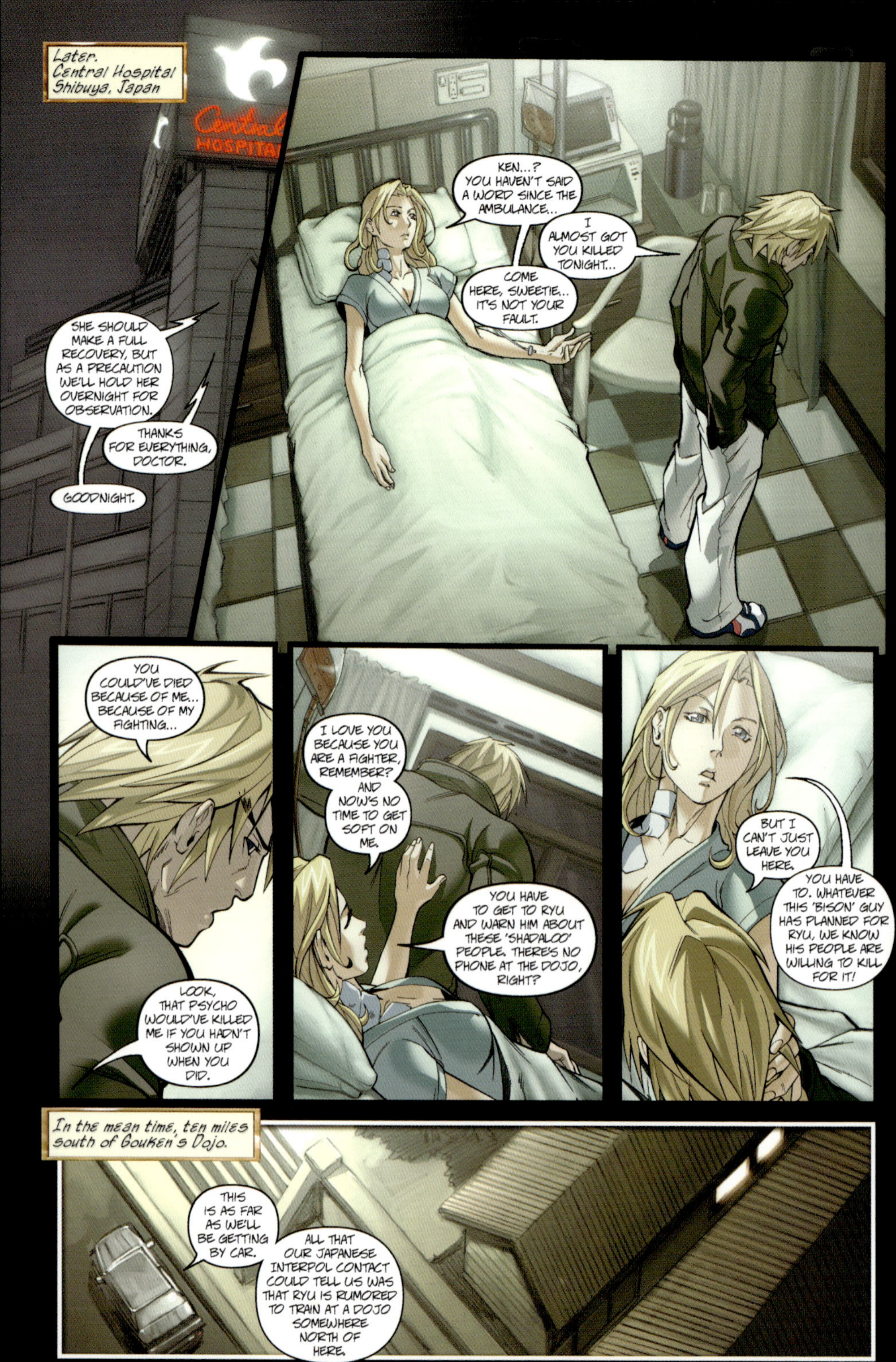
Later.
Central Hospital
Shibuya, Japan
Central
HOSPITAL
SHE SHOULD MAKE A FULL RECOVERY, BUT AS A PRECAUTION WE'LL HOLD HER OVERNIGHT FOR OBSERVATION.
THANKS FOR EVERYTHING, DOCTOR.
GOODNIGHT.
KEN...? YOU HAVEN'T SAID A WORD SINCE THE AMBULANCE...
I ALMOST GOT YOU KILLED TONIGHT...
COME HERE, SWEETIE... IT'S NOT YOUR FAULT.
YOU COULD'VE DIED BECAUSE OF ME... BECAUSE OF MY FIGHTING...
LOOK, THAT PSYCHO WOULD'VE KILLED ME IF YOU HADN'T SHOWN UP WHEN YOU DID.
I LOVE YOU BECAUSE YOU ARE A FIGHTER, REMEMBER? AND NOW'S NO TIME TO GET SOFT ON ME.
YOU HAVE TO GET TO RYU AND WARN HIM ABOUT THESE 'SHADALOO' PEOPLE. THERE'S NO PHONE AT THE DOJO, RIGHT?
BUT I CAN'T JUST LEAVE YOU HERE.
YOU HAVE TO. WHATEVER THIS 'BISON' GUY HAS PLANNED FOR RYU, WE KNOW HIS PEOPLE ARE WILLING TO KILL FOR IT!
In the mean time, ten miles south of Gouken's Dojo.
THIS IS AS FAR AS WE'LL BE GETTING BY CAR.
ALL THAT OUR JAPANESE INTERPOL CONTACT COULD TELL US WAS THAT RYU IS RUMORED TO TRAIN AT A DOJO SOMEWHERE NORTH OF HERE.

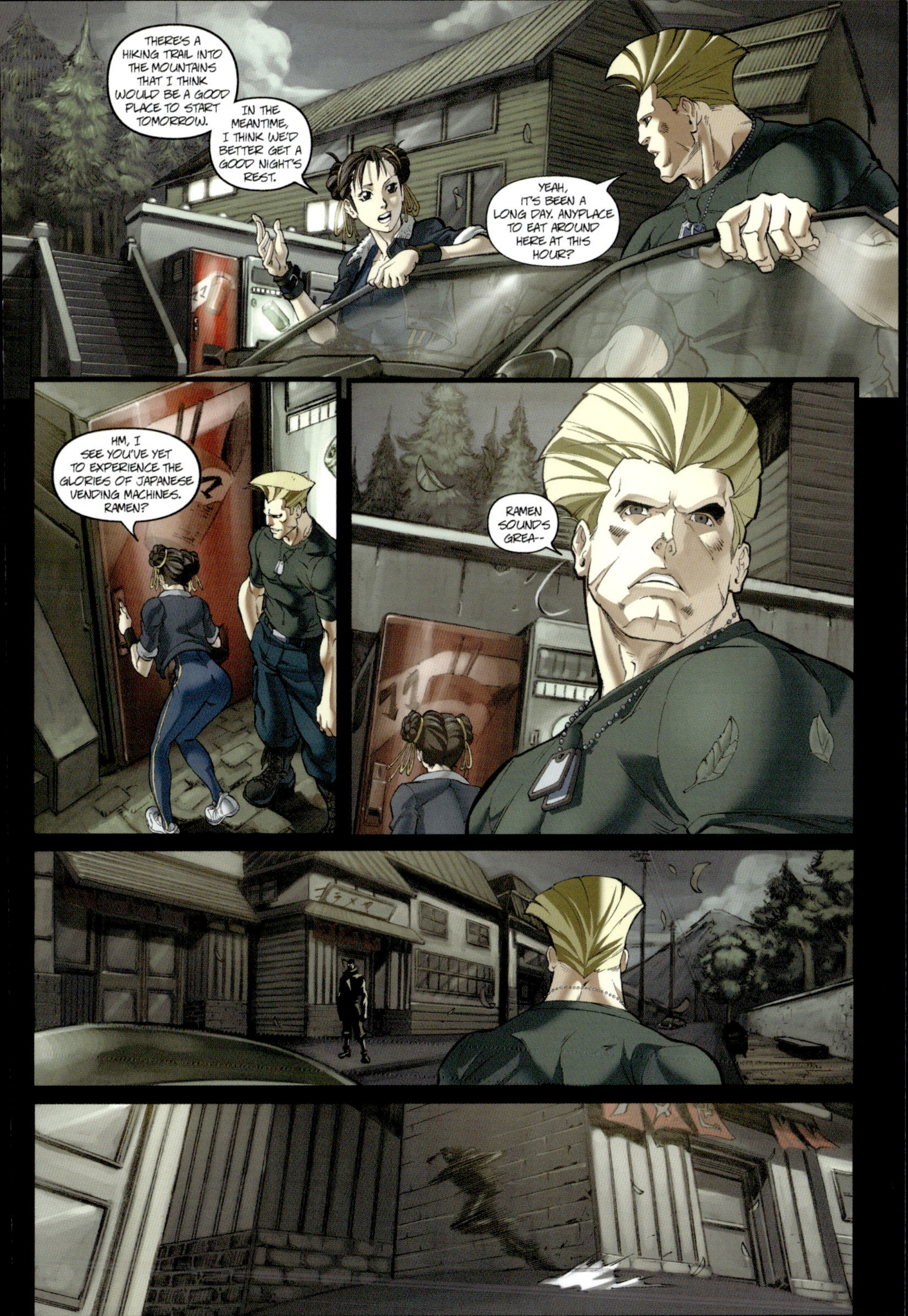
THERE'S A HIKING TRAIL INTO THE MOUNTAINS THAT I THINK WOULD BE A GOOD PLACE TO START TOMORROW.
IN THE MEANTIME, I THINK WE'D BETTER GET A GOOD NIGHT'S REST.
YEAH, IT'S BEEN A LONG DAY. ANYPLACE TO EAT AROUND HERE AT THIS HOUR?
HM, I SEE YOU'VE YET TO EXPERIENCE THE GLORIES OF JAPANESE VENDING MACHINES. RAMEN?
RAMEN SOUNDS GREA--

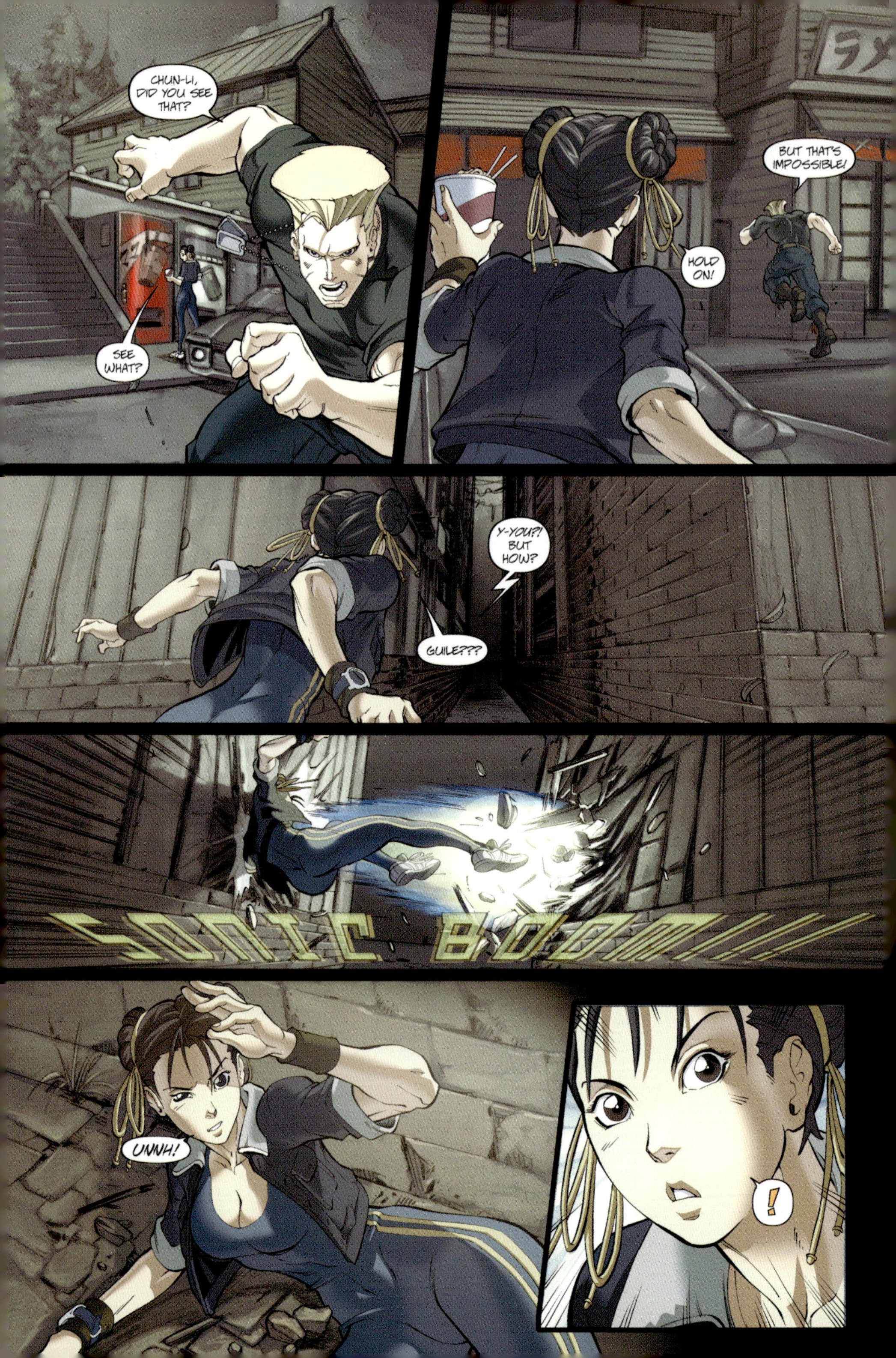
CHUN-LI, DID YOU SEE THAT?
SEE WHAT?
BUT THAT'S IMPOSSIBLE!
HOLD ON!
GUILE???
Y-YOU?! BUT HOW?
SONIC BOOM!!!
UNNH!
!

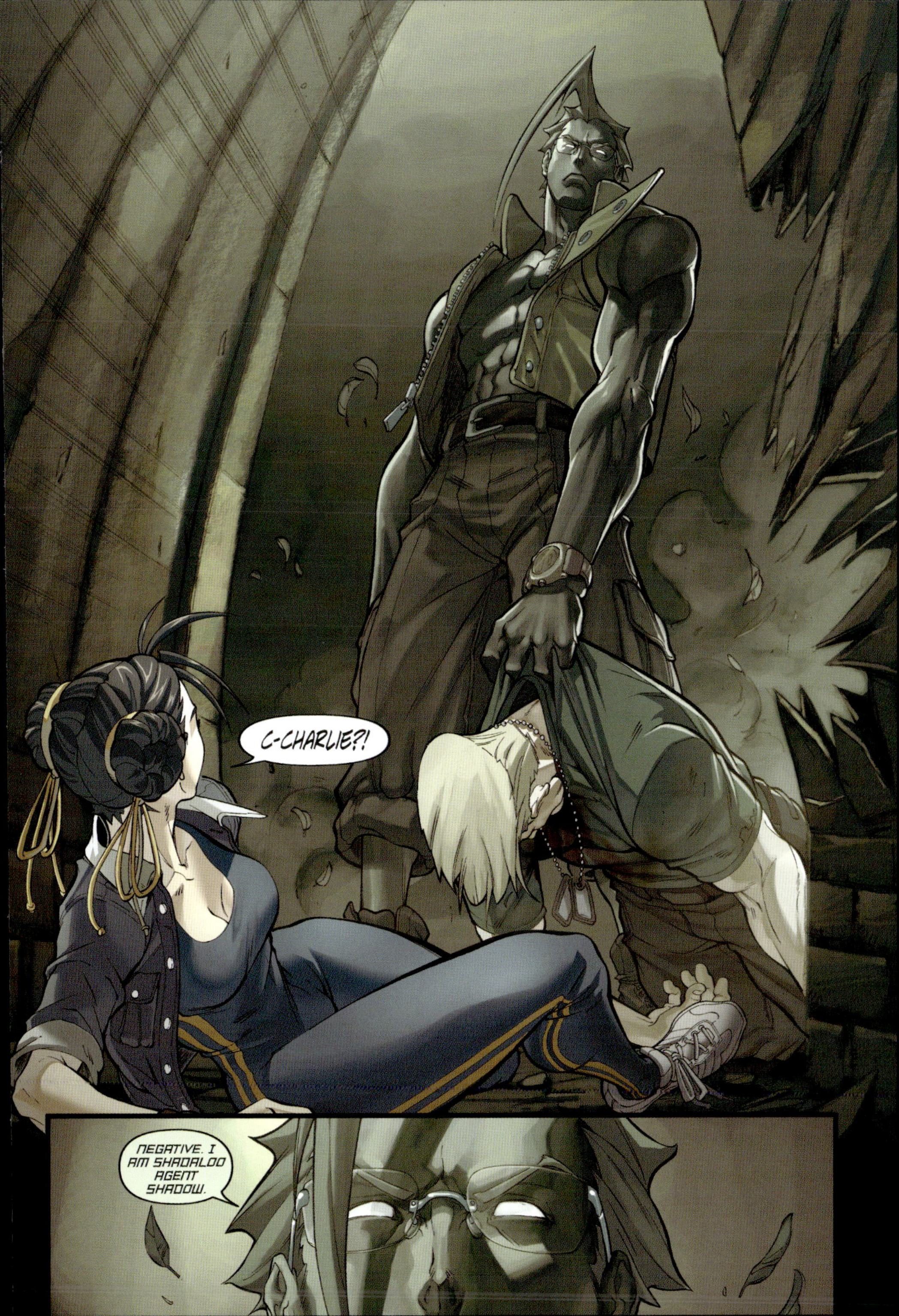
C-CHARLIE?!
NEGATIVE. I AM SHADALOO AGENT SHADOW.

Cover Art by: Alvin Lee and Arnold Tsang

Chapter 04: FROM THE SHADOWS

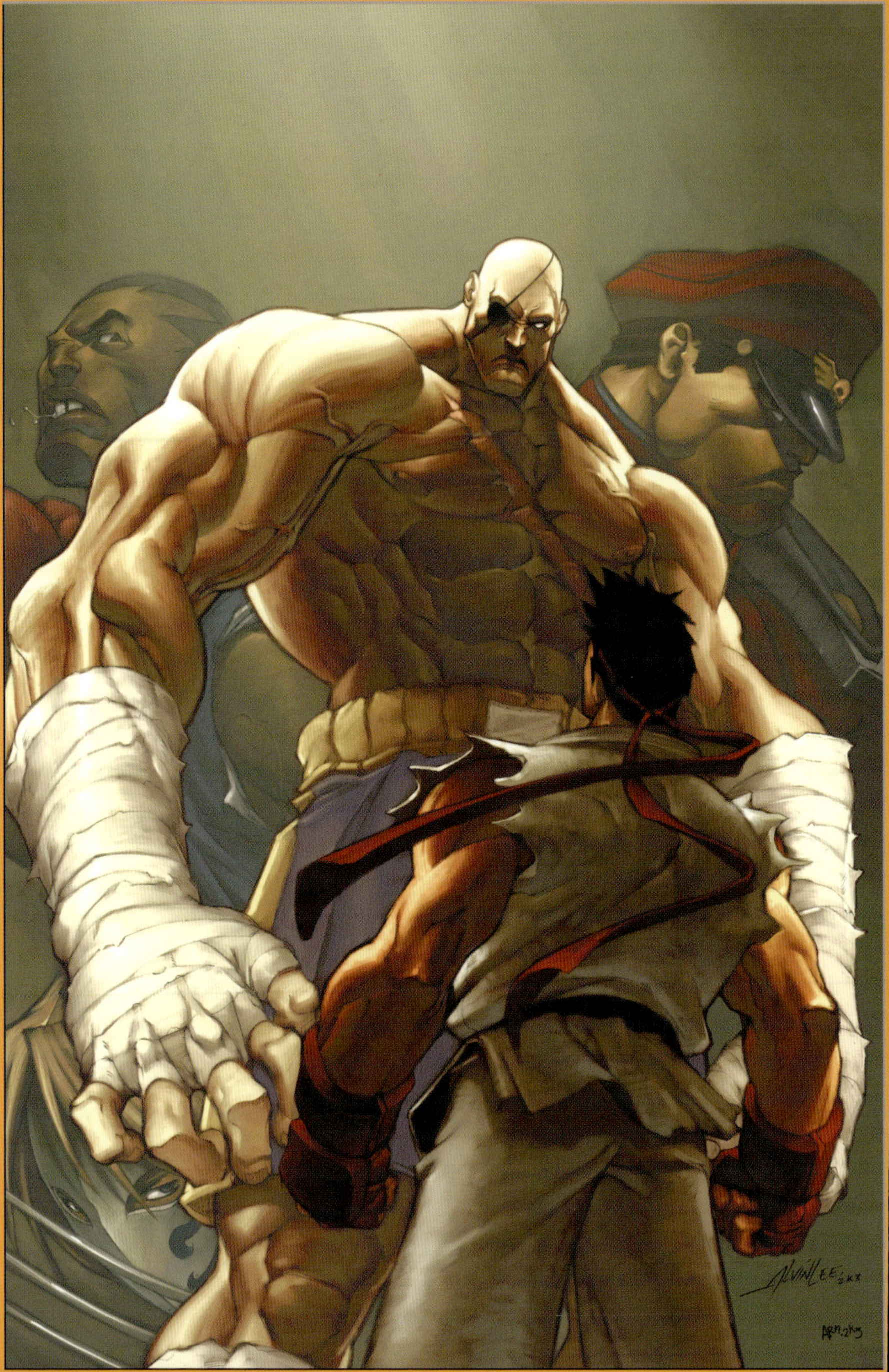

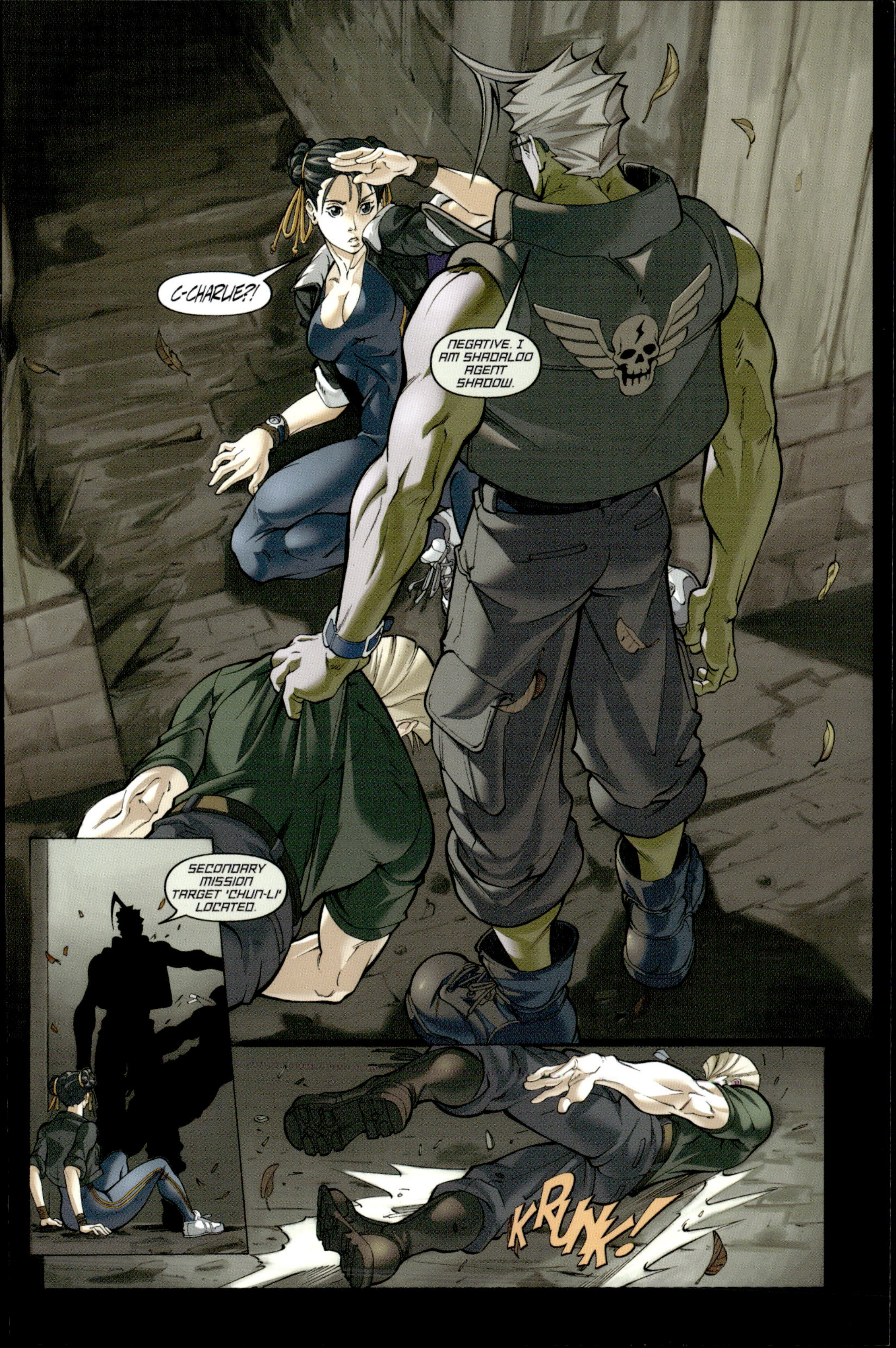
C-CHARLIE?!
NEGATIVE. I AM SHADALOO AGENT SHADOW.
SECONDARY MISSION TARGET 'CHUN-LI' LOCATED.
KRUNK!

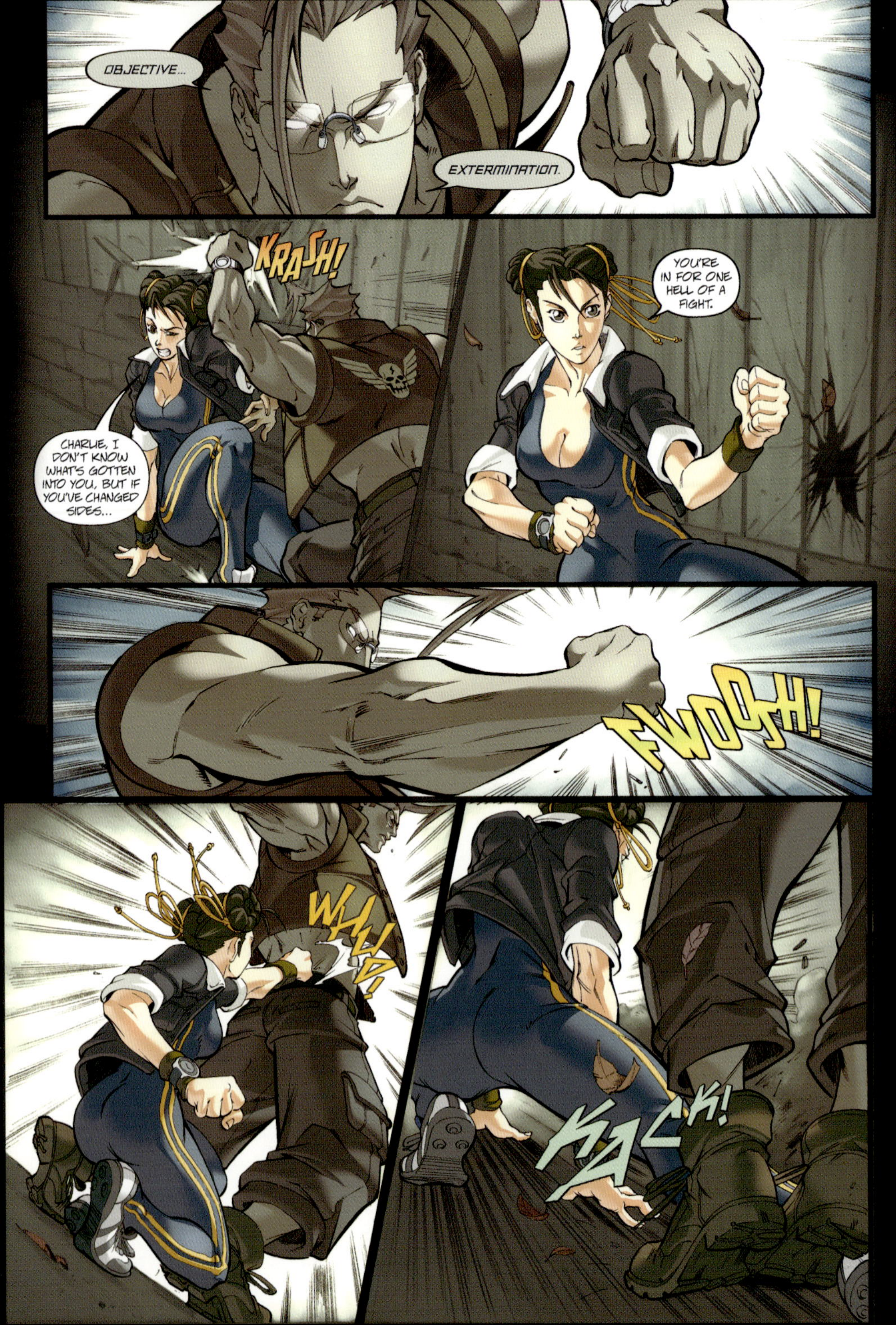
OBJECTIVE...
EXTERMINATION.
KRASH!
CHARLIE, I DON'T KNOW WHAT'S GOTTEN INTO YOU, BUT IF YOU'VE CHANGED SIDES...
YOU'RE IN FOR ONE HELL OF A FIGHT.
FWOOSH!
WHAM!
KRACK!

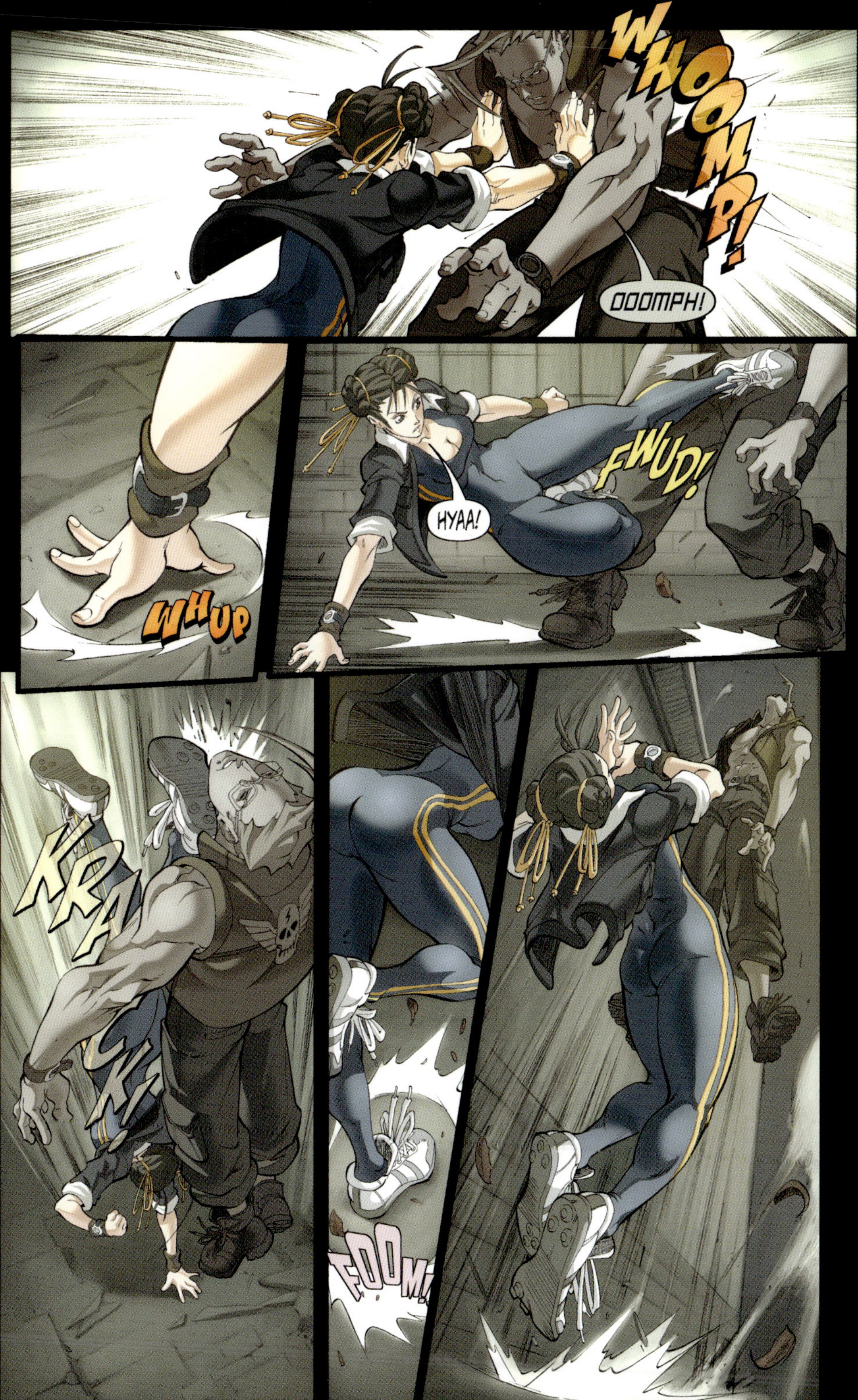
WHOOMP!
OOOMPH!
WHUP
HYAA!
FWUD!
KRAKUNK!
FOOM!

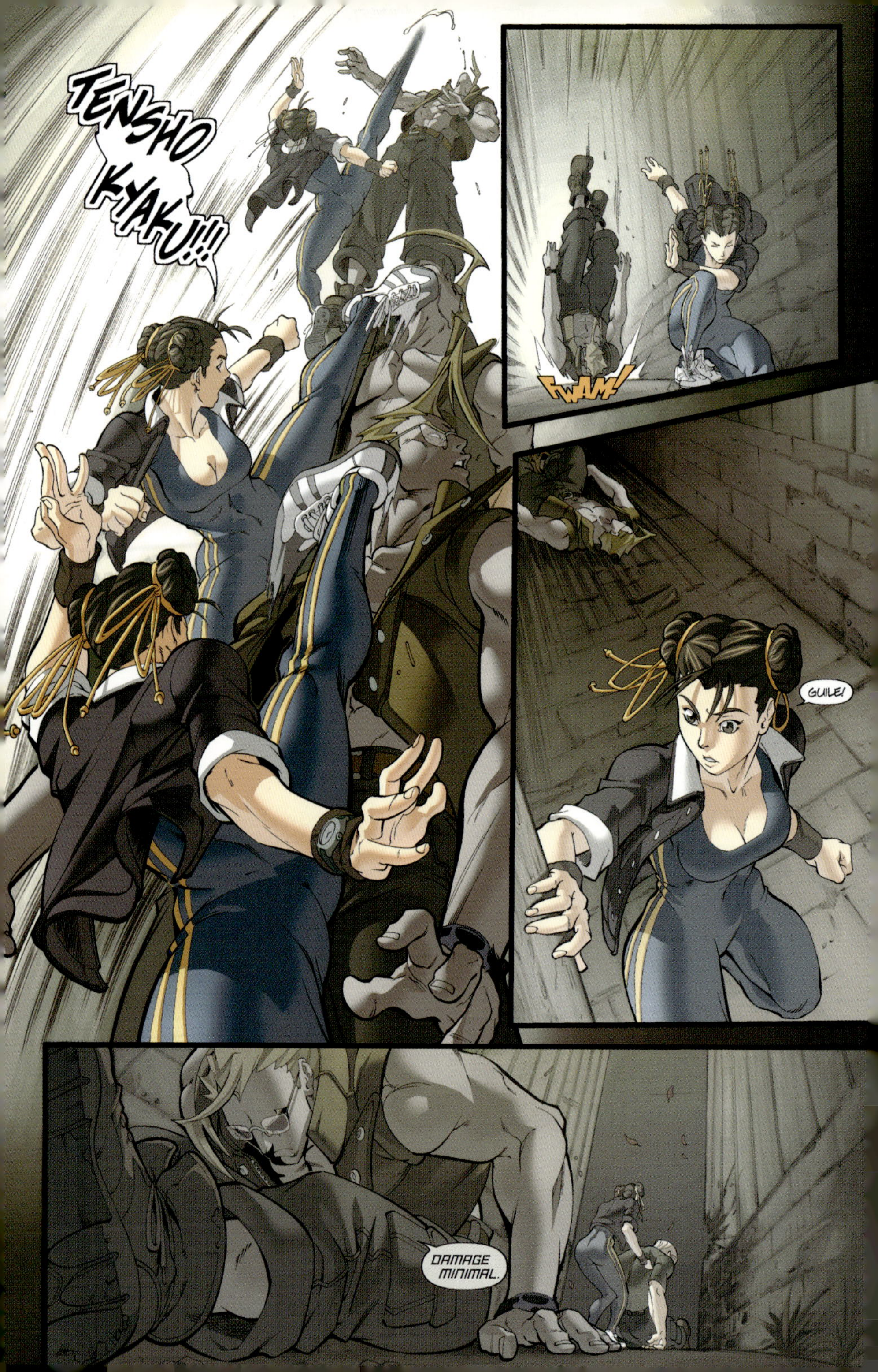
TENSHO KYAKU!!!
FWAM!
GUILE!
DAMAGE MINIMAL.

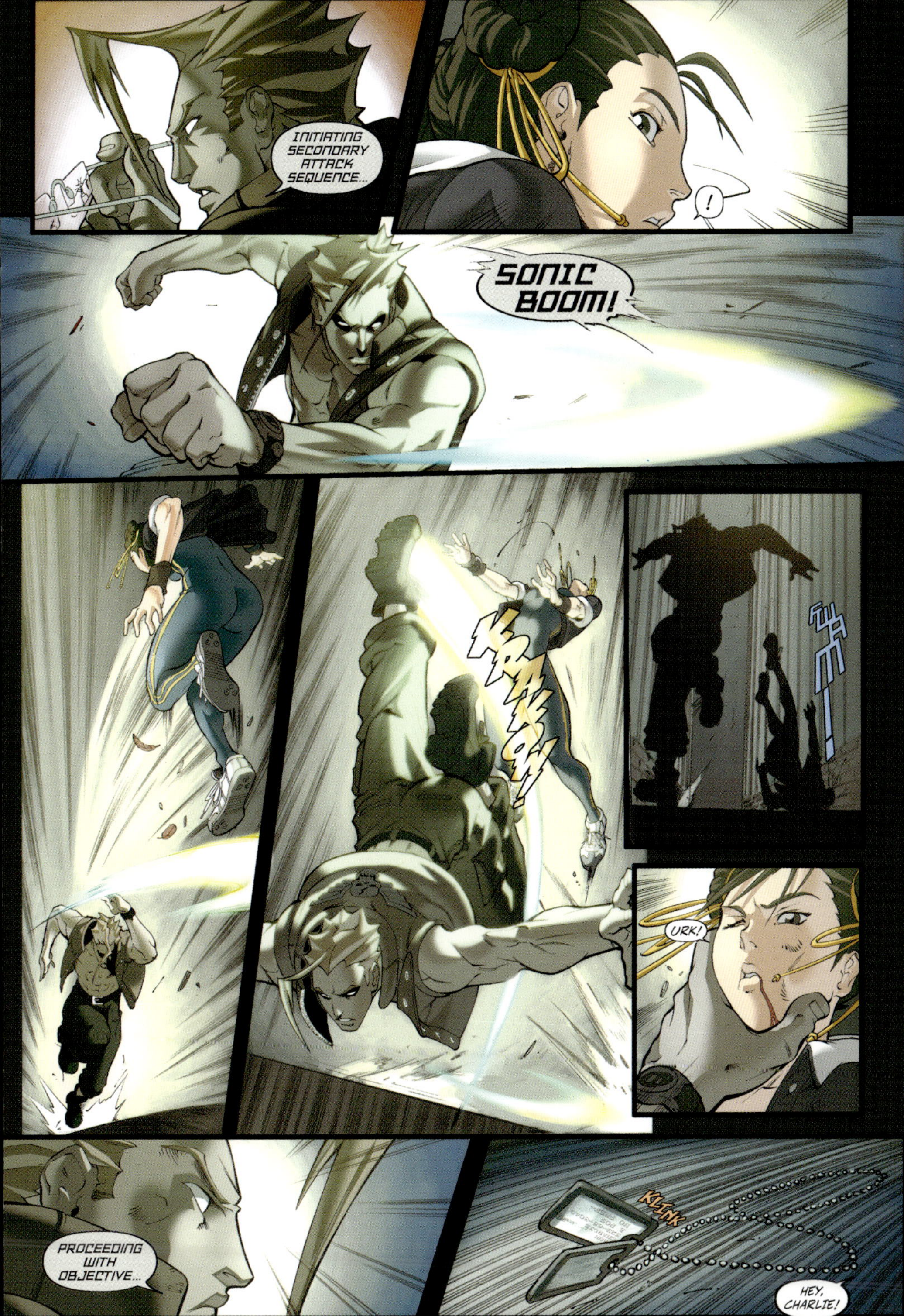
INITIATING SECONDARY ATTACK SEQUENCE...
!
SONIC BOOM!
SLAM!
URK!
PROCEEDING WITH OBJECTIVE...
KLINK
HEY, CHARLIE!

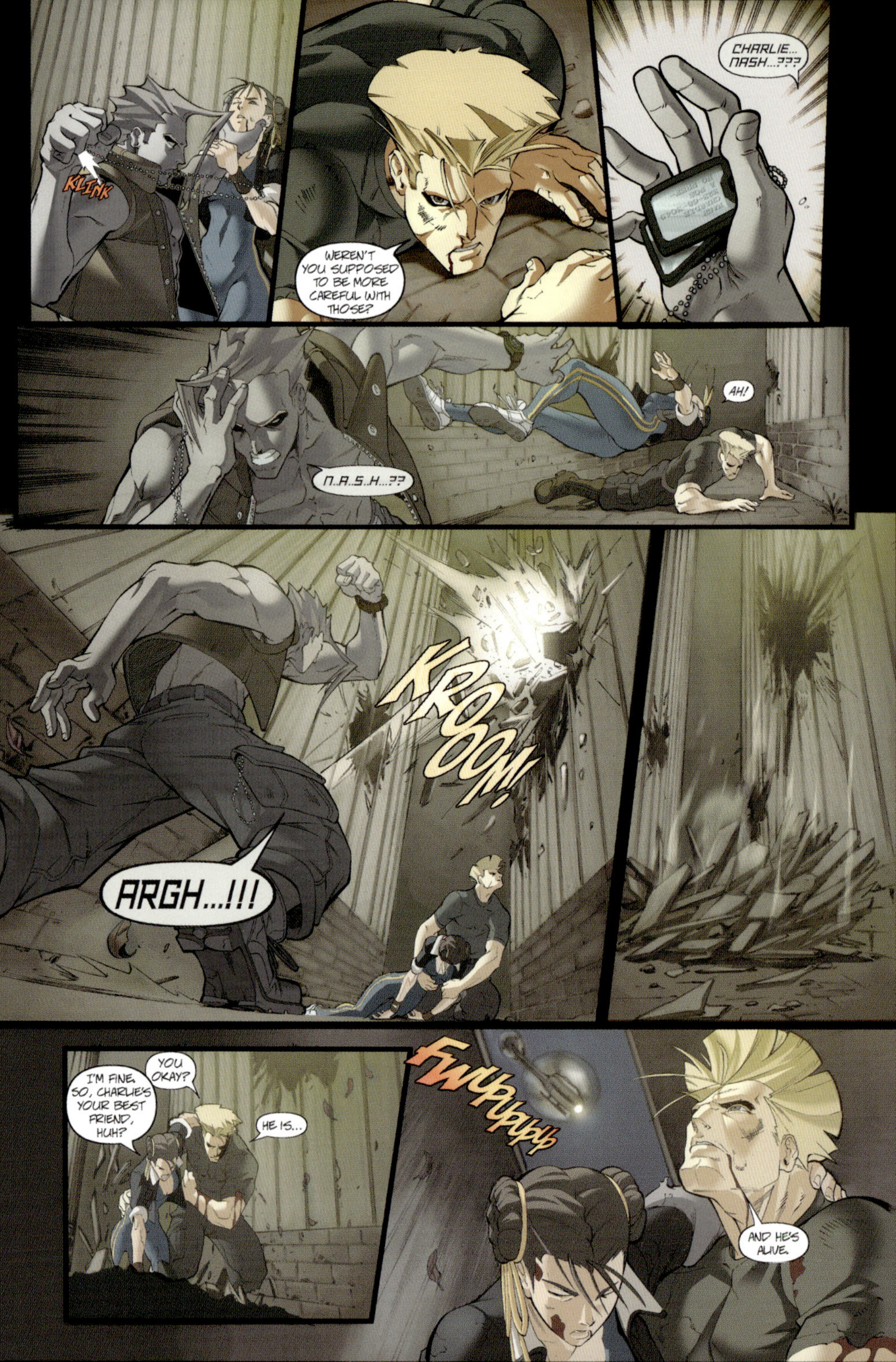
KLINK
WEREN'T YOU SUPPOSED TO BE MORE CAREFUL WITH THOSE?
CHARLIE... NASH...???
AH!
N..A..S..H...??
KROOOM!
ARGH...!!!
YOU OKAY?
I'M FINE. SO, CHARLIE'S YOUR BEST FRIEND, HUH?
HE IS...
FWUPUPUPUP
AND HE'S ALIVE.

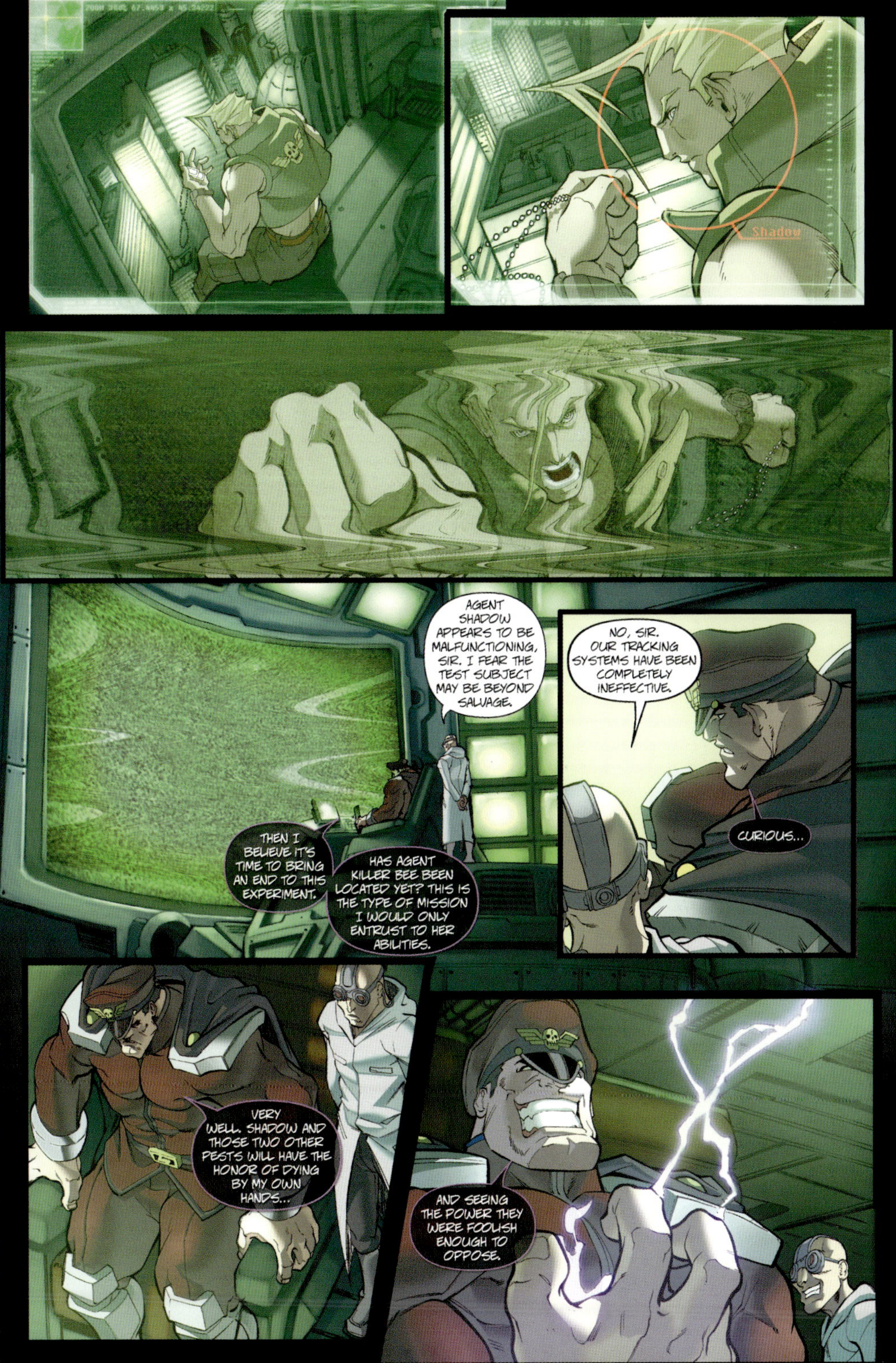
Shadow
AGENT SHADOW APPEARS TO BE MALFUNCTIONING, SIR. I FEAR THE TEST SUBJECT MAY BE BEYOND SALVAGE.
THEN I BELIEVE IT'S TIME TO BRING AN END TO THIS EXPERIMENT.
HAS AGENT KILLER BEE BEEN LOCATED YET? THIS IS THE TYPE OF MISSION I WOULD ONLY ENTRUST TO HER ABILITIES.
NO, SIR. OUR TRACKING SYSTEMS HAVE BEEN COMPLETELY INEFFECTIVE.
CURIOUS...
VERY WELL. SHADOW AND THOSE TWO OTHER PESTS WILL HAVE THE HONOR OF DYING BY MY OWN HANDS...
AND SEEING THE POWER THEY WERE FOOLISH ENOUGH TO OPPOSE.

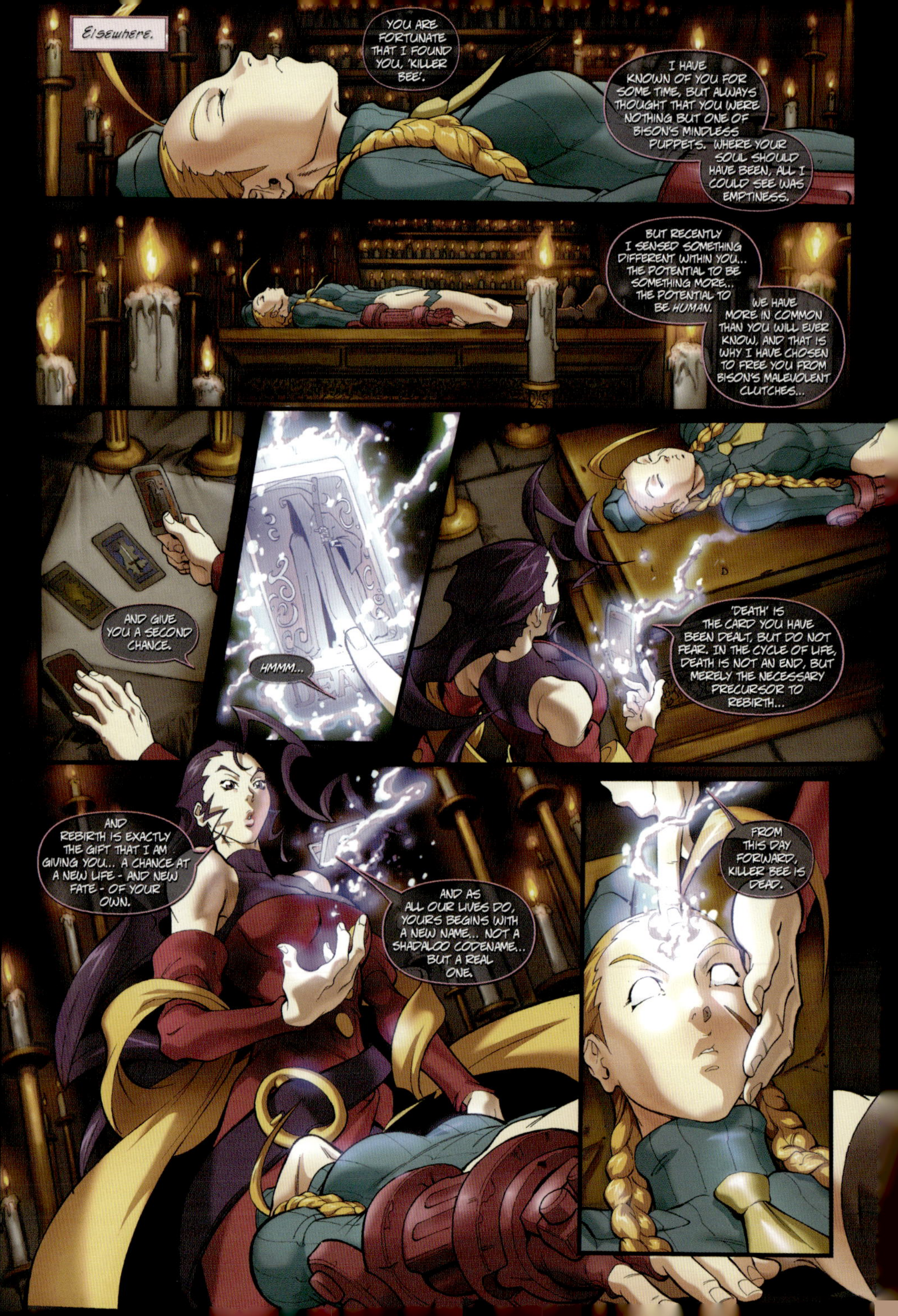
Elsewhere.
YOU ARE FORTUNATE THAT I FOUND YOU, 'KILLER BEE'.
I HAVE KNOWN OF YOU FOR SOME TIME, BUT ALWAYS THOUGHT THAT YOU WERE NOTHING BUT ONE OF BISON'S MINDLESS PUPPETS. WHERE YOUR SOUL SHOULD HAVE BEEN, ALL I COULD SEE WAS EMPTINESS.
BUT RECENTLY I SENSED SOMETHING DIFFERENT WITHIN YOU... THE POTENTIAL TO BE SOMETHING MORE... THE POTENTIAL TO BE *HUMAN*.
WE HAVE MORE IN COMMON THAN YOU WILL EVER KNOW, AND THAT IS WHY I HAVE CHOSEN TO FREE YOU FROM BISON'S MALEVOLENT CLUTCHES...
AND GIVE YOU A SECOND CHANCE.
HMMM...
'DEATH' IS THE CARD YOU HAVE BEEN DEALT, BUT DO NOT FEAR. IN THE CYCLE OF LIFE, DEATH IS NOT AN END, BUT MERELY THE NECESSARY PRECURSOR TO REBIRTH...
AND REBIRTH IS EXACTLY THE GIFT THAT I AM GIVING YOU... A CHANCE AT A NEW LIFE - AND NEW FATE - OF YOUR OWN.
AND AS ALL OUR LIVES DO, YOURS BEGINS WITH A NEW NAME... NOT A SHADALOO CODENAME... BUT A REAL ONE.
FROM THIS DAY FORWARD, KILLER BEE IS DEAD.

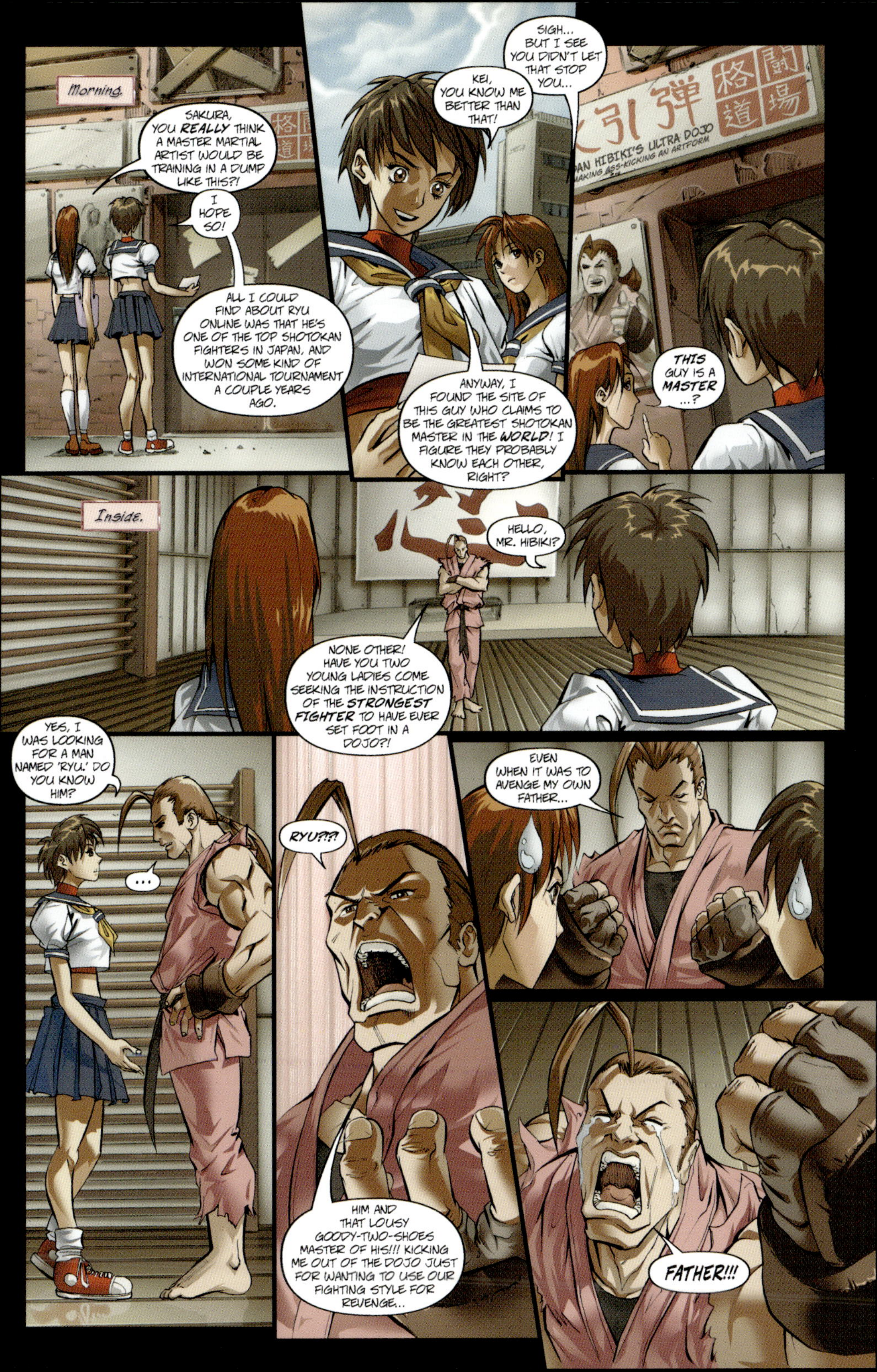

Morning.
SAKURA, YOU REALLY THINK A MASTER MARTIAL ARTIST WOULD BE TRAINING IN A DUMP LIKE THIS?!
I HOPE SO!
ALL I COULD FIND ABOUT RYU ONLINE WAS THAT HE'S ONE OF THE TOP SHOTOKAN FIGHTERS IN JAPAN, AND WON SOME KIND OF INTERNATIONAL TOURNAMENT A COUPLE YEARS AGO.
KEI, YOU KNOW ME BETTER THAN THAT!
SIGH... BUT I SEE YOU DIDN'T LET THAT STOP YOU...
ANYWAY, I FOUND THE SITE OF THIS GUY WHO CLAIMS TO BE THE GREATEST SHOTOKAN MASTER IN THE WORLD! I FIGURE THEY PROBABLY KNOW EACH OTHER, RIGHT?
弾 引
格 闘
道 場
DAN HIBIKI'S ULTRA DOJO
MAKING ASS-KICKING AN ARTFORM
THIS GUY IS A MASTER ...?
Inside.
HELLO, MR. HIBIKI?
NONE OTHER! HAVE YOU TWO YOUNG LADIES COME SEEKING THE INSTRUCTION OF THE STRONGEST FIGHTER TO HAVE EVER SET FOOT IN A DOJO?!
YES, I WAS LOOKING FOR A MAN NAMED 'RYU.' DO YOU KNOW HIM?
...
RYU?!?!
HIM AND THAT LOUSY GOODY-TWO-SHOES MASTER OF HIS!!! KICKING ME OUT OF THE DOJO JUST FOR WANTING TO USE OUR FIGHTING STYLE FOR REVENGE...
EVEN WHEN IT WAS TO AVENGE MY OWN FATHER...
FATHER!!!

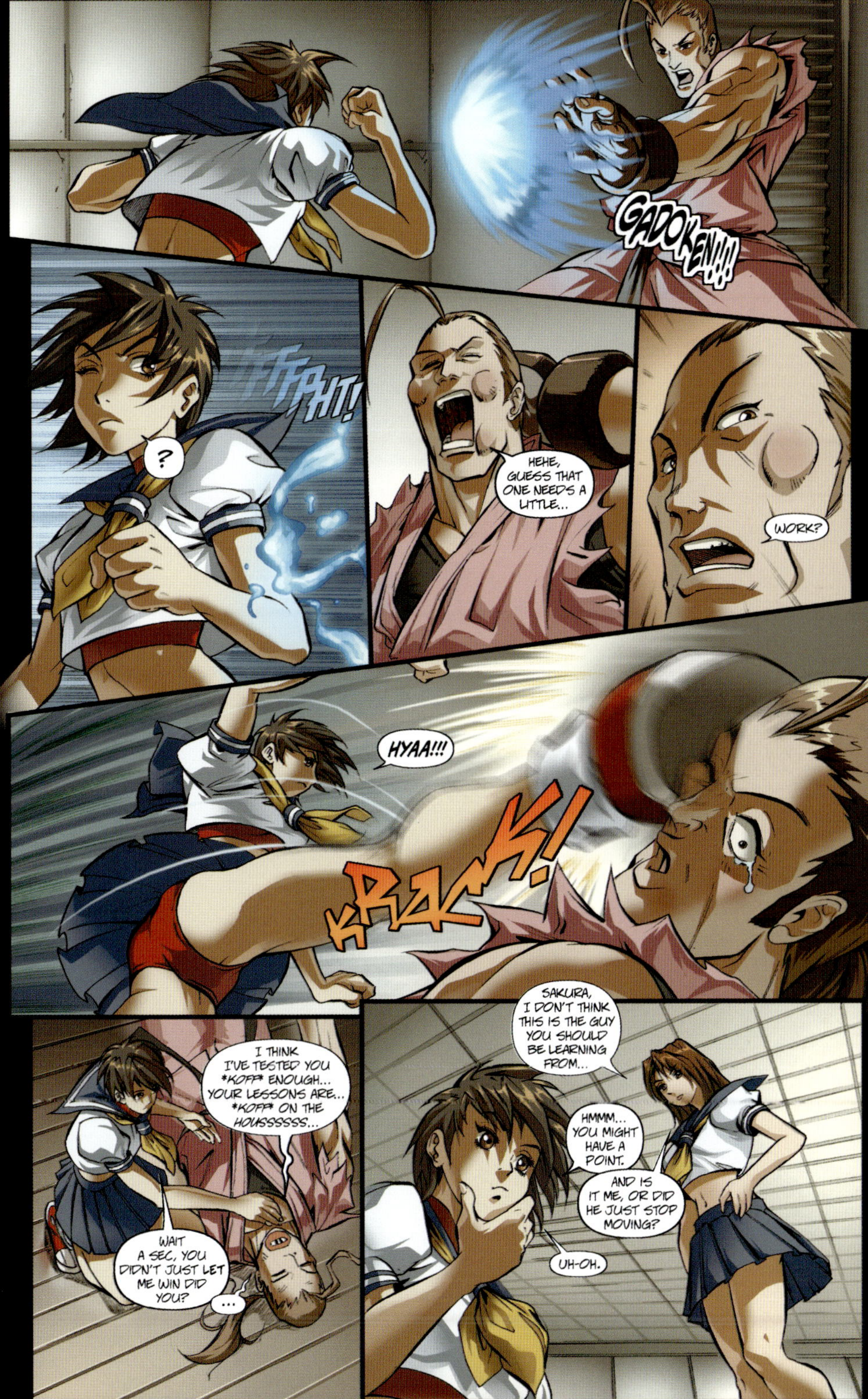
GADOKEN!!!
FFFAHT!
?
HEHE, GUESS THAT ONE NEEDS A LITTLE...
WORK?
HYAA!!!
KRACK!
I THINK I'VE TESTED YOU *KOFF* ENOUGH... YOUR LESSONS ARE... *KOFF* ON THE HOUSSSSSS...
WAIT A SEC, YOU DIDN'T JUST LET ME WIN DID YOU?
...
SAKURA, I DON'T THINK THIS IS THE GUY YOU SHOULD BE LEARNING FROM...
HMMM... YOU MIGHT HAVE A POINT.
AND IS IT ME, OR DID HE JUST STOP MOVING?
UH-OH.

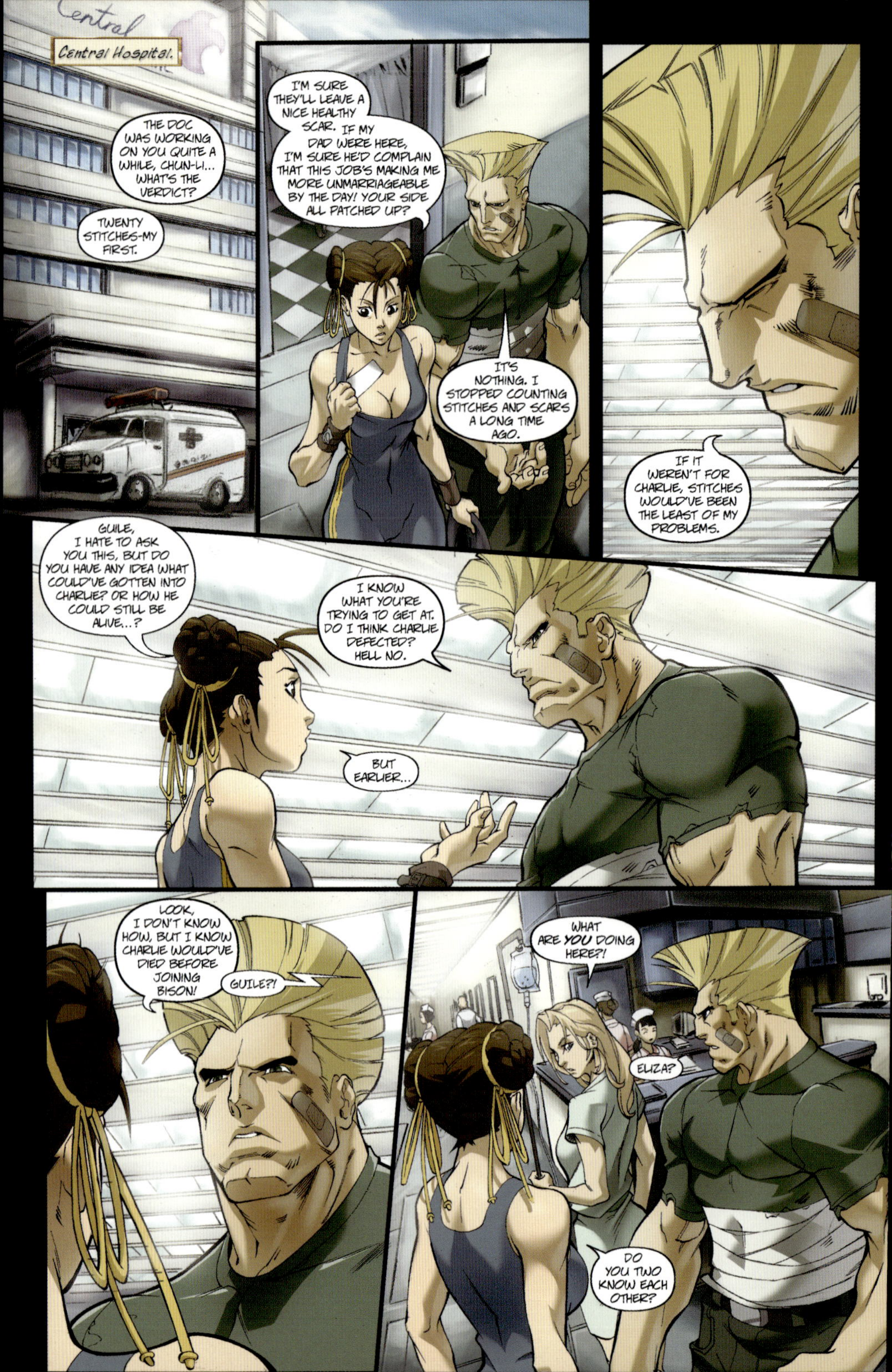
Central
Central Hospital.
THE DOC WAS WORKING ON YOU QUITE A WHILE, CHUN-LI... WHAT'S THE VERDICT?
TWENTY STITCHES-MY FIRST.
I'M SURE THEY'LL LEAVE A NICE HEALTHY SCAR. IF MY DAD WERE HERE, I'M SURE HE'D COMPLAIN THAT THIS JOB'S MAKING ME MORE UNMARRIAGEABLE BY THE DAY! YOUR SIDE ALL PATCHED UP?
IT'S NOTHING. I STOPPED COUNTING STITCHES AND SCARS A LONG TIME AGO.
IF IT WEREN'T FOR CHARLIE, STITCHES WOULD'VE BEEN THE LEAST OF MY PROBLEMS.
GUILE, I HATE TO ASK YOU THIS, BUT DO YOU HAVE ANY IDEA WHAT COULD'VE GOTTEN INTO CHARLIE? OR HOW HE COULD STILL BE ALIVE...?
I KNOW WHAT YOU'RE TRYING TO GET AT. DO I THINK CHARLIE DEFECTED? HELL NO.
BUT EARLIER...
LOOK, I DON'T KNOW HOW, BUT I KNOW CHARLIE WOULD'VE DIED BEFORE JOINING BISON!
GUILE?!
WHAT ARE *YOU* DOING HERE?!
ELIZA?
DO YOU TWO KNOW EACH OTHER?

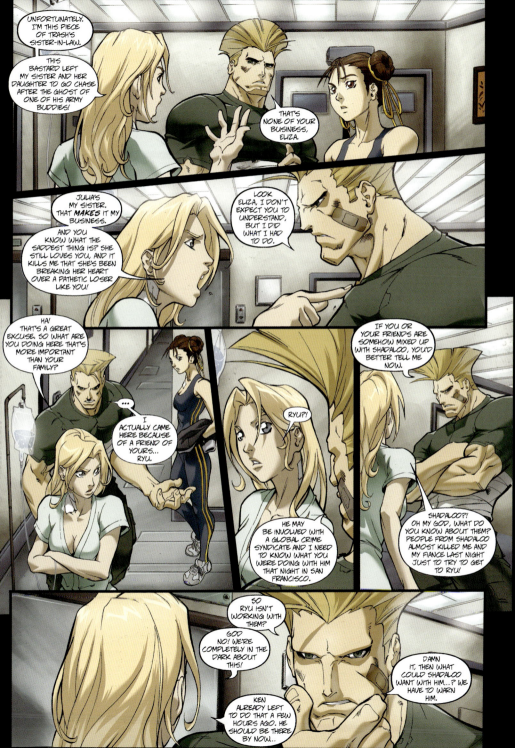

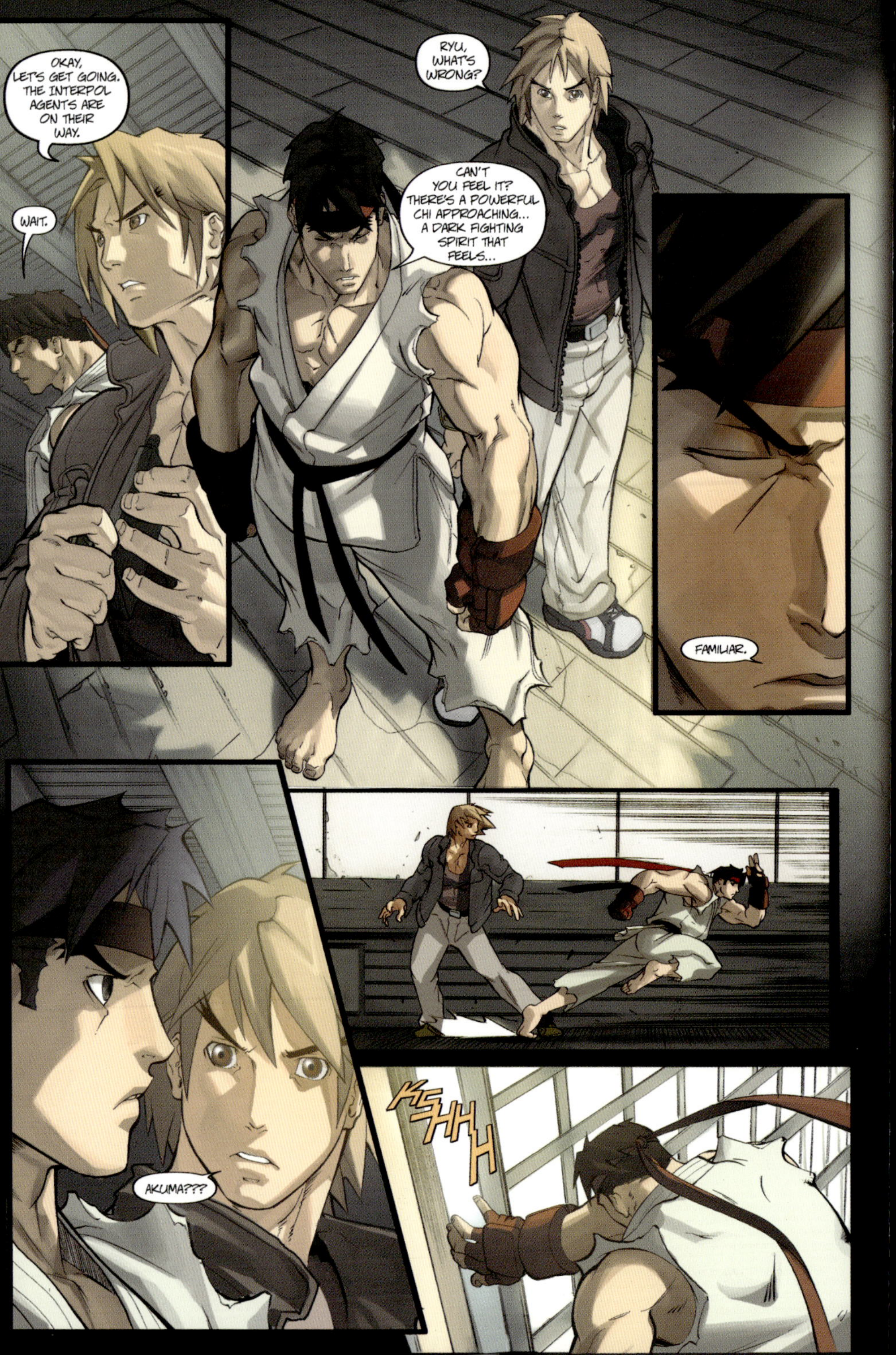
OKAY, LET'S GET GOING. THE INTERPOL AGENTS ARE ON THEIR WAY.
WAIT.
RYU, WHAT'S WRONG?
CAN'T YOU FEEL IT? THERE'S A POWERFUL CHI APPROACHING... A DARK FIGHTING SPIRIT THAT FEELS...
FAMILIAR.
AKUMA???
KSHHH

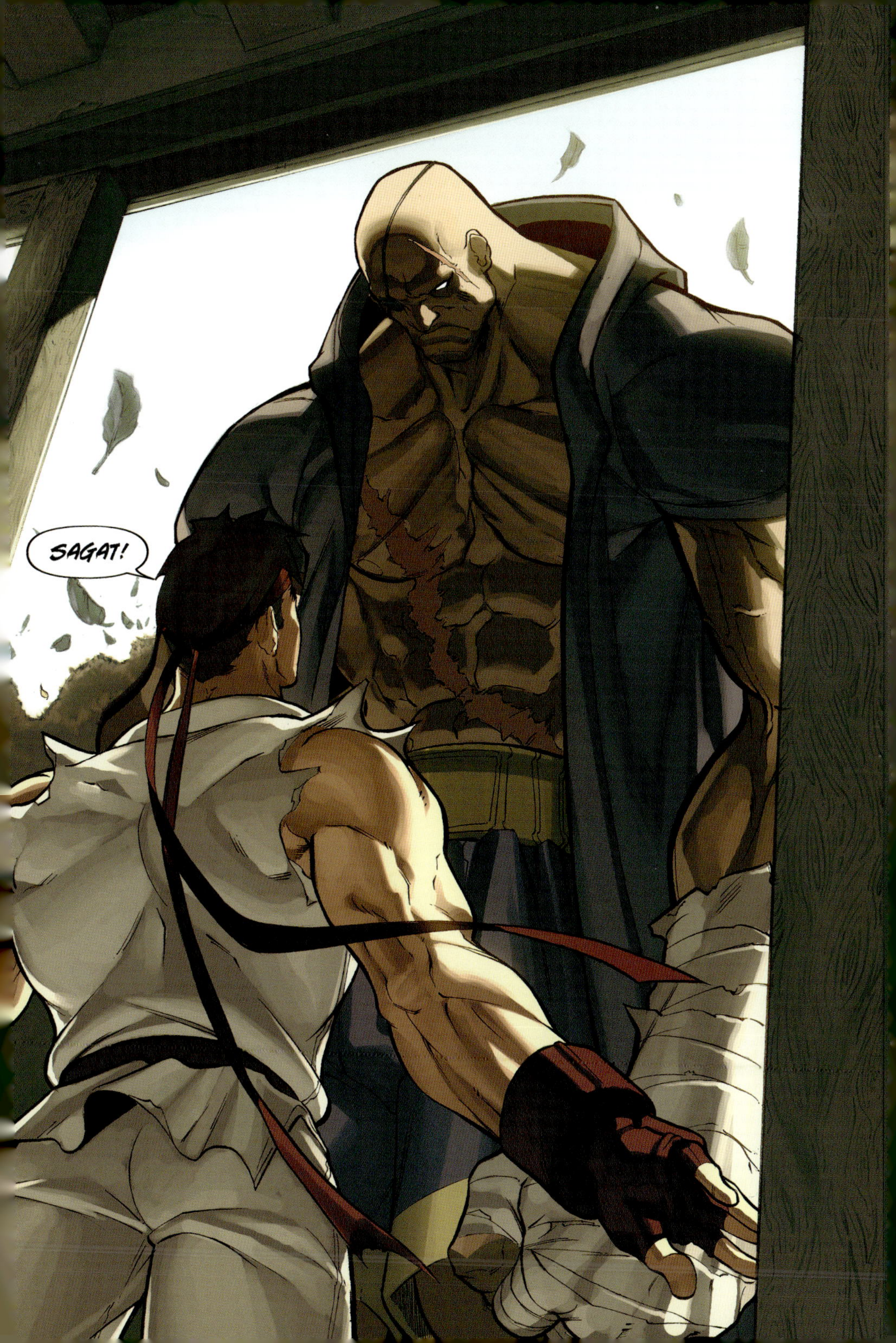
SAGAT!

Cover Art by: Alvin Lee and Arnold Tsang

Chapter 05: PSYCHO POWER

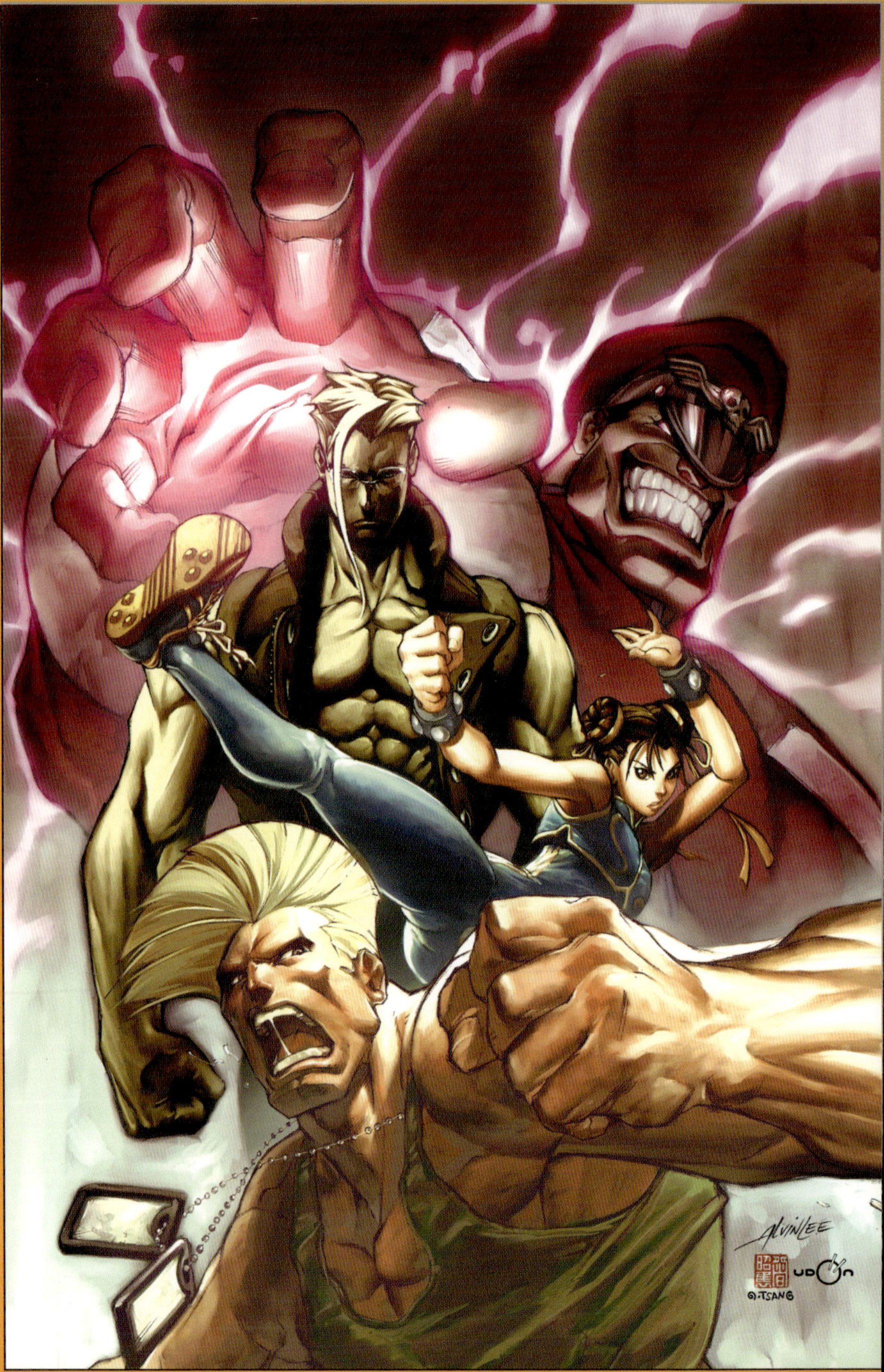

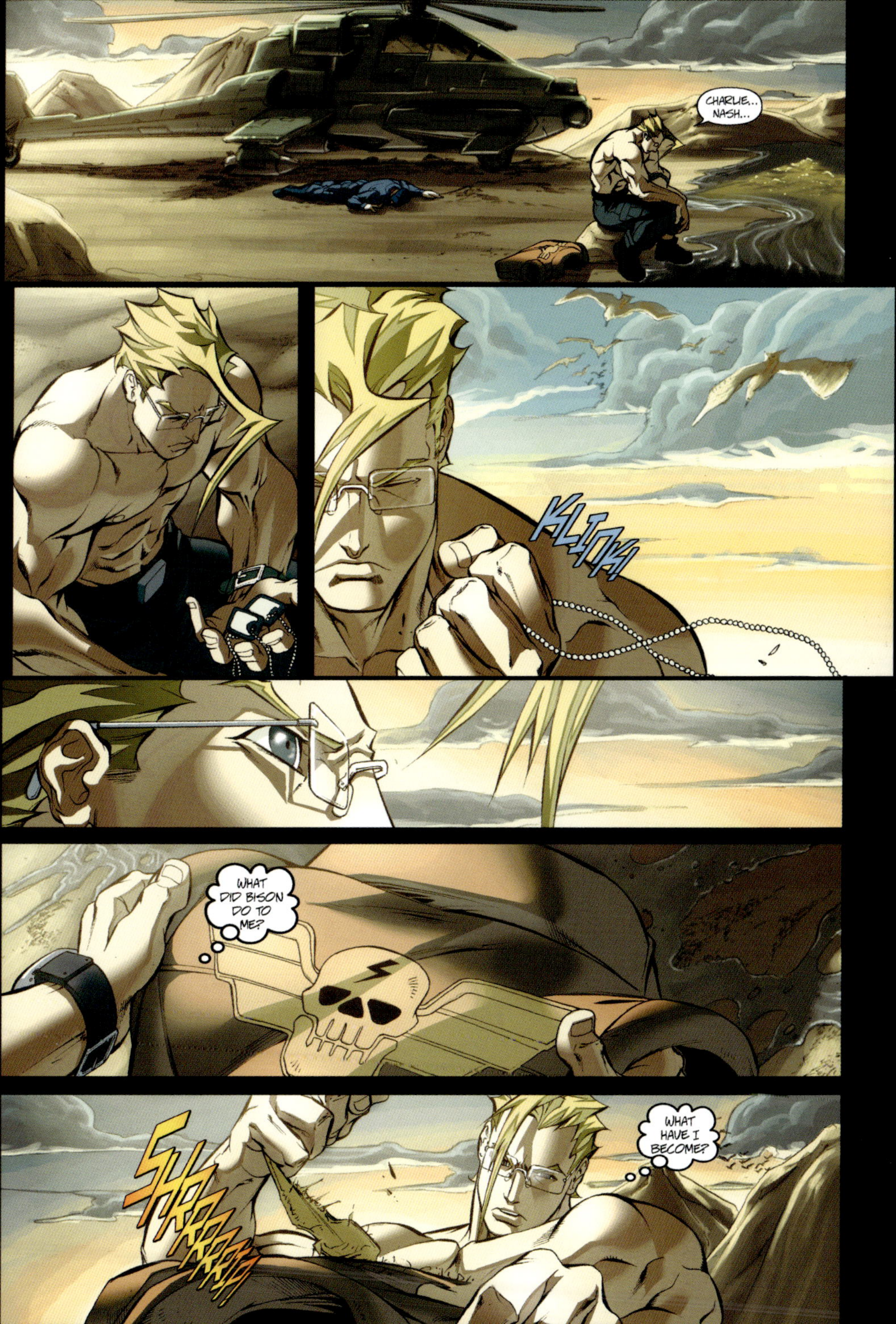
CHARLIE... NASH...
KLINK!
WHAT DID BISON DO TO ME?
SHRRRRR!
WHAT HAVE I BECOME?

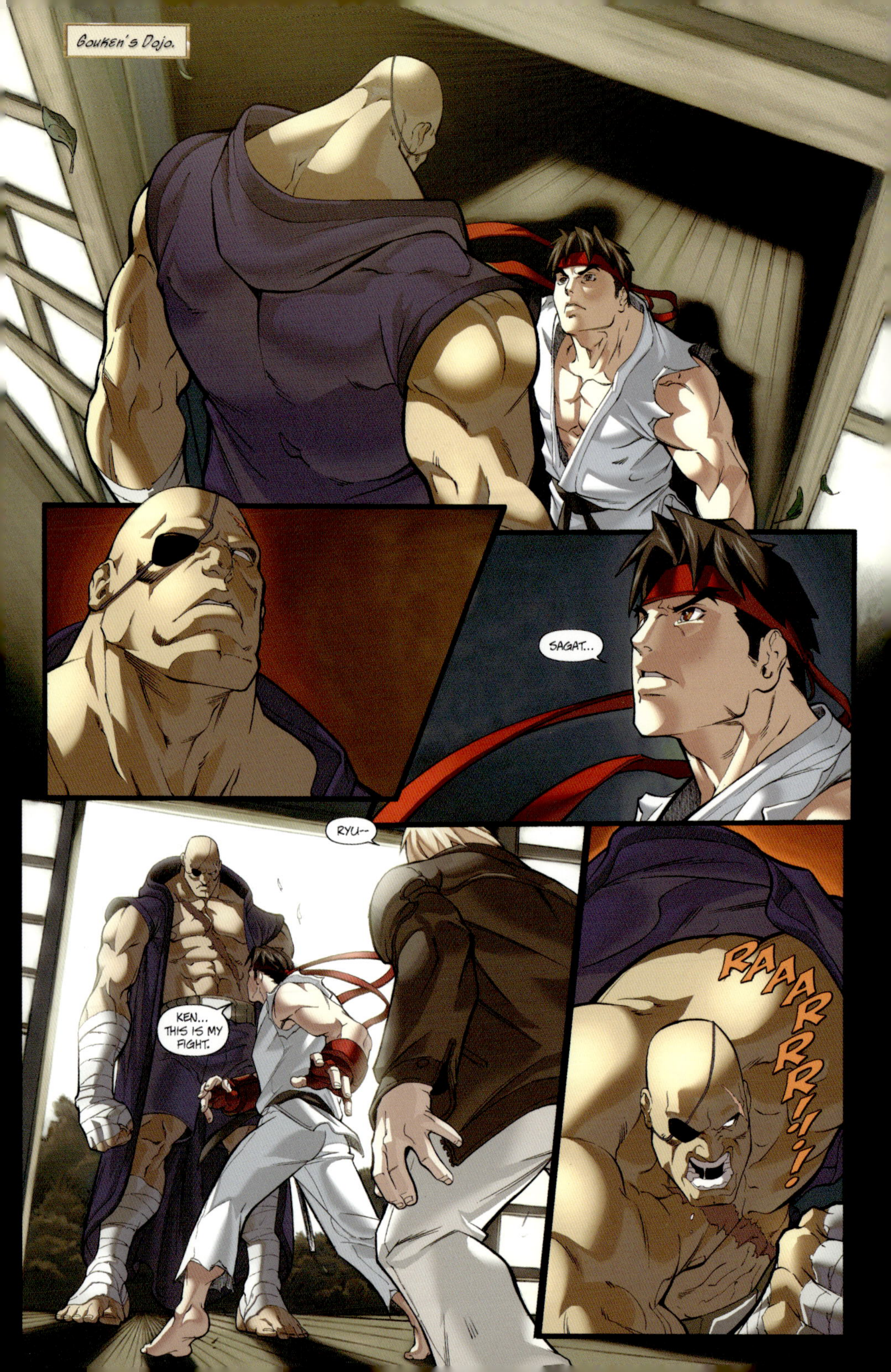
Gouken's Dojo.
SAGAT...
RYU--
KEN... THIS IS MY FIGHT.
RAAARRR!!!

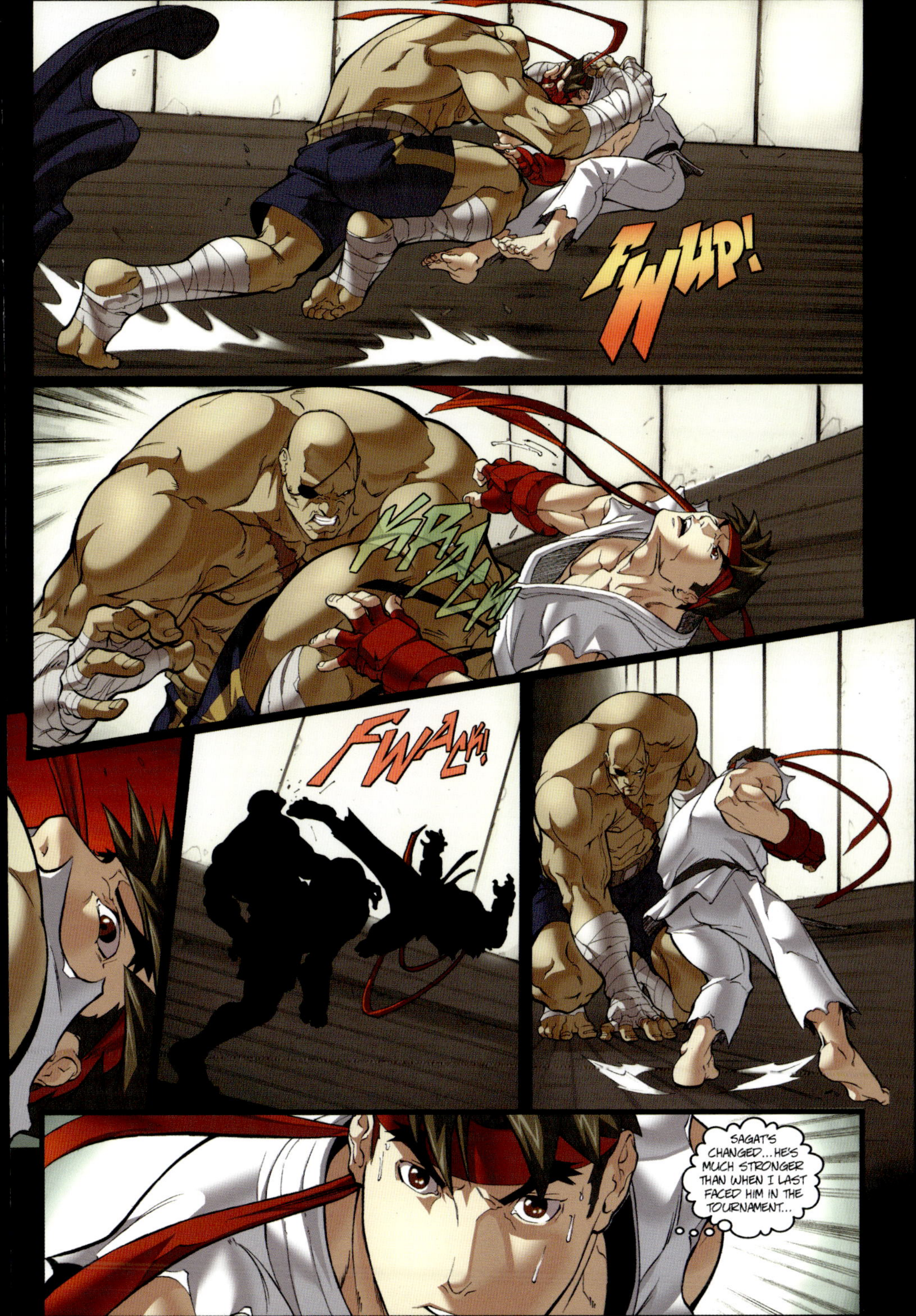
FWUP!
KRACK!
FWACK!
SAGAT'S CHANGED... HE'S MUCH STRONGER THAN WHEN I LAST FACED HIM IN THE TOURNAMENT...

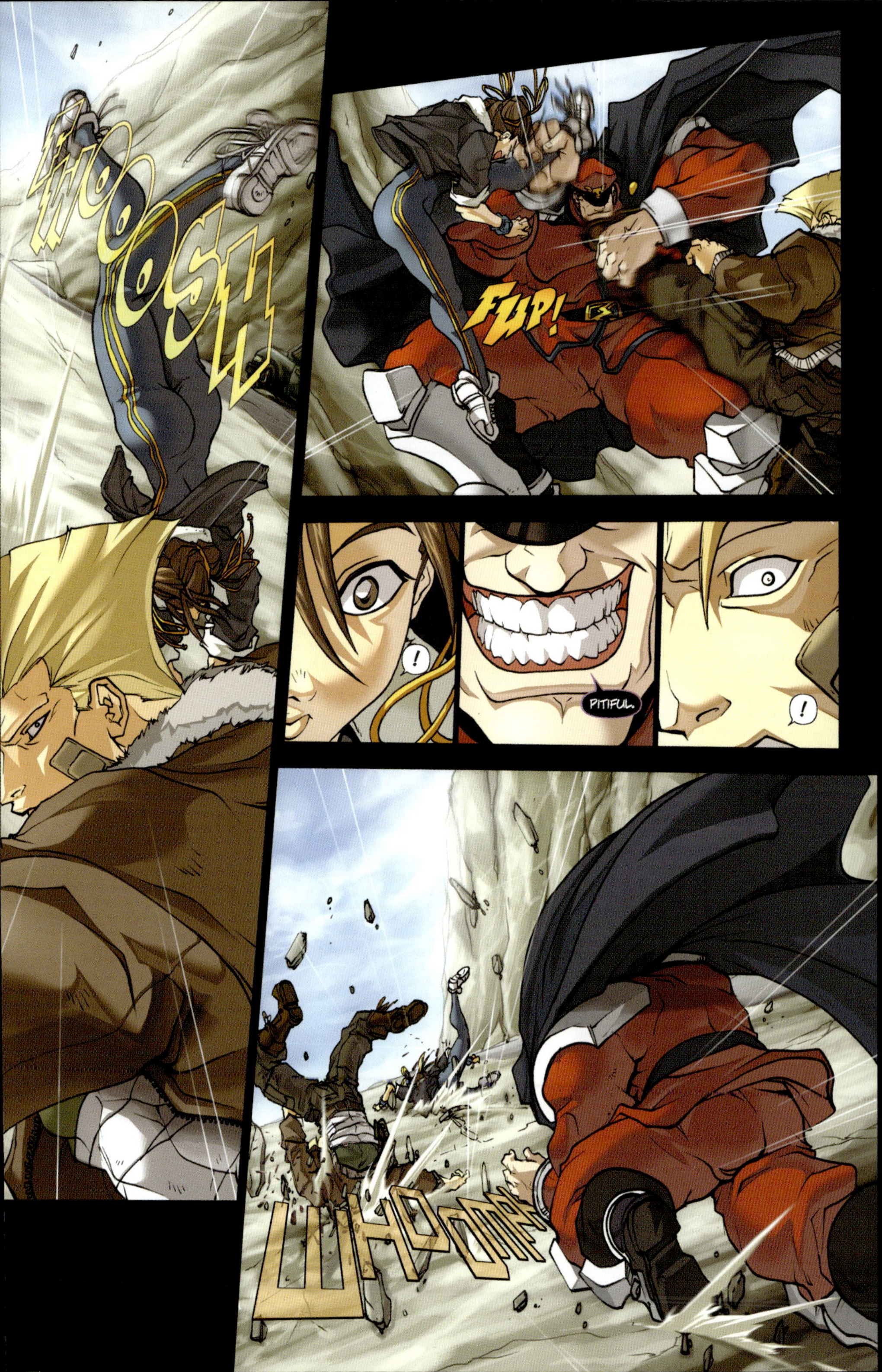
WHOOSH
FUP!
!
PITIFUL.
!
WHOOMP

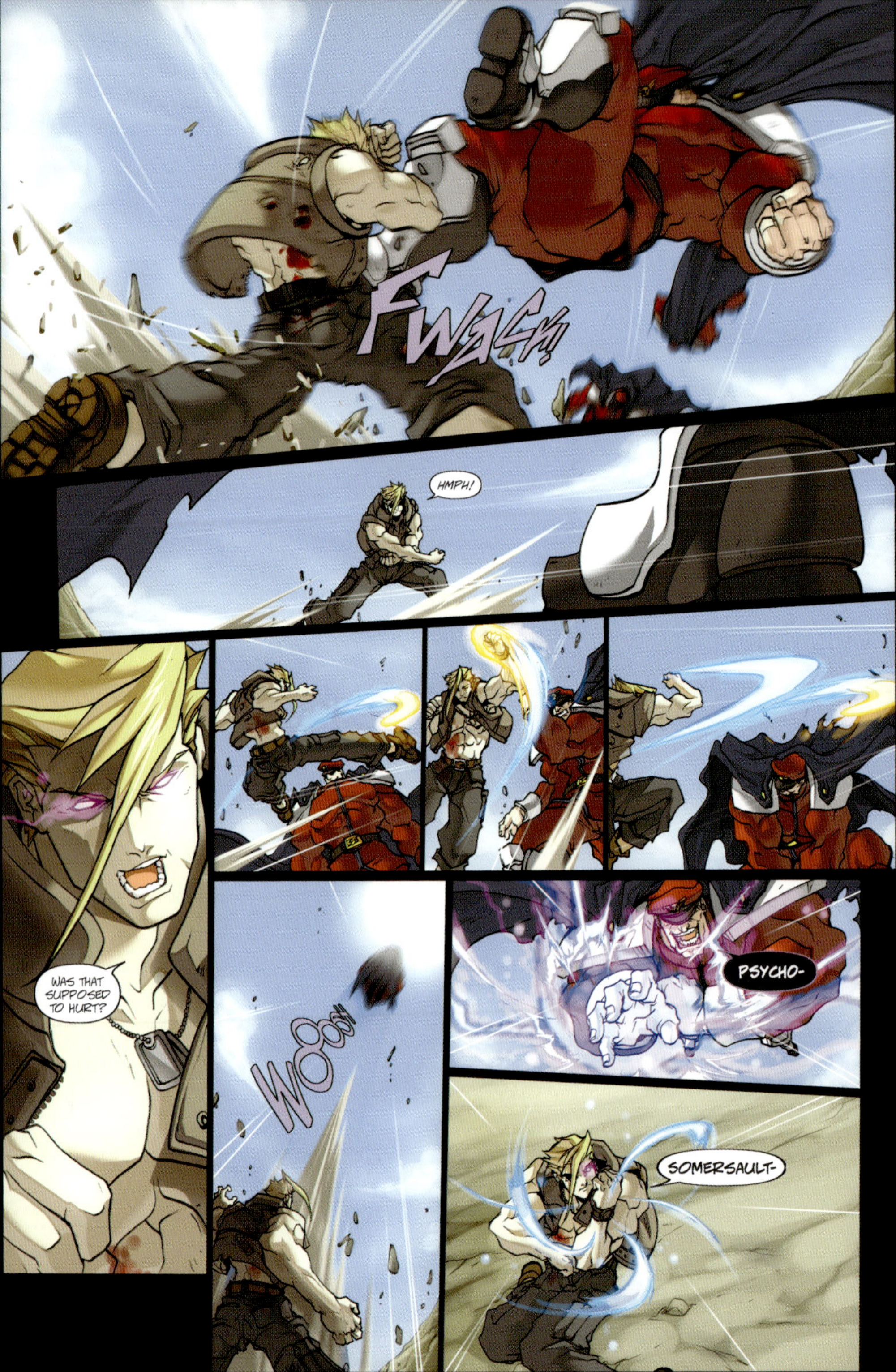
FWACK!
HMPH!
WAS THAT SUPPOSED TO HURT?
WOOSH!
PSYCHO-
SOMERSAULT-

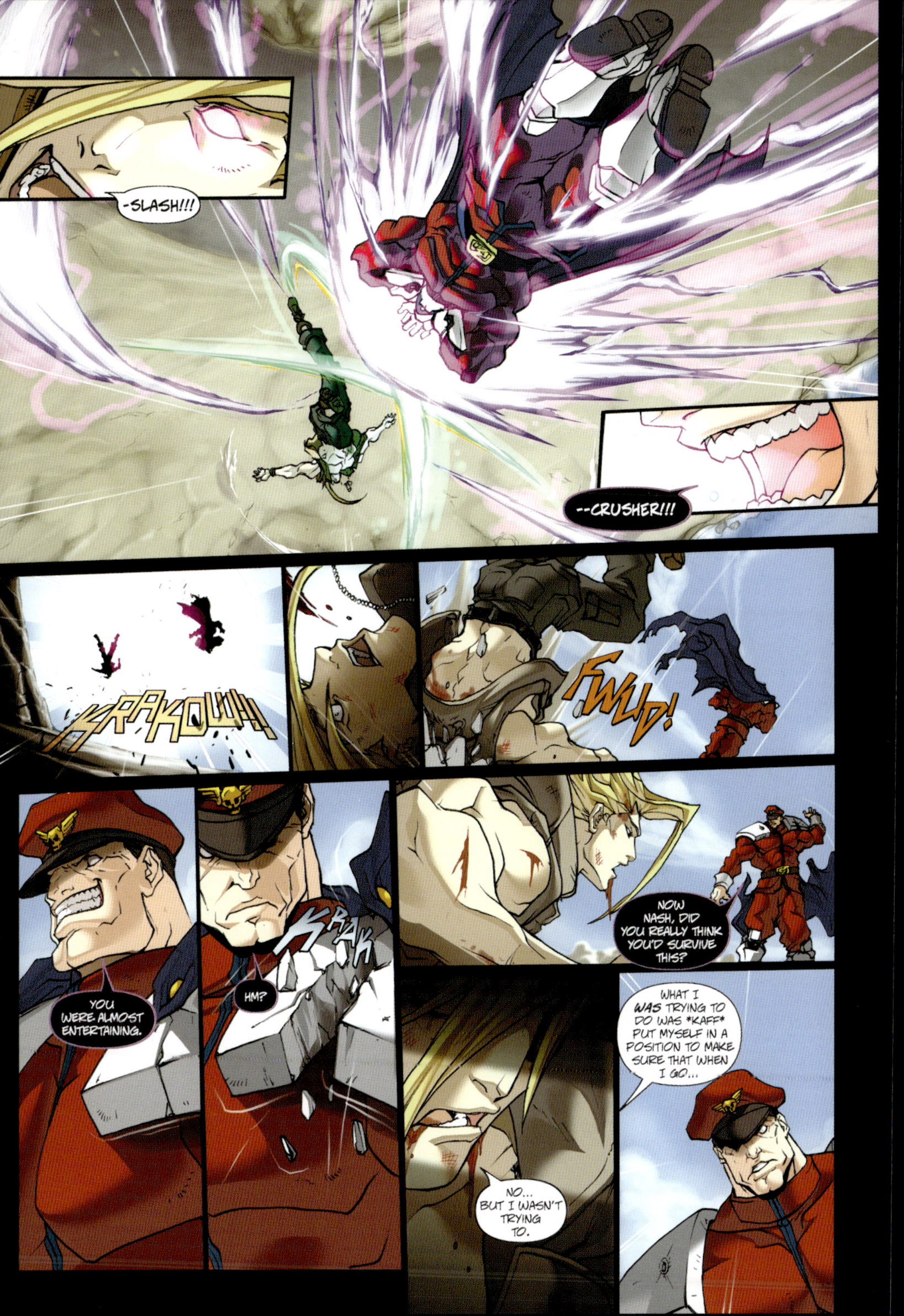
-SLASH!!!
--CRUSHER!!!
KRAKOWW!!!
FWUD!
NOW NASH, DID YOU REALLY THINK YOU'D SURVIVE THIS?
YOU WERE ALMOST ENTERTAINING.
HM?
KRAK
NO... BUT I WASN'T TRYING TO.
WHAT I WAS TRYING TO DO WAS *KAFF* PUT MYSELF IN A POSITION TO MAKE SURE THAT WHEN I GO...

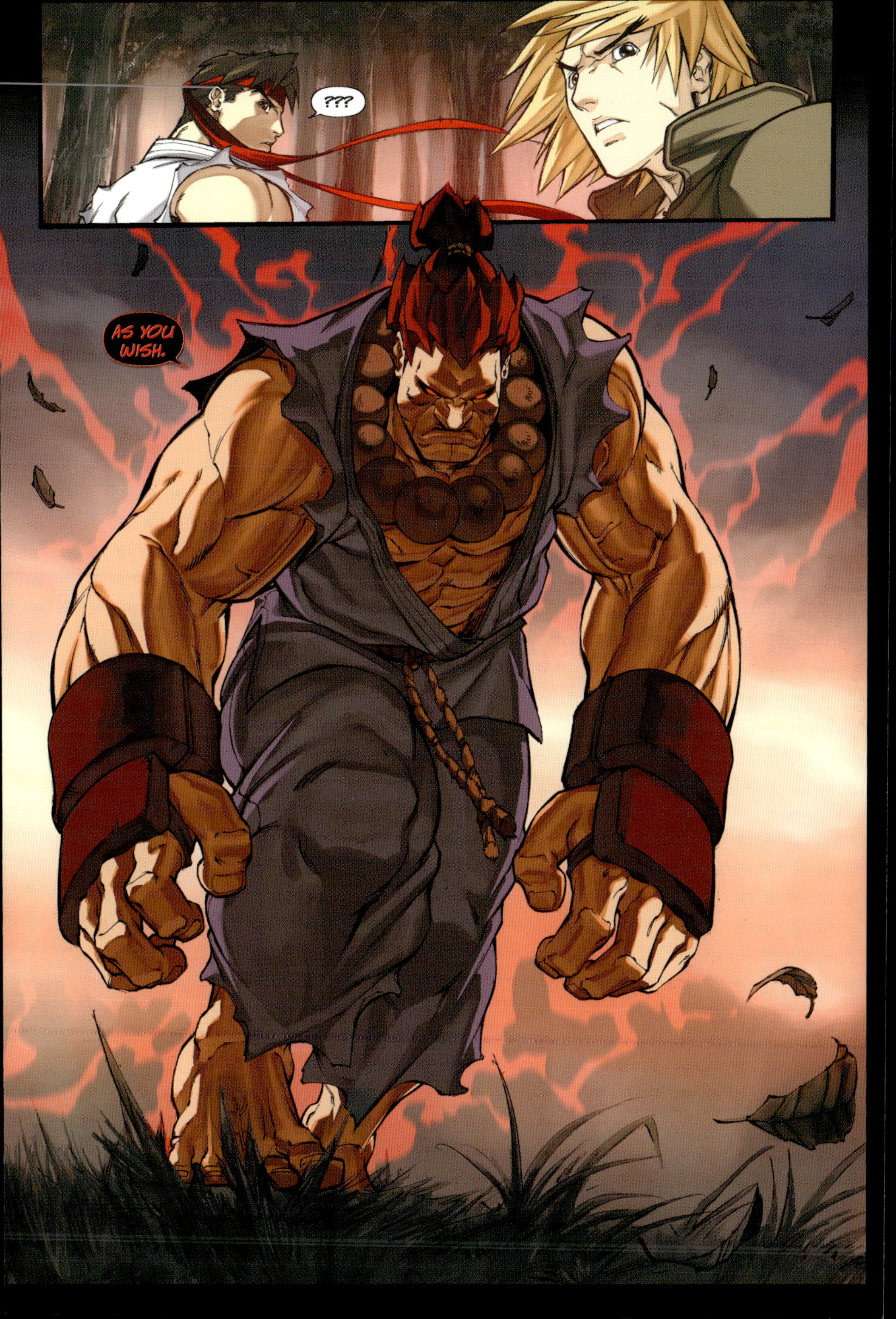
???
AS YOU WISH.

Chapter 06: THE JOURNEY BEGINS

Cover Art by: Alvin Lee and Arnold Tsang

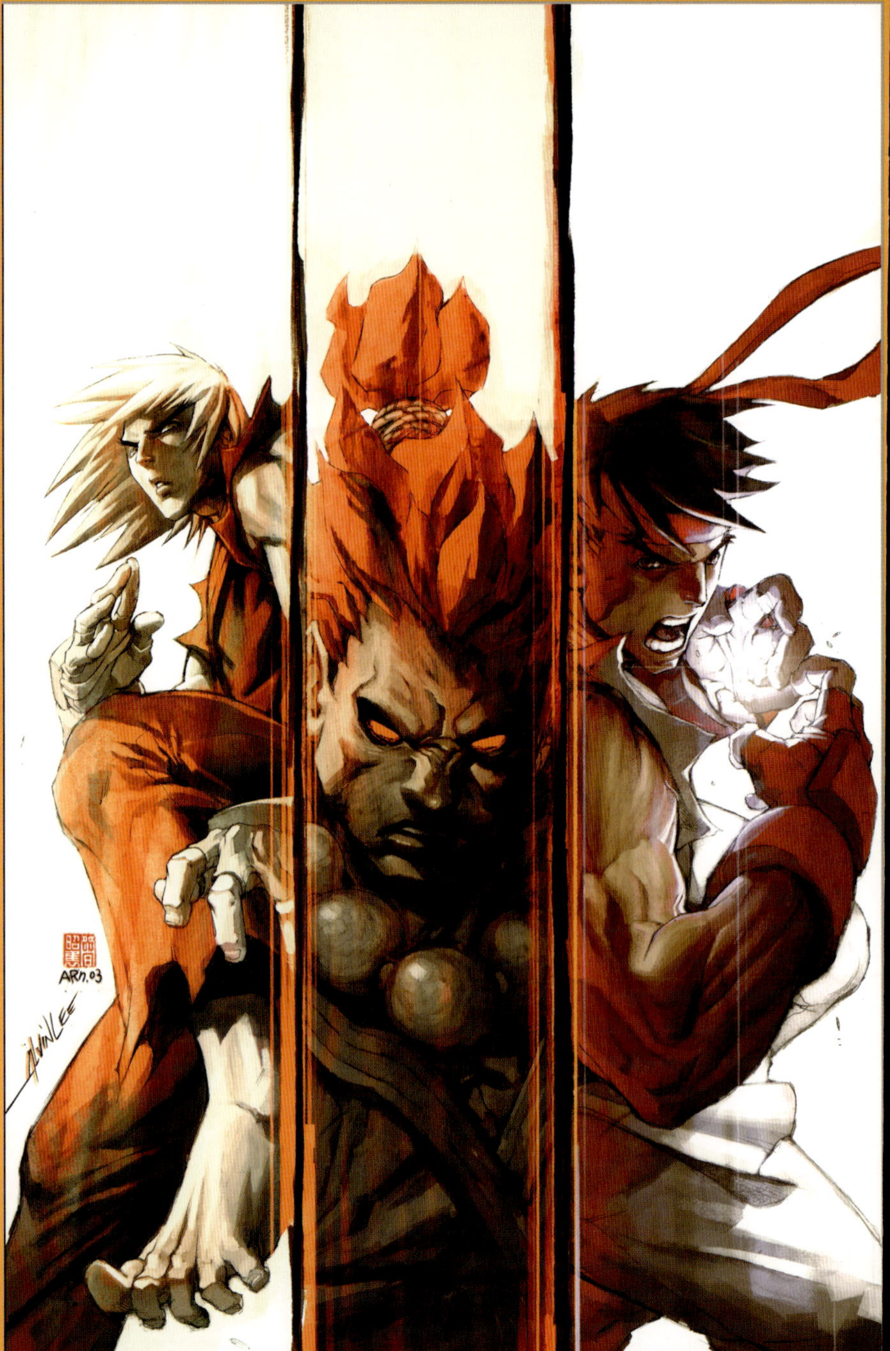

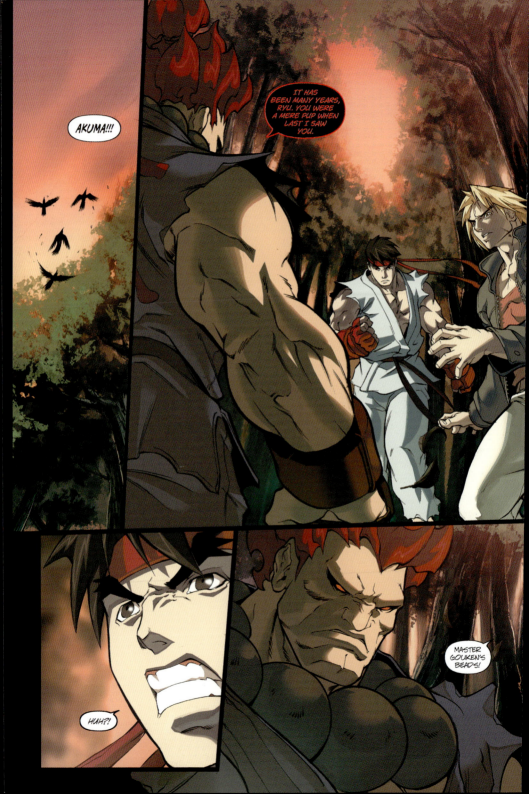

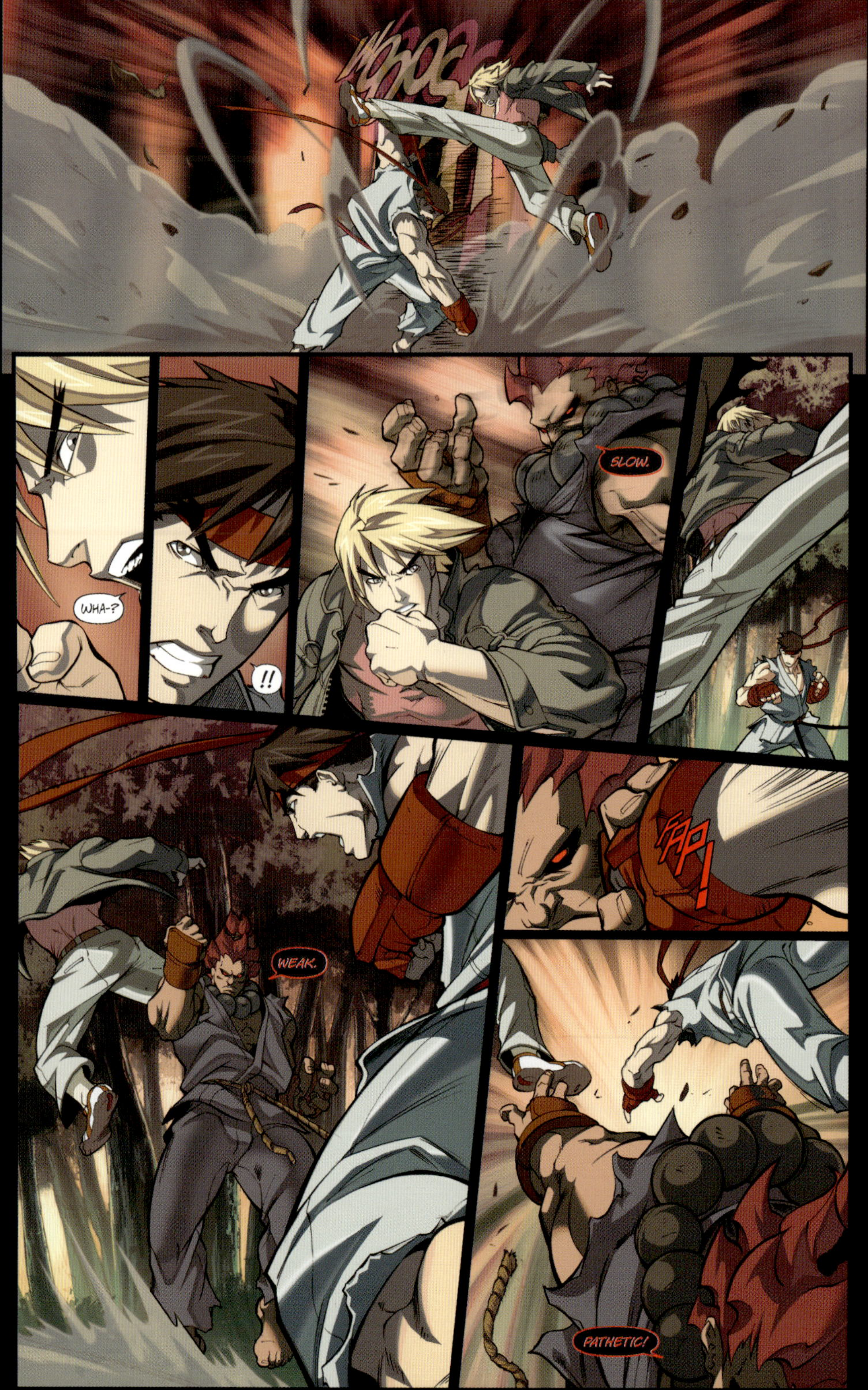
WHA-?
!!
SLOW.
FAP!
WEAK.
PATHETIC!

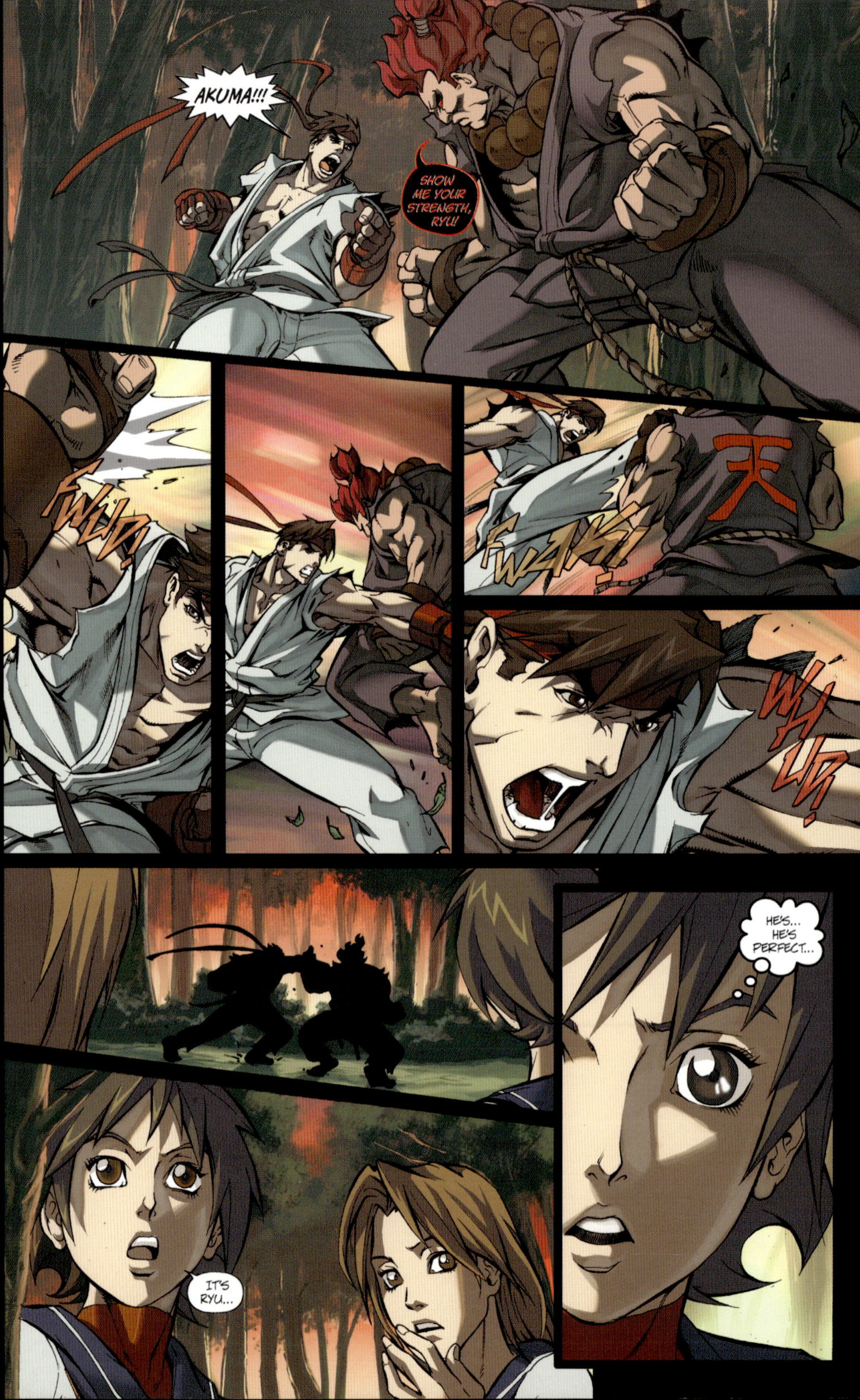

AKUMA!!!
SHOW ME YOUR STRENGTH, RYU!!
FWUD!
FWAK!
WHUD!
HE'S... HE'S PERFECT...
IT'S RYU...

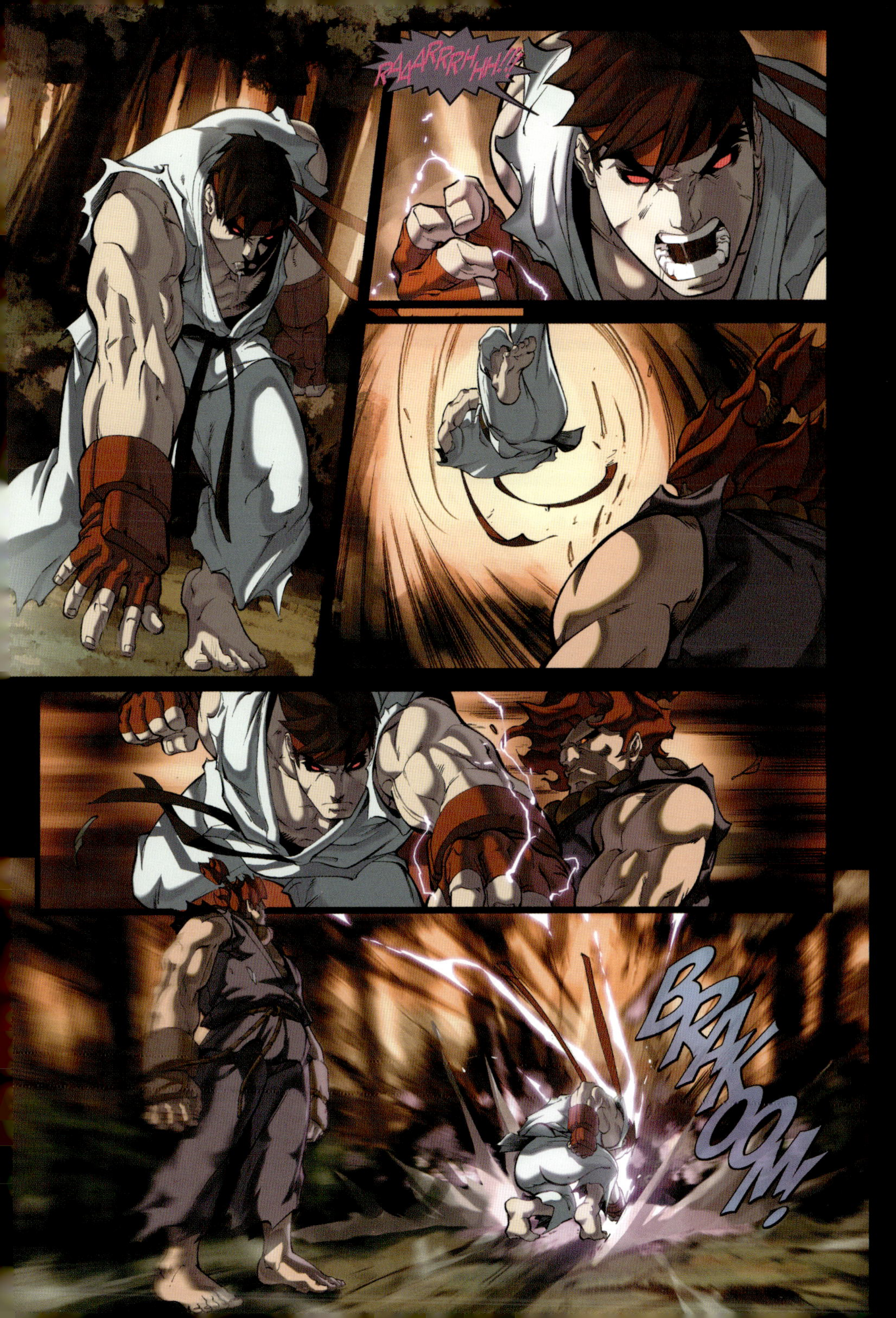
RAAARRRHHH!!!
BRAKOOM!

Additional Cover Gallery

Cover Art by: Arnold Tsang

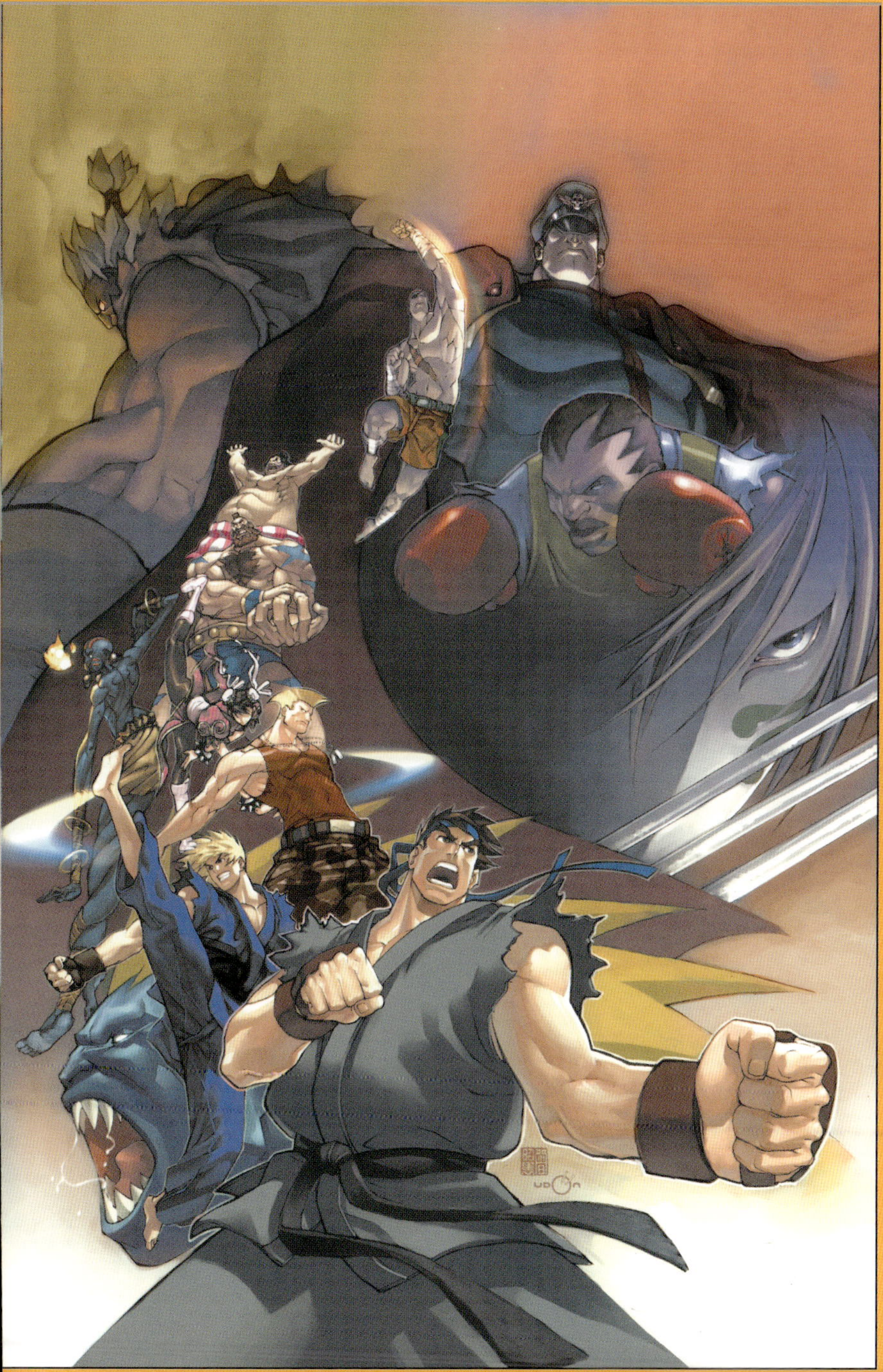

Cover Art by: Long Vo and SAKA

Issue 01: Second Printing

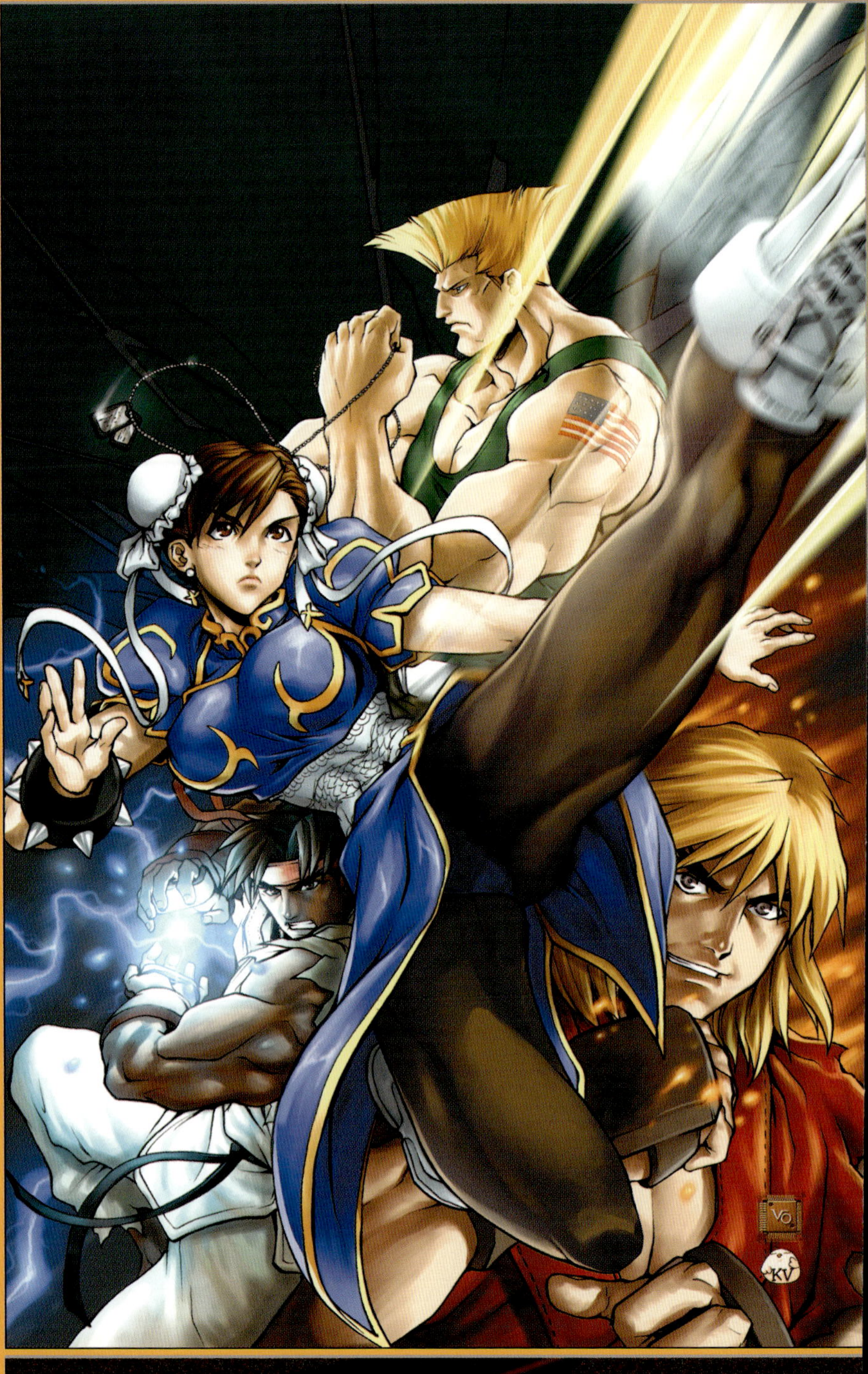

Cover Art by: Arnold Tsang

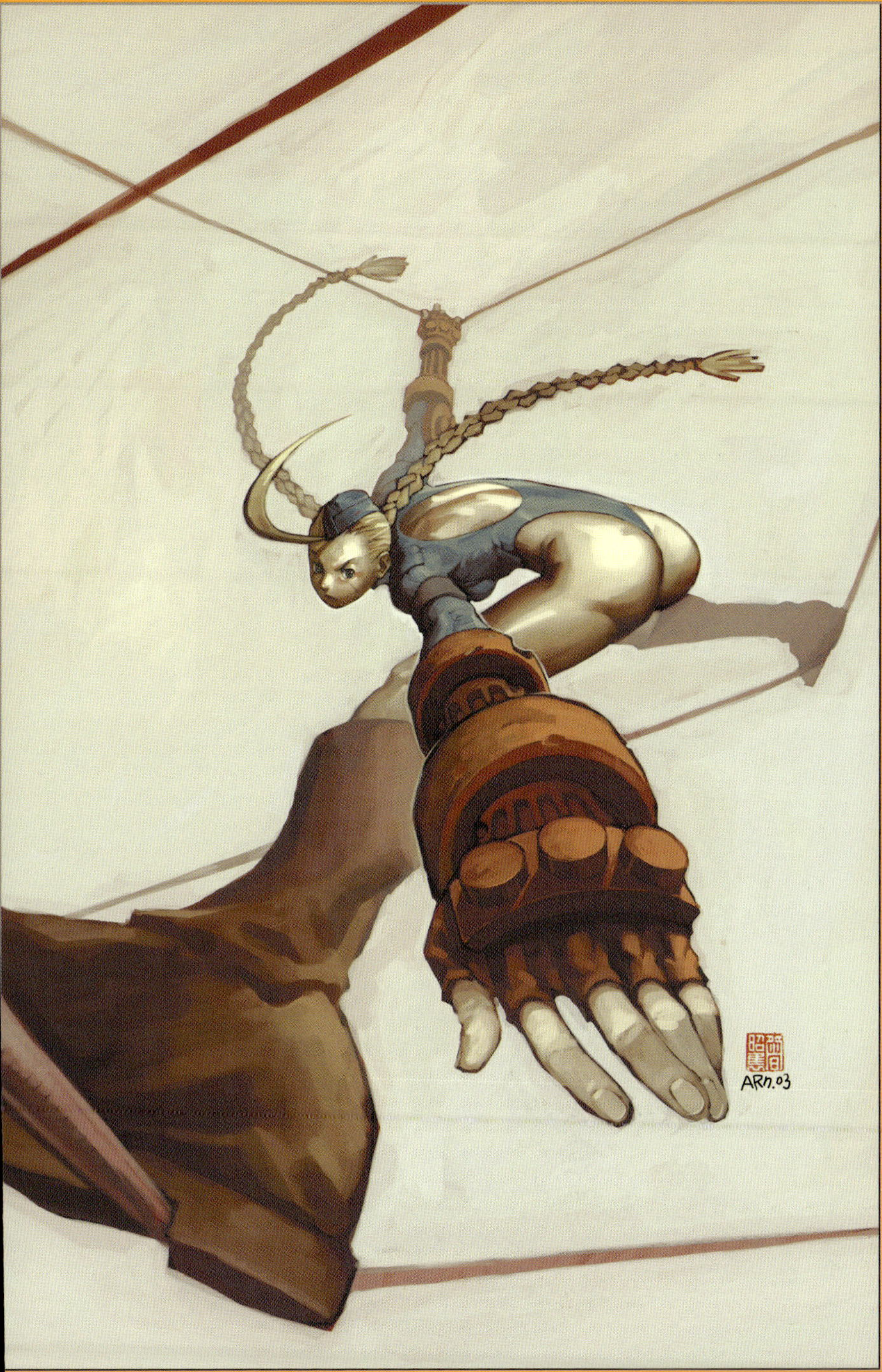
ARn.03

Issue 02: Second Printing

Cover Art by: Jo Chen

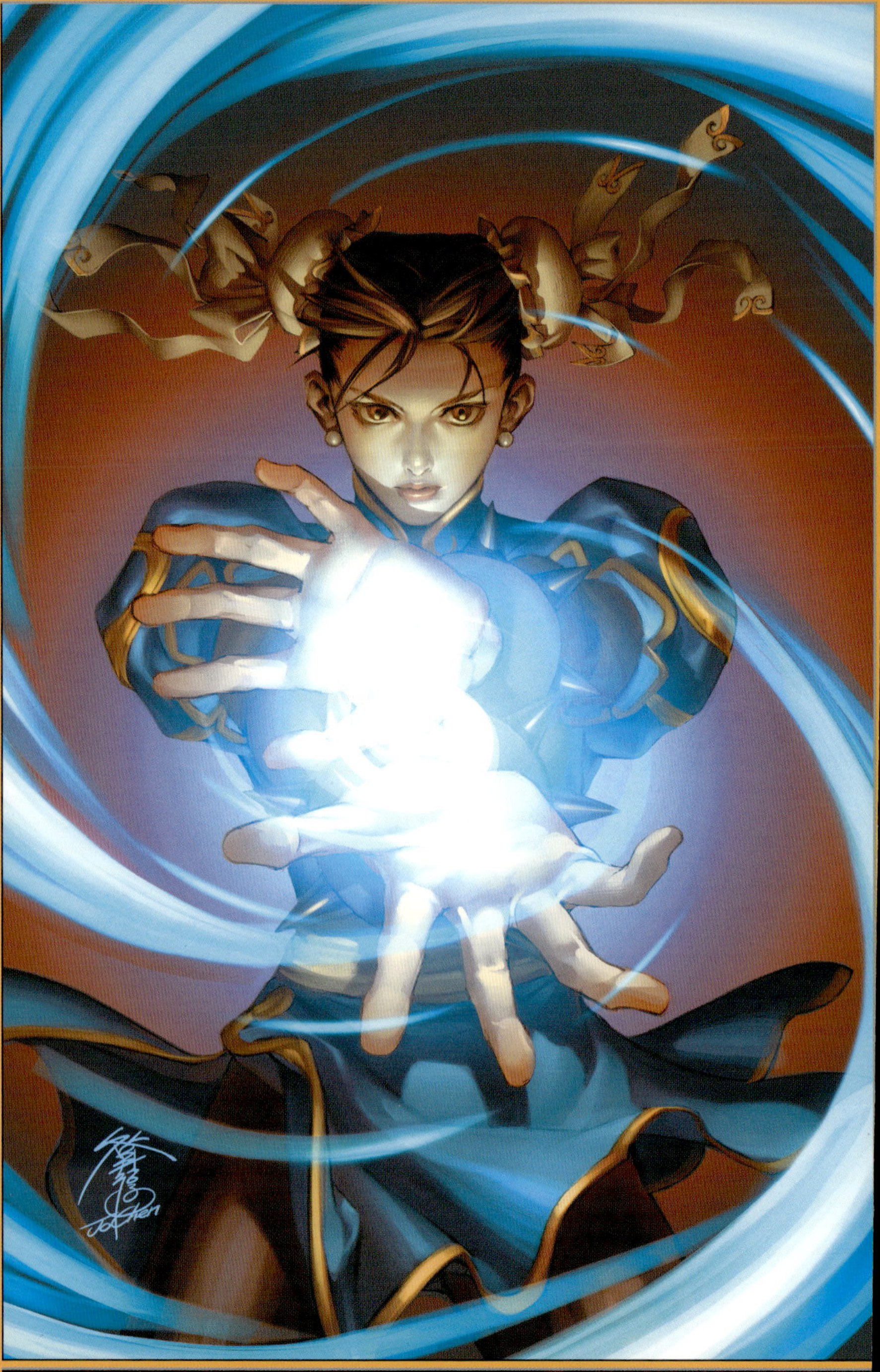

Issue 01: CHUN LI Power Foil

Cover Art by: Jo Chen

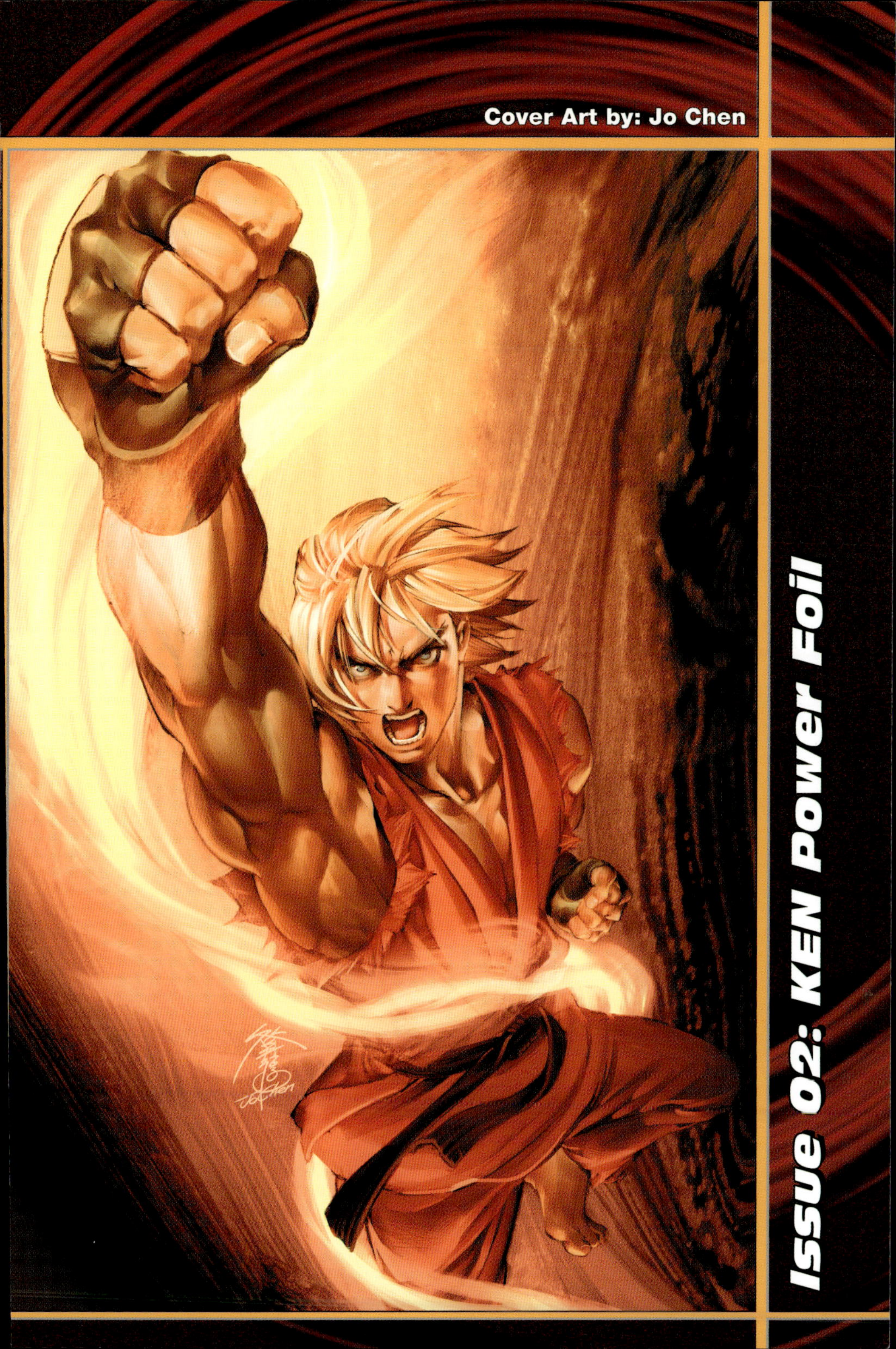

Issue 02: KEN Power Foil

Cover Art by: Jo Chen

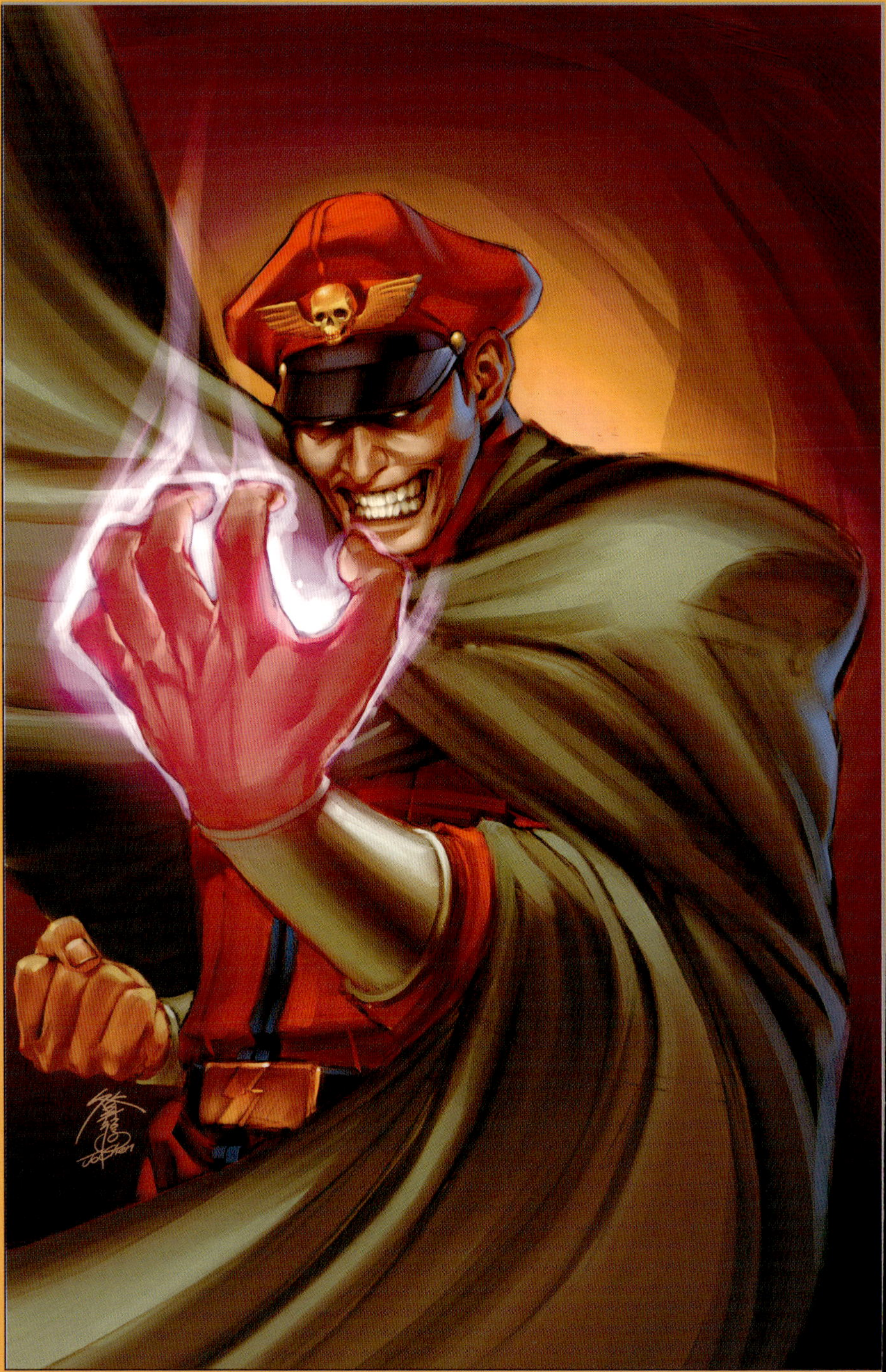

Issue 03: M.BISON Power Foil

Cover Art by: Jo Chen

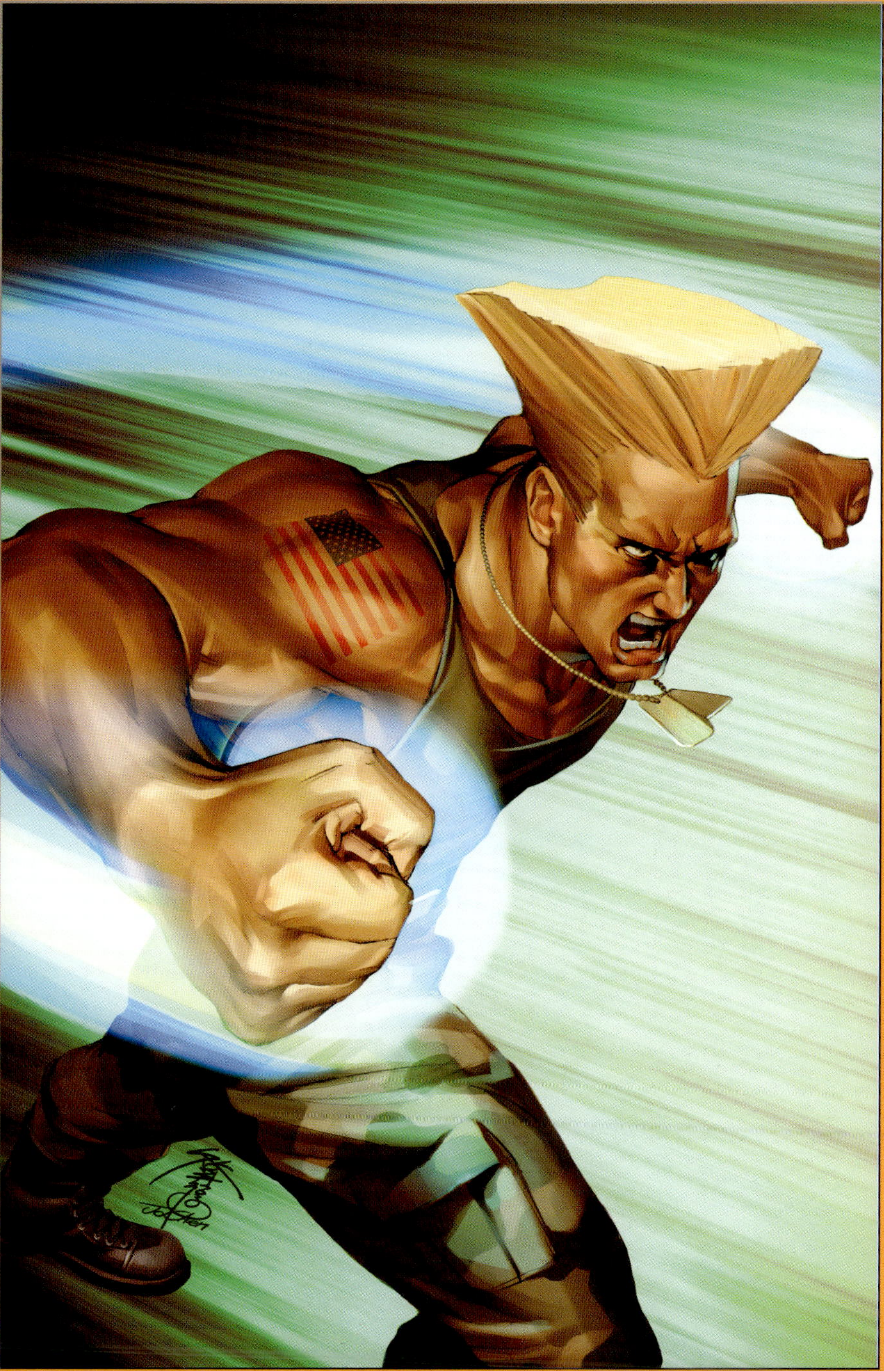

Issue 04: GUILE Power Foil

Cover Art by: Arnold Tsang

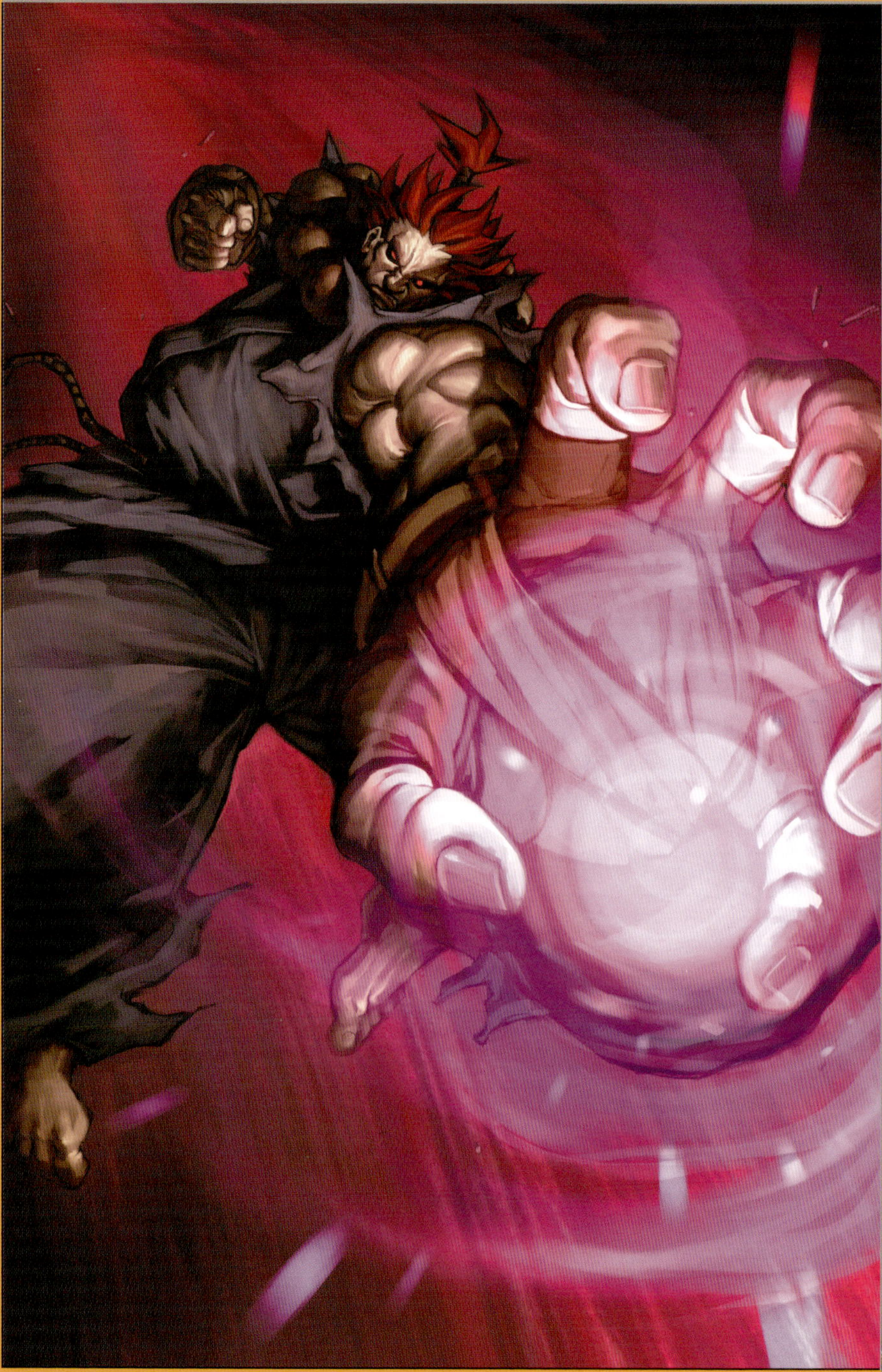

Issue 06: AKUMA Power Foil

Cover Art by: SHINKIRO (CAPCOM)

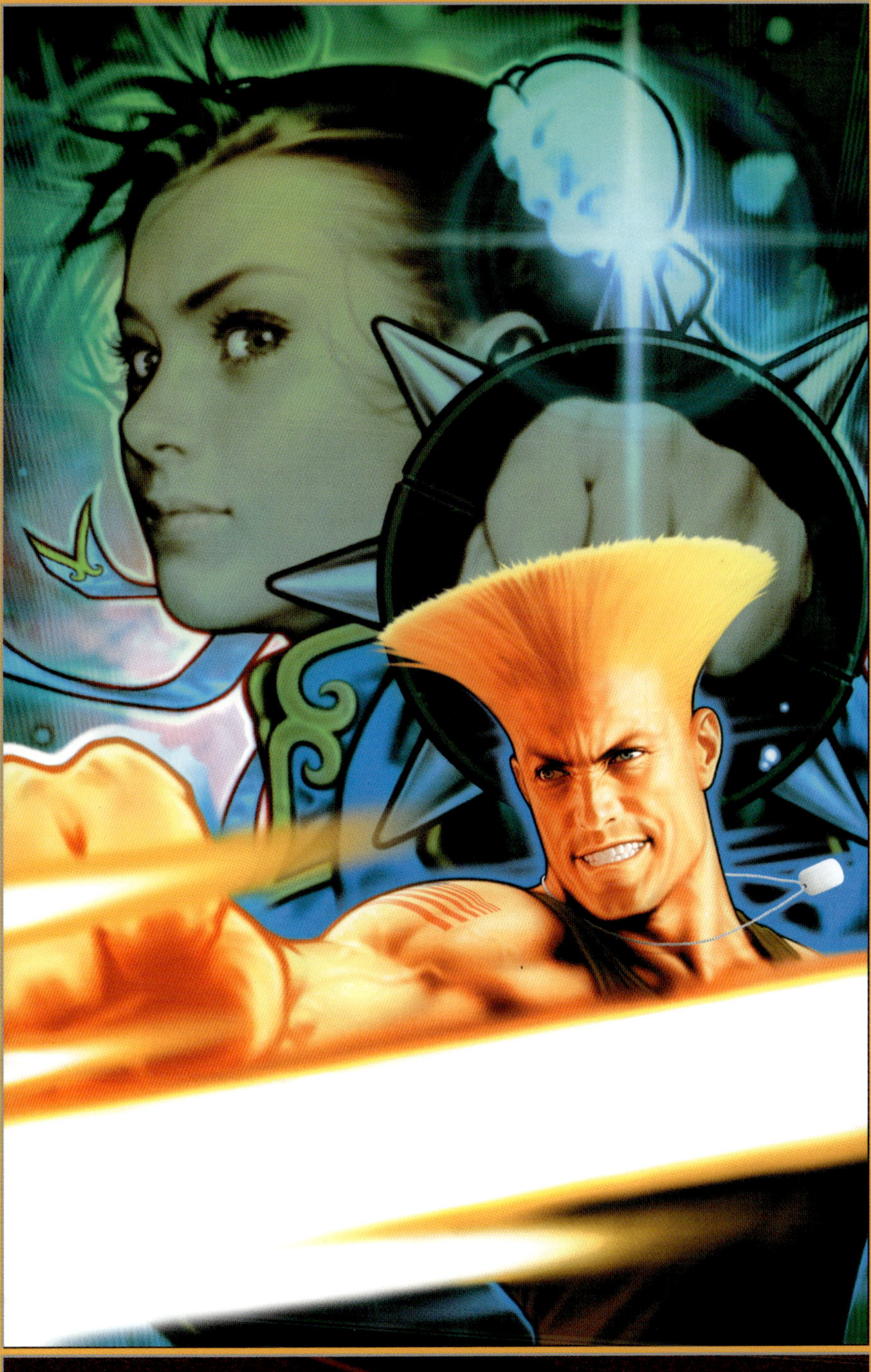

Issue 05: POWER CEL

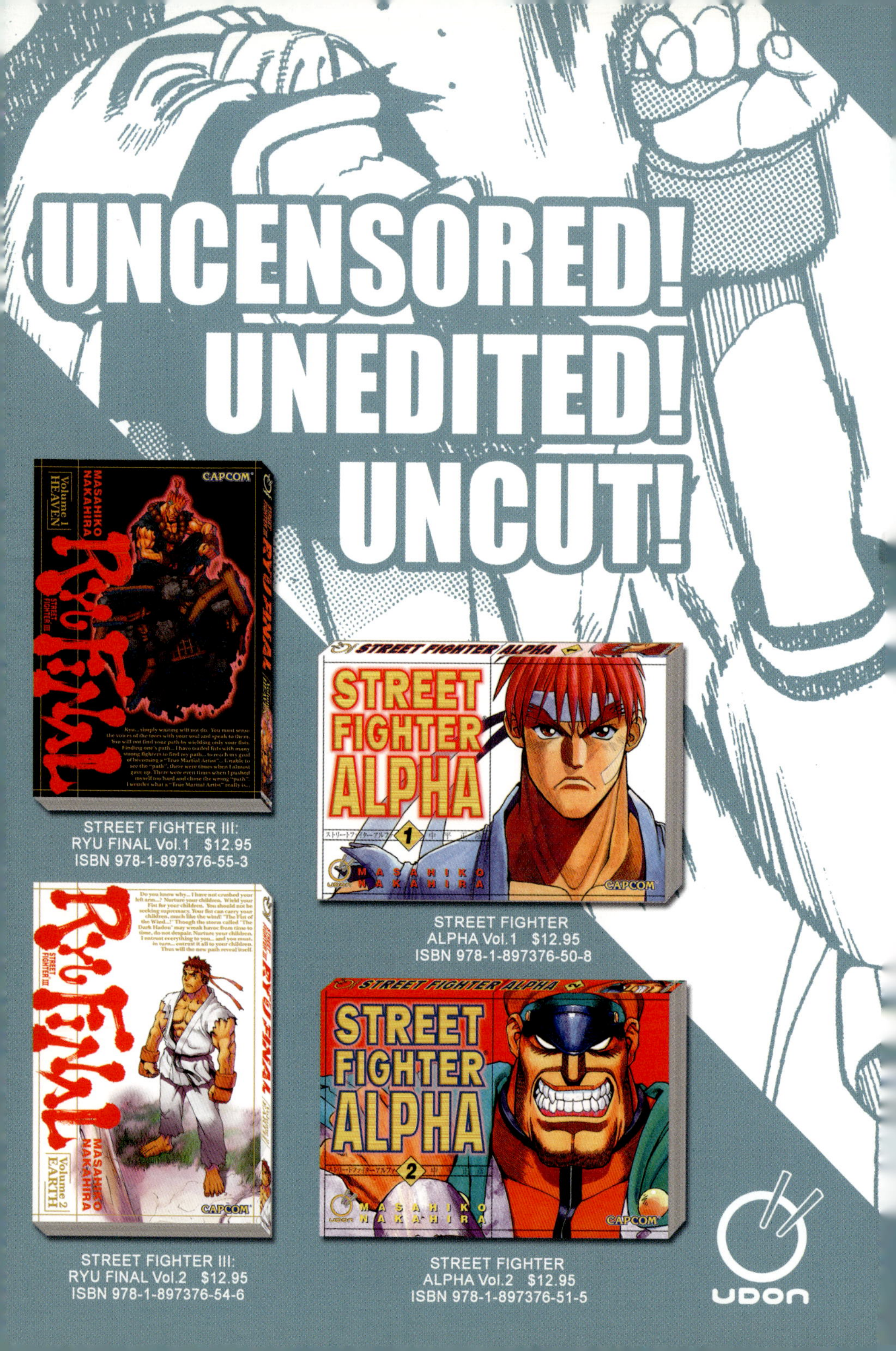

UNCENSORED!
UNEDITED!
UNCUT!
MASAHIKO NAKAHIRA
Volume 1 HEAVEN
CAPCOM
RYU FINAL
STREET FIGHTER III
STREET FIGHTER III:
RYU FINAL Vol.1 $12.95
ISBN 978-1-897376-55-3
STREET FIGHTER ALPHA
STREET FIGHTER ALPHA
1
MASAHIKO NAKAHIRA
CAPCOM
STREET FIGHTER
ALPHA Vol.1 $12.95
ISBN 978-1-897376-50-8
RYU FINAL
STREET FIGHTER III
MASAHIKO NAKAHIRA
Volume 2 EARTH
CAPCOM
STREET FIGHTER III:
RYU FINAL Vol.2 $12.95
ISBN 978-1-897376-54-6
STREET FIGHTER ALPHA
STREET FIGHTER ALPHA
2
MASAHIKO NAKAHIRA
CAPCOM
STREET FIGHTER
ALPHA Vol.2 $12.95
ISBN 978-1-897376-51-5
UDON

STREET FIGHTER II
Vol.1 $12.95
ISBN 978-0-9781386-1-5

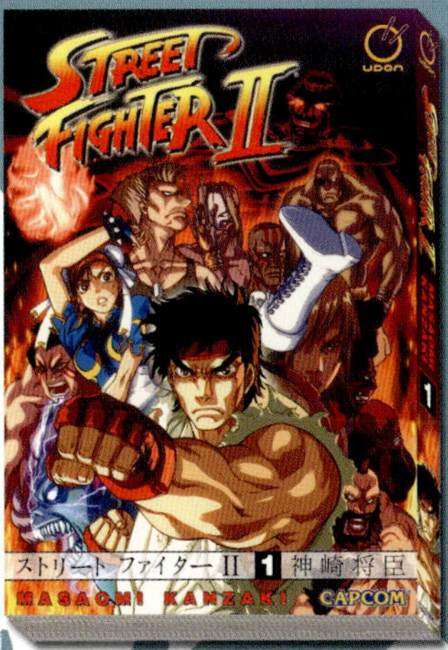
STREET FIGHTER II
ストリート ファイター II 1 神崎将臣
MASAOMI KANZAKI
CAPCOM

STREET FIGHTER II
Vol.2 $12.95
ISBN 978-0-9781386-2-2

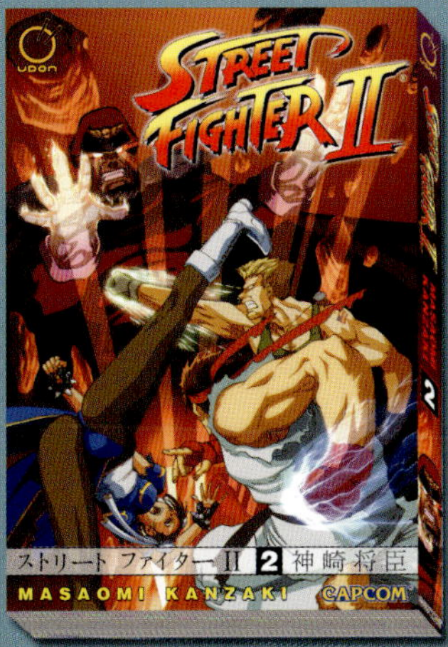
STREET FIGHTER II
ストリート ファイター II 2 神崎将臣
MASAOMI KANZAKI
CAPCOM

STREET FIGHTER II
Vol.3 $12.95
ISBN 978-0-9781386-3-9

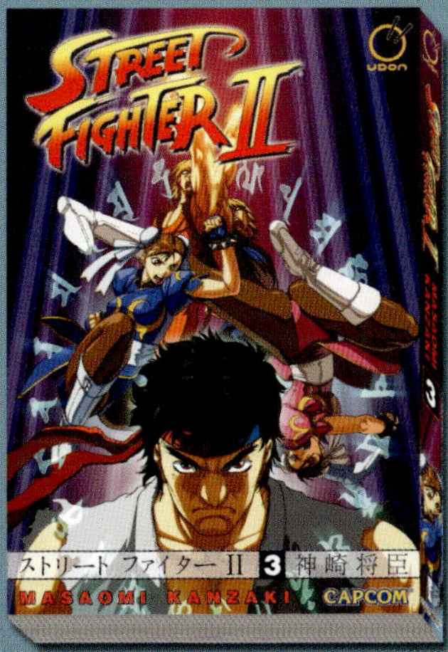
STREET FIGHTER II
ストリート ファイター II 3 神崎将臣
MASAOMI KANZAKI
CAPCOM

SAKURA GANBARU!
Vol.1 $12.95
ISBN 978-1-897376-52-2

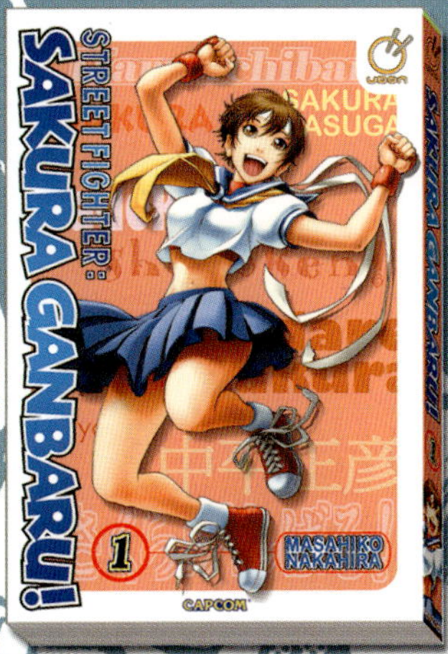
STREET FIGHTER: SAKURA GANBARU!
1
MASAHIKO NAKAHIRA
CAPCOM

SAKURA GANBARU!
Vol.2 $12.95
ISBN 978-1-897376-53-9

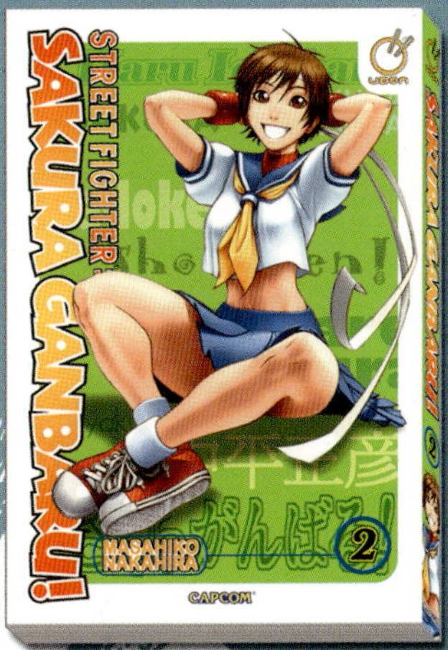
STREET FIGHTER: SAKURA GANBARU!
2
MASAHIKO NAKAHIRA
CAPCOM

CAPCOM® MANGA

Available where COMICS and BOOKS are sold!

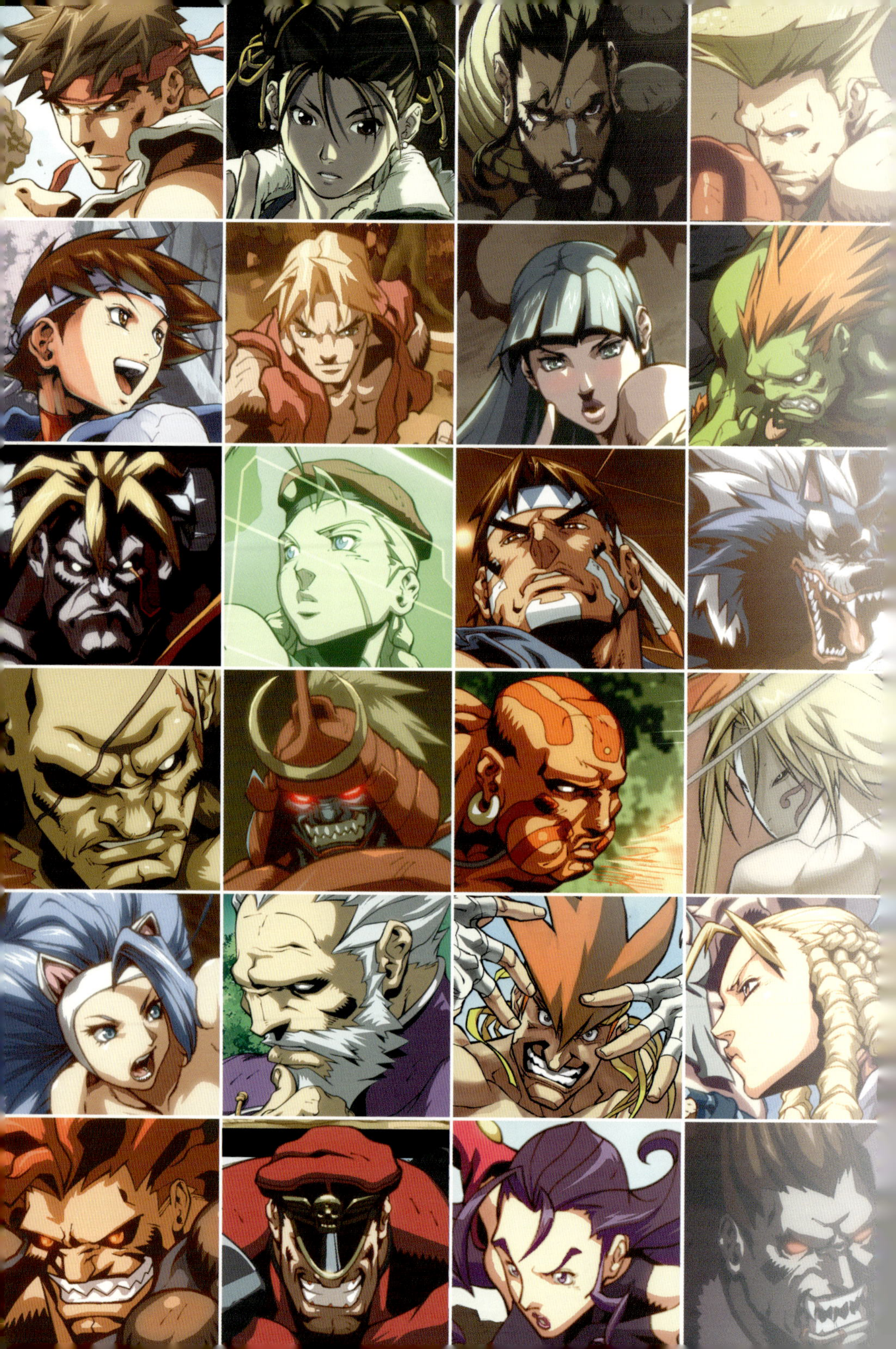

DON'T MISS THE EPIC TALES OF YOUR FAVORITE CHARACTERS!

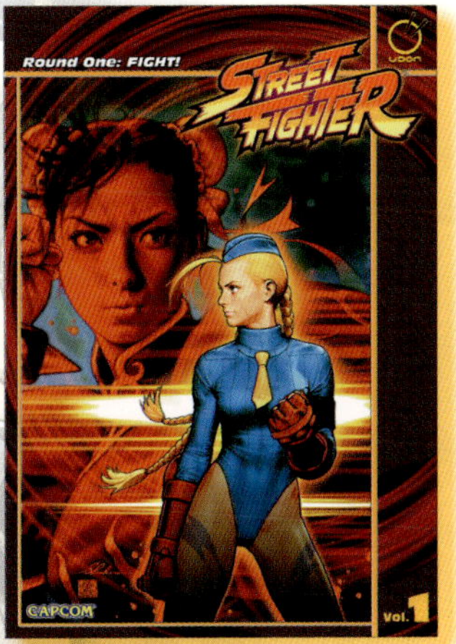
Round One: FIGHT!
STREET FIGHTER
CAPCOM
Vol. 1

STREET FIGHTER Volume 1
152 pages US$9.99
ISBN# 978-0-9738652-0-2

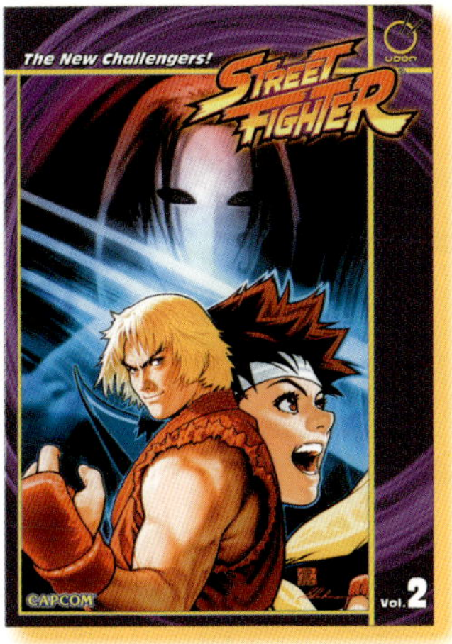
The New Challengers!
STREET FIGHTER
CAPCOM
Vol. 2

STREET FIGHTER Volume 2
200 pages US$13.99
ISBN# 978-0-9738652-7-1

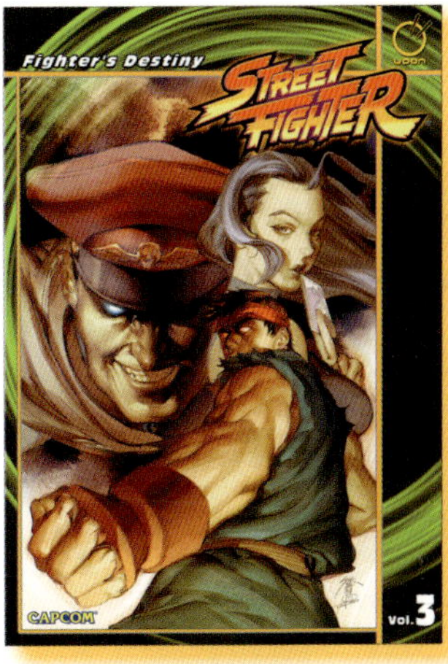
Fighter's Destiny
STREET FIGHTER
CAPCOM
Vol. 3

STREET FIGHTER Volume 3
168 pages US$13.99
ISBN# 978-0-9738652-8-8

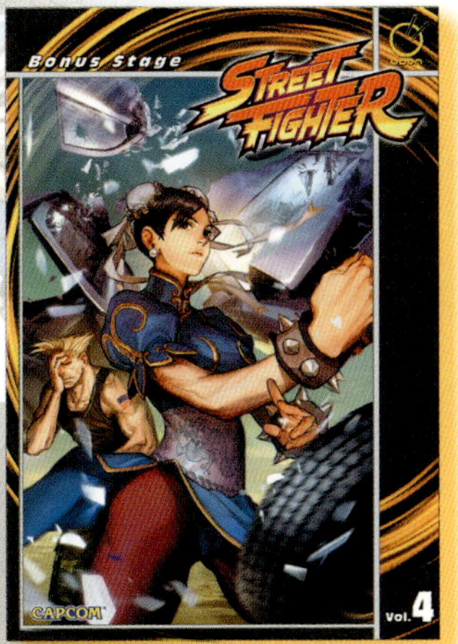
Bonus Stage
STREET FIGHTER
CAPCOM
Vol. 4

STREET FIGHTER Volume 4
144 pages US$12.95
ISBN# 978-0-897376-00-3

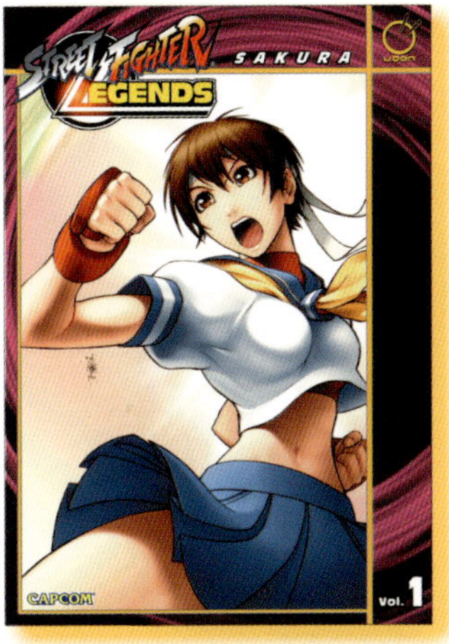
STREET FIGHTER LEGENDS
SAKURA
CAPCOM
Vol. 1

STREET FIGHTER LEGENDS Vol.1
128 pages US$11.95
ISBN# 978-0-9781386-4-6

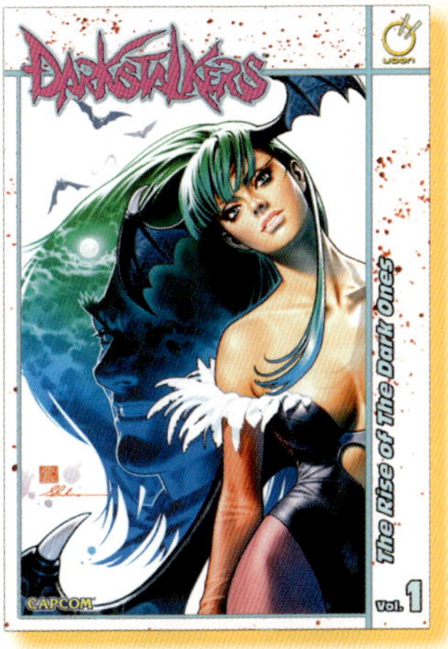
DARKSTALKERS
The Rise of The Dark Ones
CAPCOM
Vol. 1

DARKSTALKERS Volume 1
144 pages US$12.99
ISBN# 978-0-9738652-1-9

READ ALL THE CAPCOM® GRAPHIC NOVELS TODAY!

ON SALE NOW
Where books and comics are sold!

www.capcomcomics.com

UDON

these CAPCOM® posters.

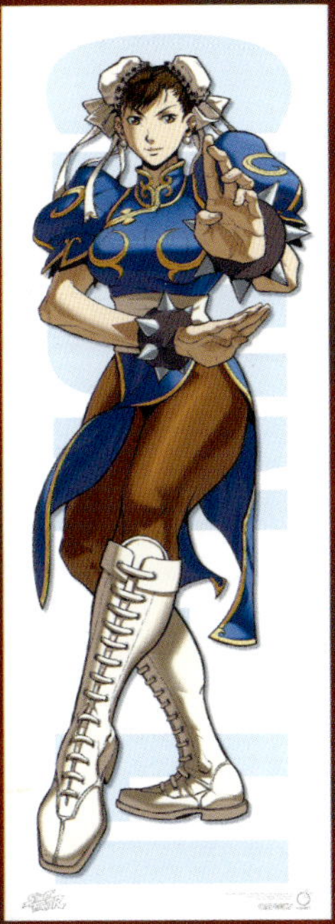

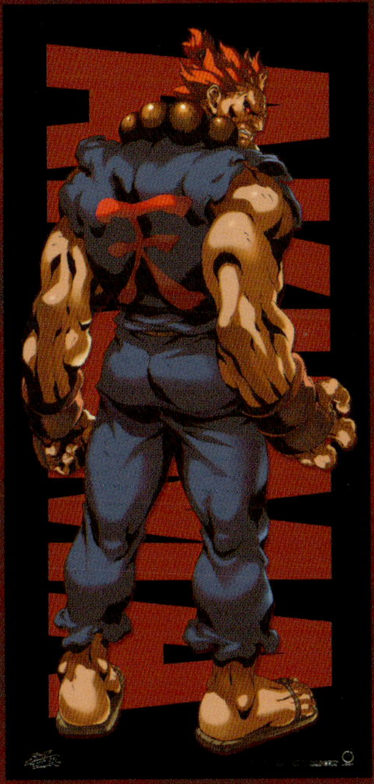

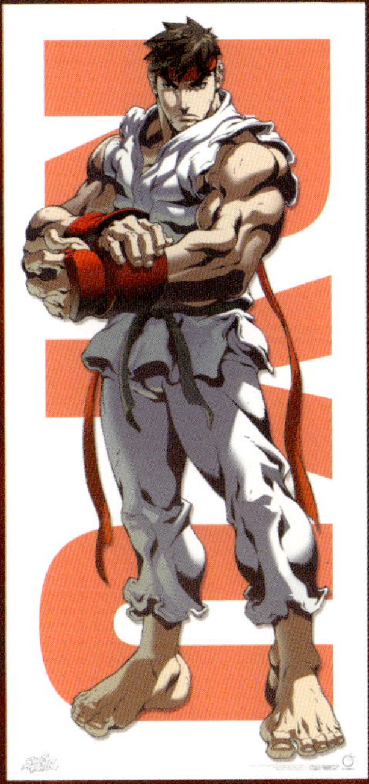

Left to Right: Morrigan, Felicia, Cammy, Sakura, Chun Li, Akuma, Ryu

←ALL DOOR POSTERS ARE 55 INCHES TALL!→

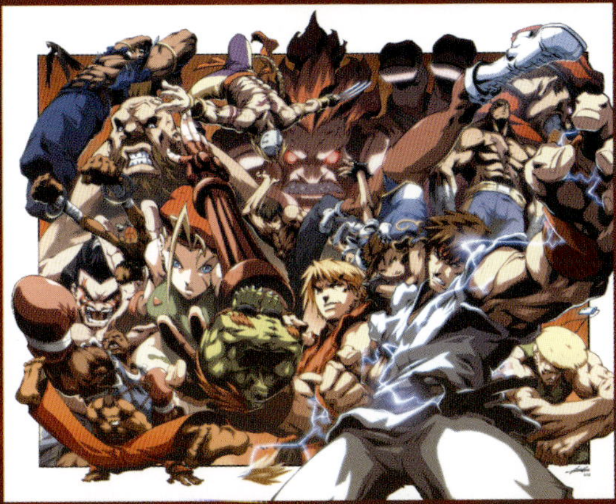

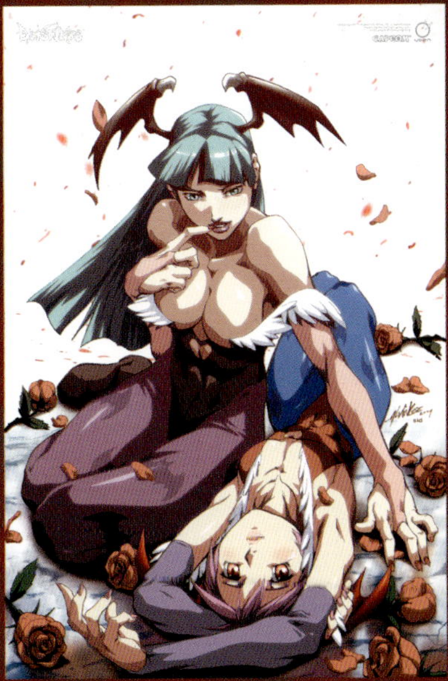

Above: Street Fighter: World Warriors (24 X 30 inches)
Right: Darkstalkers: Sisters (24 X 36 inches)

STREET FIGHTER® DARKSTALKERS™

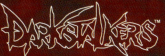

Licensed by: CAPCOM®

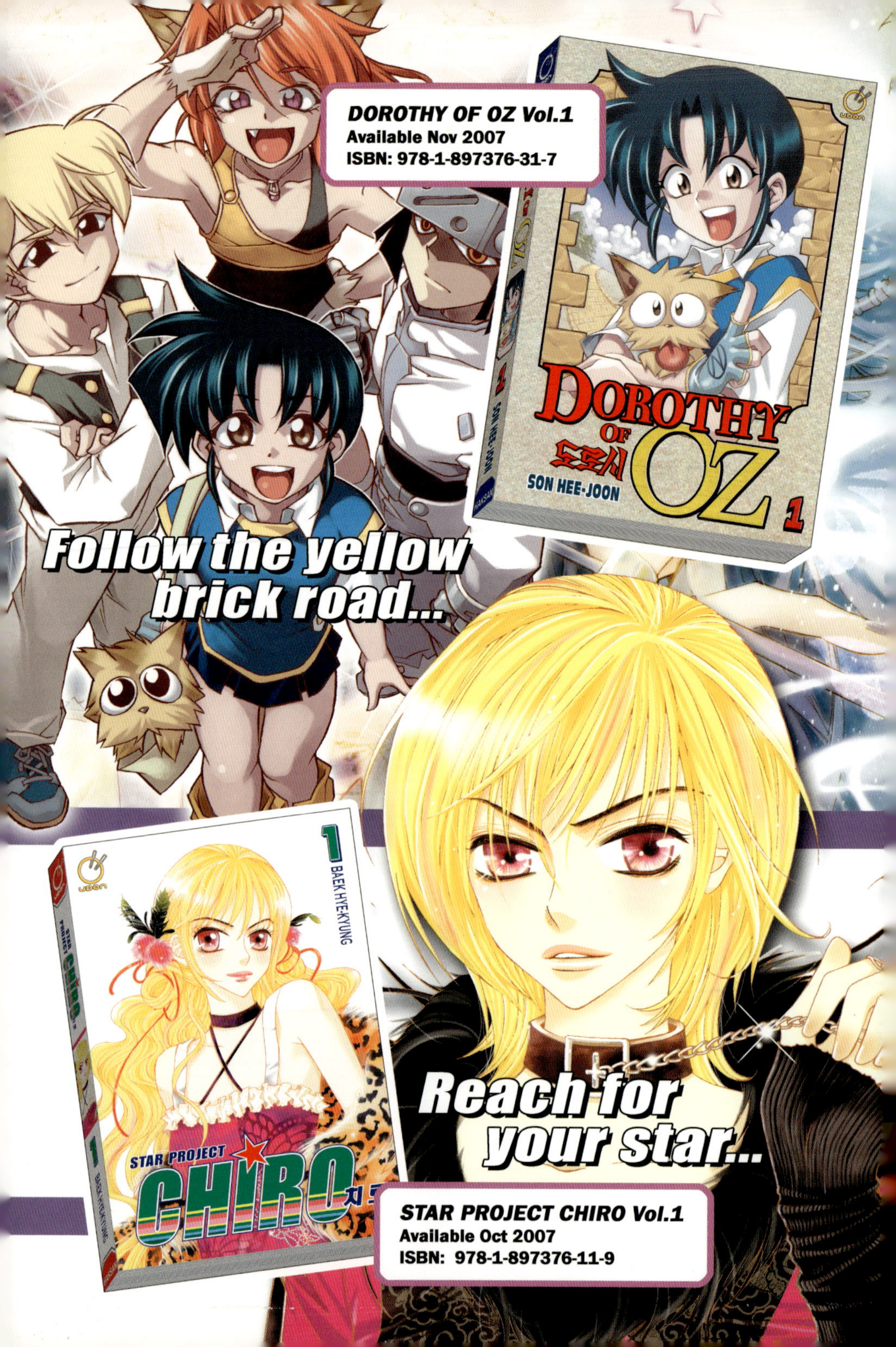

DOROTHY OF OZ Vol.1
Available Nov 2007
ISBN: 978-1-897376-31-7
DOROTHY OF OZ
도로시
SON HEE-JOON
1
Follow the yellow brick road...
STAR PROJECT CHIRO
치로
1
BAEK HYE-KYUNG
Reach for your star...
STAR PROJECT CHIRO Vol.1
Available Oct 2007
ISBN: 978-1-897376-11-9